WE ARE THE DAMNED UNITED

WE ARE THE DAMNED UNITED

THE REAL STORY OF BRIAN CLOUGH AT LEEDS UNITED

PHIL ROSTRON

MAINSTREAM
PUBLISHING

EDINBURGH AND LONDON

First published in Great Britain in 2009 by
MAINSTREAM PUBLISHING COMPANY
(EDINBURGH) LTD
7 Albany Street
Edinburgh EH1 3UG

ISBN 9781845964450

A catalogue record for this book is available
from the British Library

Typeset in Big Noodle and Palatino

Printed and bound in the UK by
CPI Mackays, Chatham ME5 8TD

FOR ROWLAND,
A PROPER FOOTBALL FAN

ACKNOWLEDGEMENTS

Grateful thanks go to the following for their generous help: Frank Gray, Peter Lorimer, Eddie Gray, Gordon McQueen, Joe Jordan, Peter Hampton, Terry Yorath, Duncan McKenzie, David Harvey, Jimmy Armfield, Peter Reid, Hugh McIlmoyle, Gary Newbon, Tommy Docherty and John Wray.

Also, in regard to copyright matters, thanks to Brian Viner, Paul Newman and *The Independent*; Paul Napier, Phil Hay and the *Yorkshire Evening Post*; Gerry Ormonde and the Dublin *Evening Herald*; Robert Galvin and the National Football Museum Hall of Fame; Duncan Hamilton and Harper Perennial for permission to reproduce extracts from *Provided You Don't Kiss Me*; the *Sunday Times*; Barney Ronay and *The Guardian*; Delia Monk, Bryan Henesey and the *Nottingham Evening Post*; Ed Reed and the *Huddersfield Examiner*; Ian Murtagh and *The Journal*; Dennis Signy; Rob Stewart; the *Manchester Evening News*; the *Daily Mail*; and the websites mightyleeds.co.uk, thisisderbyshire.co.uk, ozwhitelufc.net.au, bwfc.co.uk and leedsfans.org.uk.

Thanks to Iain MacGregor of Mainstream for commissioning the book, the Mainstream team for their exemplary professionalism, Phil Hay, one of the top two football writers outside of Fleet Street, for his camaraderie and painstaking revision of the manuscript, Neil Hodgkinson, editorial director of Cumbrian Newspapers, for his trust, support and understanding, and finally to my lovely wife Caroline for everything.

CONTENTS

FOREWORD

I write the foreword to this insightful analysis of Brian Clough's 44 days at Leeds United within 24 hours of the famous Yorkshire club being beaten by a non-league side for the first time in its history – a 1–0 reverse against Histon in the second round of the FA Cup – and Nottingham Forest creeping off the bottom of the Coca-Cola Championship table by virtue of a 1–0 win over Barnsley. How times change in the world of football that we so love and adore! Some years previously, I represented both Leeds and Forest in finals of the biggest club competition in the world, the European Cup, when the clubs were in their pomp.

If I impressed Brian Clough during his spell managing Leeds in 1974, then it wasn't immediately apparent, because he didn't include me in his plans at Elland Road. In fact, I had become a little disillusioned and was actively looking to move on, with both Birmingham City and Ipswich Town showing an interest in my services. In the event, some five years elapsed before I was to leave Leeds in a £500,000 deal that took me to Clough's Forest.

When Clough arrived at Leeds, I was one of a number of younger players tasked with maintaining the club's success in the aftermath of the Don Revie era. The great Revie team was ageing and breaking up, and the club was looking to the likes of me, Gordon McQueen, Joe Jordan and others to keep them high in the pecking order. I had joined the club, at which my older brother Eddie had already made a name for himself, as a 17-year-old midfielder and made my debut in 1973, scoring a goal in that first match. Regular left-back Terry Cooper had suffered a very nasty leg break, which was how my big chance came about. However, I was still very much learning the game then and I soon made way at number 3 for Trevor Cherry, though I was at least invited to go with the squad to Wembley for the 1973 FA Cup final against Sunderland.

I quickly found my patience being tested, because, with Trevor settled into a team that went 29 league games unbeaten and won the Division One title at the end of the 1973–74 season, my chances were strictly limited. However, a fairly regular place in the team came along and the 1975 European Cup final between Leeds United and Bayern Munich in Paris was something of a big-occasion baptism of fire, because it ended with our fans rioting after a highly controversial defeat. When I was playing in Clough's Nottingham Forest team, I was privileged to become the first player to represent two different English clubs in the European Cup final. I'm still the only player to have done so! That time, in 1980, I got a winner's medal after a 1–0 victory over a Hamburg team featuring Kevin Keegan.

I suppose Leeds were always in my heart and in 1981 I returned to Elland Road under Allan Clarke, only for the club to suffer relegation and 'Sniffer' to lose his job. My brother Eddie took over as manager and I played under him for four years without us quite being able to get out of the Second Division. I left Leeds for Sunderland in 1985 with a career record at Elland Road of 396 appearances and 35 goals and was at least able to help Sunderland to promotion from the third tier.

Internationally, I first played for Scotland against Switzerland in 1976 (a 1–0 victory). I was capped again in 1978 but didn't make it onto the squad for the World Cup in Argentina. Four years later, I was selected for the Scotland squad for the 1982 World Cup in Spain and played against New Zealand, Brazil and the USSR in the group stages, though that was the end of the road for us. I finished up with 32 caps and can safely say that in my time as a footballer I witnessed a wide spectrum of managerial ability and talent.

In analysing why a liaison between a club as mighty as Leeds United and one of the greatest managers the game has ever seen in Brian Clough should be doomed to spectacular failure, one major reason stands out above all others. It is the fact that Clough was at Leeds without the support and guidance of his great ally and assistant, Peter Taylor. They were a brilliant partnership and it was unfortunate for Clough that when Leeds came calling Taylor preferred to stay at Brighton. With Taylor at his side at Elland Road, the situation might have been much calmer. Taylor would have been a steadying influence and would have taken on board much of the disharmony within the camp, shielding Clough from it. Who knows what might have happened had Clough stayed longer, but the club went on to reach a European Cup final that season with the same squad of players who had won the league title 12 months earlier. There was no need for drastic changes, though Clough seemed to have an agenda to make them. Perhaps if he'd managed to settle things down, we might have won the European Cup.

However, somewhat cast adrift, he hurriedly brought in people he knew, like John McGovern and John O'Hare, his trainer Jimmy Gordon and striker Duncan McKenzie, and although these were 'his' people, none of them was Peter Taylor. In retrospect, Clough admitted that he had been too rash in his approach to the job. He acted too quickly. He tried to change things in a blur of activity and he later accepted that this had been a mistake. I know he regretted it.

The accusation has been levelled that the players he inherited didn't respond to his management methods, but first impressions matter and their first impressions were of a man accusing them of being cheats, of someone ordering them to throw their medals in a bin because they had been won unfairly, of someone telling a fine but injured player that he would have been shot had he been a horse. Nevertheless, a lot of players would have liked the chance to play under him for much longer than those 44 days he was in charge. Though it wasn't the case at Leeds, nearly everybody who played under Clough at Derby County and Forest liked and respected him, and if the whole scenario at Leeds could be replayed with Taylor at his side, I am sure it would be a whole lot different.

Like most in the game, I was saddened by the later estrangement between Clough and Taylor, because they had become one of the enduring football partnerships of modern times. Clough took offence when in 1983 Taylor, as Derby's manager, signed his player John Robertson from Forest. The deal was done while Clough, who had been in the process of drawing up a new contract for his favourite winger, was away on a rambling holiday, and he felt Taylor had gone behind his back. That they never made up was another of Clough's regrets.

Players are in the game to get to the highest level and win trophies, and I hung up my boots in 1992 having figured in not only two European Cup finals but also the European Cup-Winners' Cup in 1973, when Leeds lost 1–0 to AC Milan at the Kaftanzoglio Stadium in Thessaloniki, Greece, the European Super Cup in 1979, when Forest beat Barcelona 2–1 on aggregate, and 1980, when Forest were beaten by Valencia on the away-goals rule, and the Intercontinental Cup in 1980, when Forest were beaten 1–0 by Uruguayan side Nacional at the National Stadium in Tokyo. I was on the bench when Leeds were beaten by Sunderland in the 1973 FA Cup final and towards the end of my career I was a member of the Sunderland squad who took the 1987–88 Third Division title and won successive league titles with Darlington in 1989–90 (Conference) and 1990–91 (Fourth Division).

I was with Clough at Forest for only two years but that was long enough to become entangled in what, for many people, is one of life's mysteries: the secret of his success. I'm not sure there was one. Certainly, his involvement in training was rudimentary and elementary – just the basics. He didn't do a lot of coaching and when he became involved it was usually centred on a five-a-side game in which he insisted on the ball being kept down on the floor in a simple passing game. He would tell defenders it was their job to defend, midfielders that they were there both to shield the defence and feed the forwards, and forwards that they were there to score goals. Very basic. Very simple. And it was probably this simplicity that was the key. No doubt he would be of the opinion that football is an easy game sometimes made difficult by over-elaborate coaching.

Having been at Leeds since I was a boy and played nearly four hundred games for them in two spells, I obviously hold the club in greater affection than I do Forest, with whom I spent just two seasons. You can't help but wonder if the decline of Leeds in the late 1970s would have happened if Clough had had an extended run at Elland Road, and the balance of probabilities in view of what he later achieved at Forest is that they would have thrived and prospered rather than sinking into the abyss. Having managed Darlington, Farnborough Town, Grays Athletic, Woking and Basingstoke Town, I know how difficult the job can be. More often than not, Clough made the very best of it. Clough's life in football was nothing if not colourful, and the Leeds episode must go down as a short but fascinating period of failure in an otherwise highly successful career.

Frank Gray

INTRODUCTION

They say Rome wasn't built in a day,
but I wasn't on that particular job.

Brian Clough

To understand the situation that Brian Clough found himself in as manager of Leeds United, one has first to analyse the two decades at the club leading up to his appointment and the early, unlikely successes that had brought him the opportunity. In particular, a look at Don Revie's tenure at the club – considered by fans and players alike a golden age of stability and silverware – is revealing. Clough's time in charge was a complete contrast, and it would have dramatic effects that are still being discussed and dramatised today.

This book does not intend to dwell on the portrayal of events in the film *The Damned United*. That is a film based on a work of fiction by a very successful writer who knows his craft and has a vision of what he wants his story to be about. My aim is simply to discuss the details of Brian Clough's 44-day reign at Leeds United with many of the players who were there at the time, as well as others connected to the club. This is not to answer Clough's critics, or Revie's for that matter, but simply to discover what the men who were there at the time thought of the situation and how they reacted to it. Obviously, some key figures, such as Billy Bremner, are no longer with us, so I have researched their views on events through interviews, autobiographies and other sources.

I discovered that very little is known about Clough's six league games in charge of the team and what transpired in those fixtures. I believe this tells a story in itself, as they provide the background to the internal struggle that was going on at the top of the club's management structure. I was therefore very fortunate to discover contemporary match reports in the archives of the *Yorkshire Evening Post*, which the *Post* have very kindly allowed me to reproduce for the first time within this narrative.

I hope you find the story both illuminating and enjoyable, as it concerns some of the greatest players of the era, indeed of any era, at loggerheads with arguably one of the greatest managers of all time. What went wrong? Well, read on and find out what the players themselves have to say.

When in March 1961 a Leeds United board of directors alarmed by the club's slide to the lower reaches of the Second Division ran out of patience with their manager, Jack Taylor, it was to an influential member of their playing staff that they turned, in the hope of having identified greater potential than that held by Taylor to resurrect the failing West Yorkshire outfit. Don Revie, the man in question, had been signed from Sunderland by Taylor's predecessor, Bill Lambton, as a 31-year-old ex-England inside-forward, costing a significant £14,000.

Four months after Revie's appointment as player-manager, one of the best post-war English goal-poachers, by the name of Brian Clough, made the national headlines with a high-profile transfer. The Teesside legend, who had set a scoring record of 204 goals in 222 matches for Middlesbrough, was sold to regional rivals Sunderland for £55,000. He would go on to replicate his incredible strike rate at his new club, scoring 54 goals in 61 league matches. Had it not been for a horrific accident that in effect prematurely curtailed his career, Sunderland and Clough would have enjoyed a happier time together and would surely have won promotion to the top flight. However, events dictated that the club had to finish the season without him, and it failed at the very last hurdle by a single point.

On Boxing Day 1962, and with his goal tally for the season already at a sparkling 28, Clough tangled with goalkeeper Chris Harker of Bury on a terrible playing surface. They collided heavily as Clough overstretched to poke a shot at goal. It was immediately obvious to those watching that Clough had sustained a serious injury. Prostrate in the mud, he could barely move his right leg. What we see today as the curse of the professional sportsman had happened to him: Clough had badly torn his cruciate ligament. In the 1960s, this type of injury meant the end of many a player's career. Although he recovered in eighteen months and ran out three more times for Sunderland – who were by that time playing in the First Division – the reaction of the leg told him that his professional playing days were gone. Those three games were the only time he played in the elite flight.

The obvious question for a player of his calibre and ambition was what could he possibly do next in football? This was the love of his life, after all. Although offered employment outside of the game, he wanted to be involved. The Sunderland manager George Hardwick took him under his wing and allowed him to coach and run the youth team. It was in this sphere that Clough first demonstrated the leadership qualities that would take him into full-time management and eventually lead to honours in the top flight of the domestic game as well as in Europe. Ultimately, it became legend that he was the best manager England never had.

The youngsters in his charge were being guided by a genius whose incomparable record was 251 goals in 274 senior matches. In his autobiography *Clough*, he described himself as the finest goal-scorer in Britain and one of the best the game had ever seen. Who could argue with that? Who would have wanted to?

In October 1965, 30-year-old Clough became the Football League's youngest manager when he took the helm at lowly

Hartlepools United (later renamed Hartlepool United). Little did the football world realise that this was the beginning of a turbulent managerial career spanning three decades and punctuated by momentous events and controversial statements. Clough's first decision was a significant one: he brought in Peter Taylor, a friend and colleague since his spell at Middlesbrough and then manager of Burton Albion, as his assistant. Nottingham-born Taylor had been signed as a goalkeeper by Nottingham Forest in 1945, played for Coventry City between 1950 and 1955, and then moved to Middlesbrough, where, as a reserve goalkeeper, he had first encountered a young Brian Clough. In one of the first great examples of the talent-spotting for which Taylor became famed, he constantly sang the praises of the goal machine in the ranks. After 140 appearances for Middlesbrough over 6 years, Taylor moved to Port Vale in 1961. In October 1962, he was offered the manager's job at Burton and led them to triumph in the Southern League Cup in 1964.

The chemistry between Clough and Taylor was soon evident, and unfashionable Hartlepools were guided in the 1966–67 season to a very respectable eighth-place finish in Division Four. The previous campaign had seen Leeds beat Hartlepools 4–2 in the second round of the League Cup, reach the semi-finals of the Inter-Cities Fairs Cup and finish runners-up to Liverpool in the race for the Division One title. Two managerial careers that would have a huge impact on both the English game and European football were taking shape.

Elected to the Football League as comparatively recently in the game's history as 1920, Leeds United shuffled between the Second Division and First Division under a succession of managers ranging in ability from poor to moderate to only slightly above average for more than 40 years until Revie, a superstitious man who came to believe that the club's Elland Road ground was under a Gypsy curse, took over the reins and transformed the club. Prior to Revie's appointment, Leeds were off the radar of the dominant clubs in English football such as Burnley, Wolves, Tottenham and Sheffield Wednesday.

Yet Revie assumed his managerial role with some lofty ambitions and tenaciously set about achieving them. Like the rest of the football world, he was spellbound by what was being achieved in Europe by a Spanish club under the control of Santiago Bernabéu Yeste, who had become president of Real Madrid in 1945. It was under Bernabéu's guidance that Real Madrid established themselves as a major force in both Spanish and European football. The club won the European Cup five times in a row between 1956 and 1960, including a 7–3 Hampden Park final victory over Eintracht Frankfurt in 1960 that is popularly regarded as the greatest exhibition of football of all time. Having won five consecutive times in their pristine all-white kit, Real were permanently awarded the original cup and given the right to wear the UEFA badge of honour.

Ferenc Puskás, Alfredo di Stéfano et al. In all white. This was food for thought for Revie. Since 1955, Leeds had been playing in royal-blue shirts with gold collars, white shorts and blue-and-yellow-hooped socks. In 1961, Revie decided they were to change again – to all white. Three years later, a perching owl was added to the strip, a surprising choice of emblem from Revie, as one of his many superstitions was that birds brought bad luck. The owl was taken from the city's coat of arms, which itself incorporated aspects of the arms of Sir John Savile, the first alderman of Leeds.

Revie was not the only visionary talent to have taken charge at Elland Road. In the immediate post-war years, Major Frank Buckley, a Mancunian who had seen action in the Battle of the Somme, had a five-year stint in charge of Leeds, during which time he discovered the legendary John Charles and later brought in the long-serving, talismanic and, ultimately, World Cup-winning Jack Charlton, initially as a ground-staff boy. The latter's memories of Buckley are quoted at mightyleeds.co.uk:

> Unlike the pros, we got just two weeks' holidays in the summer, and while they were away our job was to remove the weeds from the pitch and replace them

with grass seed. I remember being sat out there one day with Keith Ripley, another ground-staff boy, when Major Buckley came over to us. We must have looked pretty forlorn, the two of us, and to gee us up he said he'd give us five shillings for every bucket we filled with weeds. Now that was an offer we couldn't refuse. By the time we were finished, we had filled six buckets and, cheeky bugger that I was, I marched straight up to the Major's office. And when he asked what I wanted, I told him I was there to claim my thirty bob for the weeds. He nearly blew a bloody gasket! 'Get out of here!' he bellowed. 'You're already getting paid to do that work – don't ever let me see you up here again with your buckets.'

Yet beneath the gruff exterior, he was a kind man, as he demonstrated once when I met him. My shoes must have been a sight, for when he looked down at them, he asked me if they were the only pair I had. I nodded. The next morning, he summoned me to his office and handed me a pair of Irish brogues, the strongest, most beautiful shoes I'd ever seen.

When Buckley left Leeds in April 1953, he was replaced by Raich Carter, who had enjoyed a brilliant playing career, winning 13 England caps as an inside-forward. He built his team around Charles and in 1956 Leeds gained promotion, ending a nine-year spell in the Second Division. Despite his achievements, Carter's contract was not renewed by the board in 1958. Leeds had created a stir in the transfer market by selling star player Charles to Italian giants Juventus for a record fee at the end of the previous season, and they struggled during most of 1957–58. The Leeds directors turned to Bill Lambton, who had only recently joined Leeds as an assistant to Carter having made his reputation as a fitness trainer for British boxers, to hold things together while they sought a permanent successor. Lambton was made acting manager before having what was to be a rudely cut short permanent appointment confirmed in December 1958. He fell out with the board and left in February 1959.

Lambton had little experience, and the unusual methods he tried to introduce didn't go down too well with the players and weren't a great success. Charlton remembered:

> An ex-army guy called Bill Lambton took over from Raich Carter. Bill was a nice enough man, but he wasn't a player, he wasn't a coach, he wasn't anything. If you ever saw Bill walking about, he always had a piece of paper in his hand – nobody ever found out what was written on that paper, but it made him look as though he was doing something.
>
> Bill was a fitness fanatic. I remember one windy day when we complained about the balls being too hard during a training session. Bill told us that anyone worth his salt ought to be able to kick balls in his bare feet and never feel it, so one of the lads said, 'Well, go on then.' Now Bill wasn't a pro, he'd probably never kicked a ball in anger in his life, and yet here he was running up to kick the ball in his bare feet, and of course you could see him wincing afterwards. This is the manager who's just been appointed, and he's making a fool of himself in front of his players. He finished up hobbling off the pitch, with all of us laughing at him. Bill never recovered from that day.
>
> A few weeks later we had a meeting and, after some of the lads had their say, the chairman asked if we wanted the manager to leave – and every one of the players said yes. Bill said pathetically, 'If you let me stay, we'll have a new start,' but nobody said a dicky bird. He was sacked that same day.
>
> I felt sorry for Bill. I didn't take him seriously as a football man, but I got on all right with him. I used to see him later from time to time when he was running a pub on the Leeds–Grimsby road, and he seemed much happier.

Jimmy Dunn, the Scottish full-back who played for Leeds between 1947 and 1959, agreed with Charlton's assessment of Lambton, and is quoted at mightyleeds.co.uk describing him as a 'comedian'. He continued:

> He had no experience. I remember he once took his boot off on the Fullerton Park training ground and said, 'You don't need boots when you're crossing a ball.' Eventually, there was a players' meeting in protest. It was a rebellion. Eric [Kerfoot] and I had complained about him. I can't remember exactly what we said, but it came down to the fact that he couldn't manage the club.

Although Lambton was responsible for bringing to the club the young Billy Bremner and the veteran Revie – both of whom would go on to become highly significant figures in the story of Leeds United – his spell as manager was not a successful period for the team. A 4–0 defeat at Bolton Wanderers, who three months previously had won the FA Cup, on the opening day of the 1958–59 season set the tone for what was to be a disappointing campaign, briefly lifted only by the signing of Revie. Leeds had been third from bottom in the First Division with just twelve points from sixteen matches in early November, but before the end of the month the new man took the field for the first time in the middle of a winning run of four matches that took the club to eleventh place.

Although it had become all too clear that the tough, decisive and inspirational leader the club needed to propel them forward was not going to be manifest in Boxer Bill, Lambton was confirmed as permanent manager early in December 1958. It was not a decision that found favour with the players, who had little respect for him. Chairman Sam Bolton had presumably tried and failed to attract any of the heavyweight managers of the time to Elland Road.

Soon there was open hostility, which was to be reflected on the field of play. The flicker of optimism that had coincided with Revie's arrival on the scene was soon extinguished as Irish captain Wilbur Cush resigned, to be replaced by the experienced Revie. The relationship between manager and team was deteriorating, and transfer demands were made by influential players Grenville Hair and Jack Overfield. Meanwhile, the number of outrageous reversals on the pitch began to mount. Leeds scored three but conceded four at home to Bolton on 20 December, and over the festive period there was little cheer as they encountered successive defeats, 1–0 at home to West Bromwich Albion and 3–1 at Burnley.

It was only to become worse. A thumping 5–1 defeat at Luton in the FA Cup was followed by a 3–1 loss at home to Preston in the league. Soon there would be a 6–2 humiliation at Wolves followed by a 4–0 drubbing at home to Manchester City, who were to eventually escape relegation by just one point. It could not, and did not, last. Abject misery had set in during the period of less than twelve months that Lambton had been in charge. With not only the players but also the board members becoming openly critical of him, there could be only one conclusion. There was relief all round when Lambton himself chose to call it a day, claiming to have been driven out by interference in his training methods.

His own particular brand of management did not advance his career much at his next port of call either. He went to Scunthorpe United, where in April 1959 he was to remain in charge for all of three days. At the time, this spell earned notoriety as an unprecedented example of short-termism in its field, although in view of later claims that he had taken up the position only by verbal agreement, with no contractual documentation in place, commentators may have been a bit hasty in assigning him a place in the record books. It cannot have been a happy time for a man who, after all, would find reflected glory in having been responsible for introducing the legends Revie and Bremner to Elland Road. His subsequent roles in football were low profile. By 1976, when he died at the age of 61 at his home in Nottingham, he had been out of the game for 13 years, having undertaken a short spell as caretaker manager of Grimsby Town and, finally, a 20-month stint in charge of Chester.

Upon Lambton's departure from Leeds, Sam Bolton was faced with the difficult task of procuring the services of a manager who would be capable both of lifting flagging spirits and of driving forward a club whose wider reputation was becoming subject to scorn and ridicule. It was to former Birmingham City manager Arthur Turner, then in charge of Southern League side Headington United (renamed Oxford United in 1960), that Bolton first turned, and he was sure he had got the ideal candidate in place until, at the eleventh hour, Turner had a sudden and unexpected change of mind. Next, Bolton had at the forefront of his mind the former Leeds captain Tommy Burden, who, as an all-action wing-half, had been a crowd favourite in his six years with the club before moving on to Bristol City. Burden, though, had little interest in the post, preferring to continue his playing career in the South-West. Bolton's long and frustrating search was concluded when Queens Park Rangers' manager, Barnsley-born Jack Taylor, agreed a move back to his native Yorkshire.

Taylor made an immediate statement of intent by unloading the veteran players Eric Kerfoot and Jimmy Dunn, and soon had Jack Charlton, who was having a big say in the playing ranks, onside. Charlton recalled:

> We got a manager called Jack Taylor, and his brother Frank joined the club as coach. In those days managers didn't wear tracksuits, but Frank did. He was the first guy who ever took me out on a pitch and taught me how to kick a ball properly – following it through, keeping it low, chipping balls, that sort of thing. One thing he did was to lay down two bricks and place the ball between them, then ask you to run up and hit it full on. You soon learned to keep your eye on the ball! I could talk to the Taylors about the game, and suddenly I felt I had kindred spirits within the club.

Taylor set about the task of managing Leeds by making two important additions to the coaching staff for the forthcoming 1959–60 campaign. Syd Owen, who at Luton Town had won the Footballer of the Year award and gone on to manage the Bedfordshire club, and Les Cocker, who had been trainer there with him, were to go on to enjoy distinguished careers within the game, but their start at Leeds was an inauspicious one. Along with the club they had left Luton for, they suffered a humiliating relegation.

Leeds, who as early as September had lost their free-scoring centre-forward Alan Shackleton to Everton, won just 12 of their 42 matches, despite Shackleton's replacement, Bradford City's John McCole, finding the net on 22 occasions. McCole aside, however, there was little potency among the forwards, and there was too much juggling with the defensive set-up for there to be any semblance of consistency on the park. Taylor had markedly failed to bring about the improvement sought by Bolton, and now another undesired campaign in Division Two lay ahead. It was the chairman's worst nightmare.

With Taylor aiming to restore the reputations of both the club and himself as quickly as possible, there was much summer transfer activity and the kind of optimism among fans that exists at every club with the dawn of a new season. An opening-day 2–0 defeat at Liverpool reined in expectations, however, and soon at Elland Road there would be a 3–1 defeat by Leyton Orient, a 4–1 reverse to Huddersfield and a 5–2 execution by Ipswich Town. The fans, with increasingly little to satisfy them, were turning, and where once there had been supportive noises, the mood had changed to one of contempt for players who were failing to step up to the mark.

Leeds were sinking like a stone, and with another relegation an ever-increasing threat, it became apparent to the directors that, once again, decisive action would have to be taken in an attempt to divert the club from this headlong course with disaster. Two months remained of the season and Taylor had a year to go on his three-year contract, but in a meeting with board member Harry Reynolds, it became clear to the manager that he would have to go and he duly resigned. Taylor never again took a job with a Football League team.

Bremner, a teenager then, is quoted by mightyleeds.co.uk as saying:

> It just wasn't run as a professional football club. To go to see Mr Taylor, Christ, you had to go through one secretary, then another, and finally you would get to the third secretary and she would say he couldn't see you. The only time you ever saw the manager was if you travelled with the first team on a Saturday. Training was just doing laps . . . a kickabout with a ball . . . no ball on a Friday . . . just sprints.
>
> We went to play a crucial game towards the end of the season at Blackburn Rovers. I remember wondering where we were going to eat. In the end, we stopped at a café and had beans on toast. It was all a bit of a rush . . . yet this was the most important game of the season.

Other players were similarly disaffected. One of Taylor's signings, the former Celtic half-back Eric Smith, recalled:

> The players were undisciplined. It wasn't their fault – Jack Taylor was the manager but had let things go. I certainly didn't expect what I saw in the first three or four days. We would go on long training runs and players would walk in with ice lollies in their hands.

Jack Charlton, on the other hand, felt that Taylor was not to blame:

> The other players didn't respond well to the new approach. Their general attitude was that they came into the club to do their bit of training, played their matches and then buggered off. They just weren't interested in developing their own skills or any theory or anything like that.

Now only a 'Special One' would fit the bill. In fact, that elusive being was already at the club, and within days of Taylor's departure, Don Revie was made player-manager. A new footballing era was about to begin in West Yorkshire.

Physiotherapist Bob English, also quoted by mightyleeds. co.uk, remembered:

> The club was not in a good state before Don Revie took over. There wasn't much enthusiasm, I didn't think. Jack Taylor was a nice man, don't get me wrong, but he didn't crack the whip enough. Training was slack, though Don Revie, as a player, was a great fellow as far I am concerned . . . he was one of the ones that really did train. But Taylor never came out to watch people training. I think I remember him only once getting out his tracksuit and coming out to join us. But when Don took over, he was out leading them on.

It is worth noting the parallel universe that would have been created had Revie responded positively to an alternative offer of a first job in management. As Leeds gave thought to promoting from within, south-coast club Bournemouth had already settled on the idea of naming Revie as their player-manager. Contact was made and Revie was on the verge of accepting the post. Peter McConnell, a wing-half who was on Leeds' books for the best part of a decade before joining Carlisle United in 1962, recalled the situation that nearly robbed Leeds of their most successful and revered manager. 'I remember the time when Don took over from Jack Taylor,' McConnell told the *Yorkshire Evening Post*.

> I was sat in the communal bath the day before along with another lad called Jimmy Ashall, a full-back. And Don was saying to us, 'How do you fancy going to Bournemouth?' We said, 'Bournemouth? What's going on there?' and Don replied, 'I've been offered the player-manager's job and I'd like you both – especially you, Peter – to come.' I said, 'I'll have to think about that

one, Don.' My wife was from Leeds and very, very close to her mother. I went home and said, 'How do you fancy going to Bournemouth?' I looked at her face and thought 'She's not right happy about that!' We'd just had a daughter, our Debbie. I said to Don I'd think it over and we were all sat in the dressing-room the next morning and who walks in but Harry Reynolds, the chairman. He said, 'Right, lads, settle down, you are not going training yet, I've got some news.' We were half-guessing he was going to say Jack had got the sack because we were on a bad run. He said, 'I'd like to introduce you to the new manager. Please come in.' And it was Don! That was the Bournemouth trip off.

Ray Fell, long-time chairman of the Leeds United Supporters Club, says: 'It is legendary amongst the older Leeds United fans that when relegation to Division Three threatened in 1961, the then chairman, Harry Reynolds, sat at his desk to compose a letter recommending the prowess of Don Revie to clubs that had expressed an interest in appointing Revie as manager. Harry Reynolds realised that he was recommending exactly what Leeds themselves required, tore up the letter and promptly made Don Revie the manager.'

Revie was to remain a one-club man in the managerial ranks for 13 years, making a huge imprint on the game. He built his new Leeds United on rock-solid foundations, which became the platform for the Second Division title within three years and, once promoted, the runner-up berth in the league and an FA Cup final appearance in their first season back in the top flight. By the early 1970s, the team he created would dominate English football. He was awarded English Manager of the Year three times between 1969 and 1972, and in 1970 he was given the OBE. All told, Revie took his team to two First Division titles, one FA Cup, one League Cup, two Inter-Cities Fairs Cups, one Second Division title and one Charity Shield. They also made it to three more FA Cup finals, one more Inter-Cities Fairs Cup final and one European Cup-Winners' Cup final.

THE EMERGENCE OF 'OLD BIG 'EAD'

Back in 1967, what was being achieved by Clough and Taylor in the fortification of lowly Hartlepools was not going unnoticed in the wider world. Everybody has to start somewhere, and the little cash-strapped Cleveland club, while giving Clough the chance to cut his teeth in management, could only ever be a launch pad for somebody with such intense ambition and unwavering self-belief. Aston Villa, who would be relegated to Division Two in 1966–67, and their better-placed Midlands rivals West Bromwich Albion were among the bigger clubs coveting his services, but the prize of his signature, and that of Taylor, was to go to Derby County. Tim Ward's five-year managerial reign at the Baseball Ground had seen them fall some way short of chairman Sam Longson's desire for top-tier football, and the club was in a kind of limbo, just being, doing and surviving.

It needed igniting, but little could anybody have imagined the inferno that was to develop once Longson had lit the flame in a meeting with Clough and Taylor at Scotch Corner that ended with ink on a contract. Clough started with an undertaking to Rams fans that they would better their 1966–67 finishing position in the league of 17th, and he was close: they ended up 18th.

The 1968–69 season saw the start of the Clough revolution. He had brought in John O'Hare from Sunderland and Alan Hinton from Nottingham Forest, and these very effective players were soon to be joined by Roy McFarland, who was signed as a 19-year-old centre-half from Tranmere Rovers for £25,000 and who quickly became a big influence on a club he would later manage. Kevin Hector and Colin Boulton were already stalwarts of the side, and the new Clough signings went on relentlessly. John McGovern joined from Hartlepool, Willie Carlin arrived from Sheffield United and, against all odds, Clough was able to dissuade the legendary Double-winning Tottenham Hotspur midfielder Dave Mackay from his chosen course of becoming assistant manager of Edinburgh club Hearts, where he had begun his career, and bring him to Derby instead.

A run of success that would see them race to the Division Two title began fittingly with a 3–1 victory over Chelsea at the Baseball Ground. By the end of November, Derby were on top of the pile, and they spent the rest of the season laughing over their shoulders at rivals in vain pursuit. Clough had done it – for his chairman, for the club, for the fans, for the city and for himself. He knew he could deliver, and now Derby could enjoy rubbing shoulders with the best clubs in the land.

Following their elevation to the top flight, Derby got off to a tremendous start, beating relative giants such as Everton, Newcastle and Tottenham. The newcomers were the last Division One side to lose a match. In the end, though, home losses to Coventry and Manchester City and away defeats to Leeds and Arsenal brought a sense of reality back to the club and its fans. It was at this critical point in the campaign that Clough splashed £100,000 on Nottingham Forest's Welsh international defender Terry Hennessey. It was such an inspired signing that Derby went unbeaten through their last dozen matches of the season, climbing in the process to a very respectable finishing position of fourth, thirteen points adrift of champions Everton. It was some achievement, and one that should have brought European football to the Baseball Ground. However, the UEFA Cup place that ought to have been theirs was denied Derby by an FA/ Football League inquiry into financial maladministration.

Attempting to build on his success, Clough broke the club's transfer record by paying Sunderland £170,000 for defender Colin Todd and also brought in Preston North End midfielder Archie Gemmill. Speaking to Neil Moxley of the *Daily Mail* in 2009, Todd recalled of Clough:

> He was very clever in his assessment of people. I was
> a very quiet person. He tried to provoke me. He'd play
> in the five-a-sides and he'd stand there and kick me
> whenever he could get away with it. If I snapped, then

I'd turn on him and he'd be laughing. He had achieved what he wanted. His attitude was: 'You are a defender, you need to get nasty.' He set standards for you to achieve. If you look at players now, I think there would be some who think three completed passes out of five was good. Not for Brian Clough. Five out of five and you stayed in his team for the next game. Three out of five and he'd be asking: 'What kind of standard is that? We are not looking for ordinary here. We want perfection. People who think three out of five completed passes is good, there's the door.'

A new season that had started in promising fashion with a 4–1 defeat of Manchester United in the Watney Cup petered out somewhat and a ninth-pace finish behind Arsenal was all they could muster. But Clough was kidding them, hoodwinking them. All those who thought that the rot was setting in, that Derby had got too big for their boots and were about to pay the price, could think again.

Come the start of the 1971–72 season, Mackay had gone to pastures new, taking up the player-manager position at Swindon Town, and new captain McFarland was confined to his sickbed with flu. Yet a steely, determined Derby negotiated the first twelve matches without defeat and lay in a menacing position in third place. There was a minor blip over the festive period, but there was a resilience to the team that saw them claim second spot at Easter. A breathtaking single-goal victory over Liverpool in their final game of the season shot them to the top of the league, but the odds were heavily stacked against them staying there and claiming the title, on account of the fact that FA Cup-winners Leeds United needed only a point from their game in hand at Wolves to be crowned champions. Leeds were to play this crucial fixture within 48 hours of their glorious cup final defeat of Arsenal, and the Derby contingent didn't stick around to see the outcome. Peter Taylor took the players to Majorca; Clough went on a family holiday to the Scilly Isles.

But on Monday, 8 May 1972 – with Leeds playing their third high-profile match in seven days, minus Mick Jones, who had broken his collarbone at Wembley two days previously, and necessarily fielding several injured and exhausted players – Wolves went two goals up and held on for a shock 2–1 win. Liverpool could also have claimed the title had they beaten Arsenal at Highbury, but they failed to do so and Derby, to general amazement, were the ones with the silverware.

It was the European Cup – a long way from Hartlepools – now for Clough, and there were to be no barriers to their passage on this occasion. Zeljeznicar Sarajevo were easy meat for Derby in the first round, and a stunning 3–0 defeat of Benfica at the Baseball Ground in the second-round first leg paved the way for a place in the quarter-finals. Here the Czechoslovakian side Spartak Trnava were competently dealt with and crack Italian side Juventus loomed ahead in the semis. Defeat at this stage was difficult to stomach for Clough, who went through the rest of his life believing that the West German referee was bribed and the Italians were 'cheating bastards'. Derby could finish only seventh in the league in defence of their title, and soon Clough and Longson were at loggerheads, with the chairman showing increasing irritation at his manager's high profile in the media.

Clough, it seemed, was getting as much airtime on radio and television as newsreaders and weather forecasters, and when he wasn't on air in person there were the mimics such as Mike Yarwood (as indeed there were mimics in pubs, clubs and offices) giving a mighty good and instantly recognisable impression of Old Big 'Ead.

Twelve matches into the 1973–74 season, Longson summoned Clough and Taylor to a meeting in which the resignations of the management pair were tendered. Clough would later call that 'the worst decision I ever made'. In just over six seasons at unfashionable Derby, the pair had won the Second Division championship, the Watney and Texaco cups and the First Division championship, not to mention taking the club to the semi-finals of the European Cup. They would go on, of course, to enjoy further spectacular successes at Nottingham Forest, but it remained a disappointment to Clough that he had not furthered his trophy-plundering at Derby.

While some suggested that Clough should have been offered the job of England manager in 1974, he was persuaded to join Brighton & Hove Albion, taking Peter Taylor with him, and was struggling in the Third Division, suffering a 4–0 defeat at home to Walton & Hersham in the FA Cup and losing 8–2 at home to Bristol Rovers. Meanwhile, two massive jobs were empty: Leeds United, because Revie, rather than Clough, had answered his country's call and become England manager; and Liverpool, because the legendary Bill Shankly had suddenly announced a shock retirement from the game. Clough later claimed, 'I was unlucky enough to be offered the wrong one. If I had gone to Liverpool, I would have died there. I would have become as close to that club as the paint on the walls.'

But in July 1974, to the amazement of many, he went to Leeds. And civil war between Old Big 'Ead and English football's cavaliers was declared.

1

CHANGING OF THE GUARD

I wouldn't say I was the best manager in the business.
But I was in the top one.

Brian Clough

What made Leeds United under Don Revie tick? Besides the many trophies, Revie's Leeds didn't end the season outside of the top four between 1965 and 1974. After the first of their league titles in 1968–69, the manager offered a fascinating insight into his approach to the game of football in an article entitled 'What I Expect from my Players', which appeared in the 1970 *Park Drive Book of Football*. Forty years later, Revie's remarks do not sound dated:

> Some time before Leeds United won even the first of the several honours that have come our way in recent seasons, I told a gathering of the players that if they became champions they would realise, I hoped, that there was more to it than being the top team. I cannot recall my exact words, but remember well the gist of them, which was that it was not sufficient merely to become champions; of equal importance in my book was to behave like champions, off as well as on the field.

This can have many aspects: behaviour on the field, behaviour away from it; appearance on the field, conduct off it. Many aspects, but all contributing towards the whole, the complete, educated, accomplished footballer of today.

Many years ago the great Scottish club Rangers had a foreign manager, one Willie Struth. Over the years many tales have been told about him, some perhaps embellished with the passing of time and in the retelling. But from at least one or two of them there shines a fine example of what I mean, and what I expect from a champion team.

There is the story about how he used to order any player with hair nearing his collar to attend upon the hairdresser; how he roared out two players found in the cheaper seats in a Glasgow cinema with the blast, 'As Rangers, you will occupy seats befitting your position.'

He was said to have been something of a martinet, but I doubt whether any of his players suffered because of that. Indeed, from some who served under him I have heard nothing but praise, and certainly he produced in his players a terrific pride in their club and in their profession.

That of course is how we should be. The more so today when not only the salary but also the image of the player has risen to unparalleled heights; when the public, particularly its younger members, set their sights on the footballer and their standards by him. In addition, any club enjoying a fair measure of success, and certainly any player within any such club, is subject to pressures of publicity never before experienced in the game.

So we have today a situation in which a team taking the title, indeed long before actually achieving it, becomes subject to constant survey – has the eyes of the public upon its every action, both on the field and away from it. In addition, as more and more clubs enter into European competition so the image of the British footballer, and through him the Briton himself, is spread further afield with more and more coverage through press and television.

We thus have the situation in which any club and its players are faced with the dual problem – that of winning matches and doing so with dignity on and off the field.

I could be said, perhaps, to be particularly conscious of this, because of what I still believe to be a totally unfair impression given abroad about Leeds when we first started to chase the honours. I refer, of course, to the suggestion that we were more physical than skilful. I have never subscribed to any such view, neither did I to any suggestion that we were more a defensive side than anything else. Fortunately, for my beliefs the events of the past few seasons have spoken for themselves and by now Leeds are hailed as a side containing as many skills as any, and more than most.

I recall George Best being asked last season, and just before we met them in the FA Cup semi-finals, how he rated Leeds. He replied, 'Their strength is that they have no weaknesses: they also possess a tremendous team spirit and players of great individual skills.' I like to think that George was echoing the thoughts of most of the people in football, but for a long time we had to suffer other things being said about us, and bear it with dignity. And that is what being champions is all about really – wearing a crown with dignity.

Dignified was not the description that Brian Clough would have applied to Revie's Leeds United. On the contrary, he detested their style of football and, as he would candidly admit to the squad he inherited from Revie in 1974, adhered to the idea that Leeds were indeed 'more physical than skilful'. Revie went on to address that attitude, which was not held by Clough alone, by saying:

Let me stress straight away that I am not suggesting an 'after you' type of player on the field. Perhaps it would be as well if I said at this stage what I expect from a player of Leeds United.

On arrival at Elland Road any new boy, be he a young apprentice professional or an already established star, is quick to appreciate that he should combine courage, hard but fair play and complete confidence on the field, with courtesy, good conduct, manners and humility away from it. I do not intend to speak on his need for soccer skills, already obvious or latent. That goes without saying.

To assist in this we hold our own 'educational classes' at United, with members of the staff as the tutors and the incoming teenagers as the pupils. Augmented by advice from outside professional and trade organisations, we inculcate into the lads a knowledge of dining out, checking in to and out of hotels, how to travel in comfort, even how to reply to toasts and many other things. In addition there is the emphasis upon religious advice if they want it and talks on girlfriends, male and female fans, etc. Everything and anything in fact.

The idea behind all this is to ensure that so far as is humanly possible every lad on the staff has, within a short time of joining Leeds United, been taught sufficient to feel comfortable in any kind of company, able to enter any hotel he wishes and also made aware of the temptations as well as the honours and awards that can come his way.

I have heard it said that this is not the function of a football club; that a club's sole concern should be in the promotion of a fine football side and to the winning of more matches than achieved by the opposition. But surely it is all part and parcel of the same thing.

Let me say immediately that no one is more aware than we at Elland Road of the importance of winning matches and of establishing a fine football side with which to do so. Indeed that is the major purpose behind everything we do, but there are other ancillary things to be considered.

One is that while winning matches is of vital importance, the manner in which successes are achieved must also be considered.

The other vital factor ancillary to winning matches, and winning them in the right spirit, is that the boys who obtain these honours for a club and its city, and in turn are feted by them, should be honourable representatives of that club, and that city.

As I said earlier, let there be no question of us trying to put manners before everything else. We are part of a football club, and a successful one at that, and such successes have been achieved only by a complete 100 per cent dedication – being able to match skill with sinew when required in hard but fair combat with the opposition.

But within that requirement it is possible, must be possible, for football to uphold the dignity it has brought into the twentieth century's later years. At the turn of the century and for many years thereafter this great game was considered something of a festival of the cloth-capped. That was never completely accurate. The game has always attracted the intelligentsia – though in much lower numbers it must be admitted – and now, of course, there are almost as many eggheads as those of other shapes attracted to, and attending, the game.

In turn the game has received recognition at the highest level, with Her Majesty the Queen bestowing knighthoods and other decorations (of which I have had the great honour to receive one) upon people in the game.

Football has, indeed, arrived. It is recognised for what it is – a great game for the masses, a source of entertainment for the millions and a combination of employment and enjoyable activities to the fortunate thousands earning their living from the game.

The eyes of the world are upon us and, being under such scrutiny, it behoves us all to do nothing to belittle the game.

Often I think that winning a trophy is almost the easiest part of the exercise. Retaining it, and at the same time one's sense of purpose, modesty and place in things, is infinitely more difficult.

But that's what I expect from my players.

The players nurtured in Revie's caring yet disciplined environment, those who made up the team and whose names tripped off the tongue of even the most befuddled drunk in Whitelocks, the city of Leeds' favourite alehouse – Sprake, Reaney, Cooper, Bremner, Charlton, Hunter, Lorimer, Clarke, Jones, Giles, Gray – loved Revie to a man. He drove them mad sometimes with his idiosyncratic behaviour – the superstitions, the fussy attention to detail, his daft bonding games such as carpet bowls – but they adored his father-figure persona and the family atmosphere created by the boss and his wife Elsie.

Goalkeeper David Harvey's time as a prominent Leeds player arrived in the 1972–73 season, during which he played 63 times, having spent fully 10 years as reserve behind Gary Sprake. It was also in 1962 that he had his first match as an international, helping Scotland to a 2–0 victory over Denmark (although Harvey was born in Leeds, his father was Scottish). Though Harvey must have been relieved to have a regular place on the side, the '72–73 campaign was in the end a disappointing one for the team. Within a few days, they lost the 1973 FA Cup final to Sunderland and then the European Cup-Winners' Cup final to AC Milan. However, Harvey took plenty of plaudits next season, which Leeds began with an unheard of 29 matches unbeaten. The league championship was theirs and Harvey earned his first title medal. He was then picked as Scotland's first-choice keeper for the World Cup in West Germany, not only proving the virtue of patience but also revealing the determination of Revie to maximise the potential of every one of his players.

Harvey remembers: 'Don Revie was like a second father to me and I owe him plenty. He took care of me right from the day I joined the club as an eleven year old and when my frustrations at being unable to break into the first team became overbearing, he would be a calming, reassuring influence. At one point, I became determined to get away, but, luckily for me, he wouldn't let me go. In fact, they offered me a lot of money to stay.

'Then one season it all became too much for me. I played, I think, two reserve games, and any footballer will tell you that is a nightmare scenario. Don agreed to put me on the transfer list and there I remained for all of ten months. There were constant rumours of interest from this club and that club, and indeed I had a couple of direct offers, yet each time I went to Don to ask if there had been any contact from other clubs, he would simply stonewall: "Not a thing, son." He could be as cute as a barrowload of monkeys at times. "I can't understand it," he'd say. "A player of your quality and not a single enquiry."

'One day in the dressing-room, unable to tolerate this any longer, I said to him, "This is no bloody use to me." Whereupon he seized me warmly by the throat and hung me up by the collar on a coat hook. There I stayed, unable but frantically trying to wriggle free, for what seemed an eternity and it was only the welcome entrance of the groundsman, John Reynolds, that saved me from further embarrassment, as he set me free. The next day, Les Cocker, our trainer, sought me out to tell me that the boss wanted to see me. I feared the worst, but Don apologised profusely for his behaviour, while insisting that I should not have said what he thought I'd said, which was: "This *club* is no bloody use to me." I would never criticise Leeds as a club, nor indeed Don Revie. I've always loved them and always will. It was just one of those misunderstandings where someone mishears what is being said.

'But the great Don Revie apologising to a little upstart like me? What a man. As long as you worked hard, he would do anything for you and more than once was the time he got me out of a scrape or a bit of bother.'

Revie was going now. Off to manage England. So who would replace him? Was it possible to replace him? Certainly, not least in the minds of the squad he left behind, it needed to be someone of great stature. Johnny Giles, United's midfield brainbox, was overwhelmingly the dressing-room vote. Within Leeds United, 'The Brains' was the tag given to Giles, and Revie had great respect for him, later saying, 'John was a superlative soccer technician whose ability had no limits. He had great natural aptitude but was always working hard to improve. When we finished a training session he would go off to the gym to work more on his own.' Giles wasn't the only candidate, though. Surely any manager worth his salt would climb over dead bodies to take over England's reigning champions. And Billy Bremner, the heart of Revie's squad, threw his hat into the ring. The guessing game went on into the early hours in many a household. One name was unconsidered: Brian Clough. He despised Leeds. Didn't like their departing manager. Had publicly called them cheats. No way.

Peter Lorimer, who made his Leeds United debut at the age of 15 in 1962 and went on to become the club's all-time record goal-scorer, recalls: 'Clough's dislike of Leeds went back a long way, to his days at Derby County. They were an up-and-coming side who won the league once, but we had lots of games in which we beat them and he, I think, didn't like the fact that we had the measure both of himself and of his team.

'There was certainly a great rivalry between himself and Don Revie. They hated each other with a passion. It was a bitter feud between the two of them. I sometimes wonder if it was because they both had their roots in Middlesbrough: two men the same age from the same small town with one having established a great pedigree in the game and the other looking on somewhat enviously at his achievements. He first came to our close-up attention really when we played Derby twice in the space of a fortnight in 1973. We beat them in the league on the Saturday and had been drawn against them in the FA Cup two weeks later. He made this statement that there was no way Leeds could possibly come out on top again on their home turf, but he was made to look somewhat foolish when we beat them again. He naturally had the needle with us.'

Eddie Gray was also conscious of that antipathy. Of all the players who have represented Leeds over the past 50 years, Gray is widely recognised as the most naturally gifted. A schoolboy international for Scotland, the Glaswegian signed professional forms for Leeds at the age of 16 after, it is said, Jack Charlton recommended to Revie that he snap up the youngster because he didn't fancy playing against him twice a season if he joined another club. Gray made his first-team debut on New Year's Day 1966, shortly before his 18th birthday. Over a period spanning almost two decades, the orthodox left-winger terrorised opposing defences and thrilled the Leeds fans with mesmerising footwork, a feint that dumped full-backs on their rears and pinpoint crossing of the ball. He remembers the events leading up to Clough's appointment vividly.

'In the spring of 1974, rumours began to circulate about a possible change of manager in light of England's failure to qualify for that year's World Cup in West Germany,' says Gray. 'The best club manager in the country at the time was our own Don Revie and it was no surprise, albeit a disappointment to us all at Elland Road, that the Football Association made the offer to Don and he accepted it. The general belief in the camp was that the job at Leeds would go to Johnny Giles. Indeed, he had been told he had got it. We were out on Fullerton Park kicking a ball about one afternoon and Johnny came up to Peter Lorimer and me and said, "I'm the new manager." Then it was discovered that somebody else in the camp had put in his application. That someone else was Billy Bremner. Billy, of course, was a big character at the club and quite within his rights to apply for the job, but here, now, was a dilemma for the board.

I think the chairman, Manny Cussins, and his board were wary about running the risk of having a split camp, but in fact Johnny turned it down so they weren't put in that position.'

There were other people as concerned as United's board. Fringe player Peter Hampton spent 10 years at Elland Road, making his debut as a 17 year old in the 1971–72 season and fitting in 83 first-team appearances before a £175,000 transfer fee took him to Stoke City in 1980. It was all going well for Hampton, with a first-team blooding, England youth honours and European action under his belt, though two giants of the game in Terry Cooper and Trevor Cherry, and sometimes Paul Madeley, were generally keeping his name off the team sheet in his preferred position of left-back. He was not yet 20 when, in the summer of 1974, the jungle drums started beating and word of Revie's departure became the talk of football.

'I was only on the fringe of things and, where one or two people were probably initially in the know, I had got no inkling,' says Hampton. 'All of a sudden, he's gone and got the England job. If the chance to manage your country is offered, then you're going to take it, aren't you? But I've gone through life believing that the directors of Leeds United never gave Don the credit for what he did and what he achieved, and that may have played a part in his decision-making process. They always thought, I feel, that it was down to them, and not Revie, that Leeds had done so well. Directors are like that, though, aren't they? Always have been. It's that blazer mentality. It was without a shadow of a doubt Don Revie who built, engineered and crafted the great Leeds of the '60s and '70s. His choice and treatment of his staff, his empathy with his players and his acquisitions were spot-on. He was truly one of the greats. Yet in modern-day pontifications and summaries about the giants of our game, he is never mentioned, and that, to me, is both surprising and shocking.

'The obvious thing for the directors to have done when Revie left was to appoint John Giles as his successor. That is what I would have done and it was what many of the players wanted.'

Numerous other players share the view that the very thought of Clough's appointment at United came as a shock, among them Joe Jordan, Leeds' former striker. As Jordan would doubtless agree, any debate about the best, most enduring and most prolific strike partnerships the English game has ever seen would naturally include the one enjoyed by Allan Clarke and Mick Jones in Leeds United colours as the 1960s turned into the '70s. Jones had scored 63 goals in 149 appearances for Sheffield United and earned two caps for England when he joined Leeds in 1967 for £100,000 with Blades manager John Harris lamenting that allowing the transfer would be the biggest mistake the South Yorkshire club had ever made. Clarke joined Leeds from Leicester in 1969 for a then British record transfer fee of £165,000 and his first-season haul of 26 goals gave birth to the nickname 'Sniffer'. His match-winning diving header goal in the 1972 centenary FA Cup final against Arsenal is still the favourite of many Leeds fans. The potency of the pairing is evident in statistics that show a joint haul of 221 goals in a combined 585 appearances. For this partnership to be dislodged, any newcomer would have to be both very good and lucky. Joe Jordan was both.

He was a teenager when he was spotted by a Leeds scout while playing for Greenock Morton in his native Scotland. A £15,000 fee took him south, but the youngster was to endure months turning into years of frustration as he saw his way into the first team barred by the exploits of Jones and Clarke. He consequently became all too familiar with reserve-team football. There was the far from inconsiderable inconvenience, too, of an introduction to English football which saw his facial features rearranged and transformed into something out of a Hammer horror film. In a reserve match at Coventry's Highfield Road, he went up for a ball with an opposing player and came down minus his four front teeth. Jordan, now first-team coach at Tottenham, says of the incident, 'I don't remember much about it or the name of the culprit. All I know is that it was a big defender who was very brave.' Jordan had to have dentures fitted, but he always removed them before matches. Without them, he looked frightening enough to earn the nickname 'Dracula' and his gap-toothed roar is an abiding image of football in days gone by.

His first-team chance at Leeds came when Jones began to suffer badly from a knee injury that was to shunt him into premature retirement at the age of 30. The 1972–73 season saw Jordan make sixteen league starts in which he scored a very handy nine goals. He was left out of the team that contested the FA Cup final against Sunderland only to get the call-up a few days later for the European Cup-Winners' Cup final against AC Milan. In what was a memorable month of May for Jordan, he was given his Scotland debut in a 1–0 defeat to England at Wembley. The lad from Carluke, Lanarkshire, had well and truly arrived on the scene. Jordan was a regular in the following season, when Leeds took the league title. He scored seven goals in twenty-five league games and before the season's end he'd earned nine more Scotland caps and scored two goals for his country, including one against England at Hampden. This excellent run of form earned him a place on the Scotland squad for the 1974 World Cup finals, where he scored two goals. By the end of his international career he would be the only Scottish player to have scored in three World Cups – a record that still stands today. While Jordan was in West Germany, back at his club headquarters in Leeds cataclysmic events were unfolding.

Jordan recalls: 'It was more of a shock than a surprise when Don Revie left Leeds United for the England job. Good managers are always in demand, whether it be by rival clubs or on the occasion when your country comes calling, and it is beyond question that Don was a good manager, a top manager. Leeds were never out of the top four over a ten-year period under his command and what makes that record extra special is that, unlike in modern-day English football, where the battle for the Premier League title is between three clubs – Manchester United, Arsenal and Chelsea – in those days you had Leeds fighting it out with Manchester United, Manchester

City, Liverpool, Everton, Arsenal and Derby, to name but a few of the great teams of the era. Not long before Don had established Leeds as a formidable force, you had titles won by Burnley, Tottenham and Ipswich, so by and large it was always extremely keenly contested by several clubs and took an awful lot of winning.

'That Don had Leeds competing every single year must have impressed the Football Association and that is why, when it came time for them to make a change, it was no surprise that he was their choice. The shock element comes with the realisation that you have lost your manager and the accompanying consternation about who his replacement might be – and to what extent you may or may not figure in his plans.

'For my own part, I was only 22 years of age, but in the summer of 1974 I was comfortable in the knowledge that my fledgling career was going very well. I had been in good form in the qualifiers for the World Cup, scoring a crucial headed goal against Czechoslovakia; I played a full part in Leeds winning the championship that season; then in the Home Internationals, I was on target when we beat England 2–0 at Hampden Park, and at the World Cup itself I scored the second goal in a 2–0 win over Zaire in the first group game and a last-minute equaliser in a 1–1 draw with Yugoslavia. Unfortunately, while Scotland finished the group unbeaten we went out of the competition at the group stage on goal difference, and my return from that tournament coincided with a certain pending appointment at my club.'

Don Revie was appointed the new England manager in succession to Sir Alf Ramsey on 4 July 1974. Sixteen days later, Brian Clough left Brighton to become the new Leeds United manager, accepting a five-year contract worth a reported £20,000 a year. Peter Taylor chose to stay at Brighton as the new boss.

Harvey sums up the mood in the camp, saying: 'Like the rest of us, I was devastated when Don left the club to take up England duties. The mood of desolation he left behind was hardly lifted when his successor was announced.'

Where Revie had gone to great lengths to explain what he expected of his players, a rather more succinct overview of Clough's requirements can be found in the manager's player rule book that was in place during Clough and Taylor's time at Derby. It included the following instructions:

- Smoking on the Ground or in the Dressing Room during training hours strictly forbidden. Players must also refrain from smoking in the coach or train prior to the Match.
- The players shall at all times obey the orders and instructions of the Manager or Trainer.
- Disciplinary action will be taken against any player absenting himself without leave.
- Players will be allowed to go to dances up to and including Tuesday (except when a mid-week match is to be played). And also Wednesday if permission is granted by the Trainer.
- No player is allowed to order sports gear or goods of any kind for himself from any shop or store without the prior permission of the Manager or Secretary.
- No player will be allowed to have direct or indirect connections with a licensed premises.
- No player will be allowed to ride motor-cycles.
- No player must under any circumstances make statements to the press appertaining to Club matters without the prior permission of the Manager.

On the one hand, a caring, arm-round-the shoulder approach; on the other, a hard-hitting list of don't-dos. Come what may, there was going to be a stark change in the atmosphere at Elland Road. The appointment promised to be interesting.

2

'FORGET REVIE'

I call myself 'Big Head' just to remind myself not to be.

Brian Clough

Well, he'd been appointed. But where was he? On holiday with his family somewhere. And that's where Brian Clough was staying until he was good and ready to grace Elland Road, home of the champions, with his presence. The disdain Clough had shown for the club in the past meant that he was far from likely to receive an enthusiastic welcome. Peter Lorimer relates: 'I first came across him and discovered his true feelings when, in the early 1970s, I won the Sports Personality of the Year award at the Yorksport dinner under the auspices of Yorkshire Television at the Queens Hotel in Leeds. This was a prestigious award, voted for by Yorkshire Television viewers, that had previously been won by the Formula One racing driver Jackie Stewart and the golfer Nick Faldo. There was a lot of kudos attached to it and there were always important figures invited to present the awards. On this particular occasion, the man handing over the trophies was no less than the prime minister of the day, Yorkshireman Harold Wilson. The guest speaker was Brian Clough.

'I duly received my award from the Prime Minister but missed out on the pleasure of listening to Old Big 'Ead on this Sunday evening because we had a cup replay against

Manchester United at Villa Park the following evening, and while Don kindly allowed me to collect the award, he ensured that there was a car waiting outside to whisk me straight to Villa Park to join up with the rest of the squad. I was therefore in blissful ignorance about what was such a diatribe that it quickly gathered notoriety for its ridiculous content. These were the days when there were no mobile telephones, of course, and thank goodness for that, because that night the phone at our team hotel never stopped ringing with requests from reporters wanting to speak to someone about Mr Clough's outburst concerning Leeds United and me at the dinner in Leeds.

'Even before he was due to make his scheduled speech, he got up and told a packed auditorium that he had sat there and listened to a load of codswallop about the greatness of Leeds United and the brilliance of Peter Lorimer. It was time now, he asserted, that he had his say. He had had enough of being made to sit through all this bullshit. But before he embarked on his speech, he said, the audience could sit there and wait patiently, just as he had done, until he had paid a visit to the lavatory. Well, of course, with the Prime Minister and all the local dignitaries of the city of Leeds being there, this sudden announcement of an unscheduled break in the proceedings did not go down too well. When he returned, he launched full throttle into an undisguised attack on Leeds United. Calling us "cheats", he said that we had never won anything fairly.

'As for me, he held that the Sports Personality of the Year award had gone to the wrong man. I wasn't a sportsman, he said. I was a cheat. I was always diving. Always trying to get the opposition into trouble with the referee. It amounted to a full-frontal assault on both the club and me, in front of a largely partisan audience in our home city. Of course, he got shouted down. People were on their feet and telling him to sit down. The boos started and he never got to finish his speech. It must have been quite funny on the night. I wish I'd been there. I quite enjoy a bit of banter and, of course, people are entitled to their opinions. There is no way I would have responded, however. I would merely have enjoyed the surrealness of it all.'

This, as many within the footballing community came to understand, was Clough's unique and unequivocal style. Someone who knew by word of mouth about this reputation was the much-travelled Hugh McIlmoyle, who is rated by many as the best header of a football the game has ever seen and scored a career total of 180 goals in some 500 games for Leicester, Rotherham, Carlisle, Wolves, Bristol City, Carlisle again, Middlesbrough, Preston, Morton and Carlisle for a third time in a career spanning 1959–75. Like Clough, McIlmoyle was a Middlesbrough hero. In the 1970–71 season, he and John Hickton were the scourge of Division Two defences, plundering 38 goals between them for Middlesbrough. For McIlmoyle, scoring goals was second nature, as simple as peeling an orange, and yet there is awe in his voice when he considers the predatory exploits of the man who preceded him as a Boro striker.

At Ayresome Park on 26 September 1970, McIlmoyle produced such an outstanding performance in a 6–2 defeat of Queens Park Rangers, who featured swanky players like Rodney Marsh and Terry Venables, that it has always been known on Teesside as 'the McIlmoyle Match'. Boro were two goals down inside five minutes and floundering until McIlmoyle, a Scot, took the game by the scruff of the neck. Scoring two bullet headers and laying on a hat-trick for Hickton, McIlmoyle so wound up the rattled visitors that there were to be personal repercussions. The striker ended the game with a badly broken nose, inflicted by a head-butt from QPR defender Dave Clement.

Boro's fans had not seen a one-man display like it for a long time; not since, in fact, the glory days at the club of that other prolific striker Brian Clough, who had departed in acrimonious circumstances nine years previously.

'Brian Clough was so good a manager,' says McIlmoyle, 'that his playing career is barely mentioned. But when you consider that he scored 204 goals in 222 games over a 10-year period at Boro – and five of those came in one game, a 9–0 thrashing of Brighton on the opening day of the 1958–59 season – then he has to have been just about the best striker Britain has ever seen. That record almost defies belief.

'When I joined Middlesbrough, the left-back and captain there, Gordon Jones, had played with Cloughie, and he told me that he was a difficult person if not to like then certainly to get to know. He was something of a loner. Normally, footballers mix quite well, and that was evident in the 1950s in the fact that players would enjoy a game of bridge or a round of golf together. But Gordon's view was that Clough was a bad mixer. He could come across as selfish, aloof and arrogant. He certainly was not well liked in the dressing-room. Where the rest of the boys would get changed together and exchange banter, this isolated figure would be in a cubicle on his own. His one close friend in the club was the goalkeeper, Peter Taylor.

'When I joined, there also remained a lot of bitterness in the club about the way Clough departed Boro for a new career with local rivals Sunderland. They felt he had let Middlesbrough down. In those days, players didn't move between clubs like they do now. Many were one-club men, and it was seen as an act of betrayal if they turned their back on one club in favour of another. People thought he'd abandoned Middlesbrough. The £55,000 transfer fee was a record at the time, and you do wonder what figure such a devastating finisher would have commanded in today's inflated market. I think that as far as his personality goes, he was the same as a young player at Middlesbrough as he was when he became a manager: abrasive, self-centred and opinionated. I was told that Clough had created friction within the camp by publicly accusing his defence of deliberately leaking goals. This led to punch-ups and, ultimately, to several members of the team signing a petition to get him demoted as captain. He was a complex person. But both as a player and manager, he was consistently able to produce the goods. He didn't just let his mouth run away with him. He knew what he was talking about.

'If ever you did see him, he was never quiet. He was the sort of bloke who had to say something. He couldn't just walk by. If he saw an old woman crossing the road he'd have to help her along, chatting from pavement to pavement. And if he saw somebody doing something wrong, he'd be just as quick to tell them off. I liked him. I did. And I'm sure everybody in the media liked him, too. He was news and he didn't shy away from making it. I liked the way he called a spade a bloody shovel, and I think anybody who engaged with him on that level couldn't fail to get along with him.'

There were elements of the ridiculous about Clough; his way of operating could seem thoroughly peculiar and was unique to him. Though McIlmoyle never played under Clough, he witnessed his quirky personality on numerous occasions. 'When Clough was managing Derby,' he recalls, 'I went down there as a Carlisle player in 1967 and we beat them. In the tunnel afterwards, there was no need for him to speak to me, because I didn't even know him, but he said, "Well played, young man. You gave our centre-half the runaround today, and that's no mean feat because he's going to be the England centre-half sooner rather than later." This was Roy McFarland. Clough must have been disappointed at being beaten at home but still found a kindly word for an opposing player.

'The next time I met him was at the Scotch Corner Hotel, where the A1 meets the A66. I was a Middlesbrough player by this time, and I'd got off to such a good start there that the local newspapers had begun doing articles comparing Clough and me. The routine was that I would drive to the hotel from home to be picked up by the Middlesbrough team coach. Derby must have been meeting there too, and as I was sitting alone drinking a cup of coffee, Clough presented himself in front of me and said, "I've been reading in the papers that you are a better player than I ever was. Let me tell you that you will never be as good a player as I was. And you'll never score as many goals as I did." I said, "Well you're probably right, Mr Clough," to which he came back, "I know I'm right, young man.

On both counts." Then, as quickly and unexpectedly as he had arrived, he was gone. In the normal course of events, you'd expect someone coming up to you when you're sitting there minding your own business to introduce themselves, exchange a pleasantry or two and then say what they've got to say. Not Cloughie. He was straight in there. That's the way he was. He'd come out with these one-liners and you'd be so taken aback that you didn't have a chance to respond.

'I recall training for a couple of weeks at Leicester when I was carrying an injury as a Middlesbrough player. I knew a lot of the backroom staff at Leicester and they were telling me how Clough had come over from Derby to buy David Nish, a very talented left-back, and wanted at the same time to buy Peter Shilton. This is where you marvel at Clough's audacity. Apparently, he pulled up in the car park, breezed through reception without a word, climbed the stairs to the boardroom and without so much as a cursory knock at the door simply burst in and demanded: "Right, then, how much do you want for David Nish? I am not leaving this boardroom until you have sold David Nish to me." Then and there they sold him, actually for a then British transfer record of £225,000. Nish was to go on and win England caps, once again typifying Clough's eye for a player he knew he could mould into something a bit special. But the way he bought him was outrageous. You imagine, from his ability to gatecrash a board meeting like that, that he would have the daring to romp unannounced into a television studio and commandeer the whole network!'

For Lorimer, however, his first experience of Clough's forthright demeanour did not inspire optimism about a future friendship. Clough was indeed outrageous. And now he was Lorimer's boss – *in absentia*.

'In came Cloughie, only not straight away,' says Lorimer. 'He was on a family holiday in Majorca when his appointment was announced and he let it be known that he would arrive at Leeds when he was good and ready. He was certainly not going to interrupt a holiday abroad and everyone could just wait.

Straight away, then, he showed no great desire or commitment, which you could perhaps understand, though even then only to a minimal extent, if you were talking about a third- or fourth-tier club with only naked ambition at stake. With Leeds, you were talking one of the biggest clubs in Britain, Europe and the world. We had just won the league title, for goodness sake, with a European campaign beckoning. What message, then, did "Leeds can wait" give out? This was no doubt his way of letting everyone know that he wasn't daunted by the task at hand. "Leeds? So what?"'

Big defender Gordon McQueen, who made his United debut against Derby in March 1973, recalls: 'If it was no great surprise when Don Revie walked out of the door at Leeds, then it was certainly a huge shock to see Brian Clough strolling in through the other door. Stories had been circulating for some time linking Don with Everton and various other clubs, and the feeling was that he was perhaps looking for a big pay day, which duly came his way when he was offered the England job.

'But Brian Clough as his replacement? There was incredulity around the place given the bitter rivalry between himself and Leeds, the disparaging remarks he had made about the club, the manager and the players. Revie had loved to beat Clough's sides and vice versa, and Clough's appointment at Leeds had a distinctly uneasy feel about it from the start. From my own perspective, I was just a young lad of 22 when Clough took over and not so set in my ways as the older players like Johnny Giles, Peter Lorimer and Eddie Gray. Clough had already made a big name for himself in the game through winning the championship with Derby County, and for me it was quite exciting to have someone with such a high profile at the helm.

'Cloughie was always fairly positive towards me. I remember Billy Bremner saying to me as soon as Clough arrived, "It won't be long before you're in there asking for a pay rise." Too right! There were no agents in those days and you fended for yourself. Here was I, just a young boy from Scotland in amongst a World Cup-winner in Jack Charlton, the Scotland captain in Billy

Bremner and a whole squad packed with international players, and if you were going to be starry-eyed, this was the place for it. Of course I was going to dare to ask the new manager for a pay rise and he duly delivered – a tenner a week I think. That was the bumptious youngster at work. I had no preconceptions, no fear, really. But I could understand the antipathy towards the new manager from these giants of the game who had built their club into the most feared side in the land and one of the most respected throughout Europe and the world. Cloughie was something of a loose cannon. It was a staggering decision to appoint him, and the Leeds board of the time had a lot to answer for. Both Johnny Giles and Billy Bremner were good candidates for the job, and maybe the directors couldn't make up their minds between the two and fudged the issue by going instead for someone with a track record in management.'

As the squad awaited Clough's arrival, the media were having a field day. Testimony to his lifetime's work as a humble journalist and seeker after truth at Leeds United are sufficient newspaper cuttings to wallpaper every room of John Wray's neat detached house in the Leeds suburb of Horsforth. Meticulously kept over a period spanning more than four decades, they amount to a seamless historical commentary on a football club that, whether it intends to or not, whether it likes it or not, has for many years been in the habit of producing newsworthy items on an almost daily basis. It is a club with a long tradition of attracting publicity, whether it be for the right or wrong reasons, and it has rarely failed to live up to the advice given to John as a young man setting out to report on them. 'If you're covering Leeds United,' a senior journalist told him, 'you won't have to go looking for stories. They'll come looking for you.'

The Clough episode gave rise to some of the most colourful to emerge from Elland Road over the years, and few are better placed to speak with authority on the subject than John. The headlines and John's words, from his reports for the Bradford *Telegraph & Argus*, tell the story as vividly as a motion picture:

IT'S OFFICIAL – FA ASK FOR REVIE'S RELEASE

The Football Association have officially asked Leeds United to release Don Revie for the England manager's job, though neither he nor the Leeds board of directors will breathe a word about this not altogether unexpected development.

DELIGHTED CLOUGH TELLS OF 'EXCITING PROSPECT'

In his first exclusive interview since becoming Leeds United's manager Brian Clough talked to me about the 'exciting prospect' of inheriting League football's top job in management. 'Leeds United is a superbly run club with immense talent both in the dressing-room and among the backroom staff. I don't envisage any problems.'

LEEDS ALSO WANTED TO RECRUIT TAYLOR

Leeds United, jubilant at clinching the services of Brighton manager Brian Clough to succeed Don Revie, were at the same time bemoaning their failure to land Clough's assistant Peter Taylor. Until today it was thought the pair were inseparable and when Leeds chairman Manny Cussins travelled to Brighton yesterday to persuade Brighton to part with Clough he had a mandate from his directors to get Taylor too.

ENIGMA WHO WILL MOVE IN WITH REVIE'S GHOST

Some call Brian Clough 'Rent-a-Gob'. Others are even less complimentary about the man Leeds United have chosen to succeed Don Revie. Yet it is impossible to sum up in one phrase the enigma that is Clough. Many have tried and failed. Indeed it is my experience that the critics who have pilloried him most are those who have never met him.

CLOUGH BREEZES IN FOR HIS FIRST DAY

A bronzed Brian Clough breezed into Elland Road to start his new job as manager of League champions Leeds United today and immediately set about making up for lost time. Shrugging aside a suggestion that he should have been with his players ten days ago when he was appointed manager, instead of flying back to Majorca to continue his holiday, Clough said: 'No one has yet accused me of that to my face so I'm not prepared to discuss it.'

Wray, who charts his career in the media in the hugely entertaining 2008 book *Leeds United and a Life in the Press Box*, recalls: 'My first sighting of Clough at Leeds was when he drove into work on his first day – I remember it being a very wet morning – in what I thought was a Mercedes but turned out to be an Audi. Embarrassingly, I filed a story mentioning a Mercedes, but my excuse was that the logos were very similar! It was just like a Hollywood legend arriving, with a battery of cameras and media figures from all over the country forming a real scrum. It was such a big story. He got out of the car with his two little lads and Manny Cussins, the chairman, welcomed him. They walked towards the main entrance. Manny was first of all to show his new manager the dressing-rooms. The media pack followed and it all became a bit unwieldy. Clough took umbrage, turned on Manny and boomed, "So this is how you run your football club, is it?" They were off on the wrong foot straight away.'

Old Big 'Ead was here now. And so to the job in hand. Says Eddie Gray: 'When Cloughie came, he brought with him a little, for want of a better word, trainer – not a coach – in Jimmy Gordon. Don't forget, I wasn't training because of my injuries, but I was watching with interest from the sidelines. Under Don, we were used to reporting for training at ten o'clock precisely and when ten o'clock came it was all systems go. Jimmy would come up, fair play to him, at ten o'clock, but he would simply jog the boys around the park, avoiding doing anything until Cloughie came up. The boys thought, "What's going on here?"'

Peter Hampton, a defender who joined Leeds as an apprentice in 1971, relates: 'On his second day at Leeds, Clough organised a practice match at Fullerton. He wasn't there to blow the whistle for the kick-off, but we decided to start without him and kick off we did. It was some time later when he emerged up the steps with his two young boys, and without so much as a sideways glance, he went over with them to the pitch next door and started kicking a ball about. He completely ignored this practice match. So what were we to deduce from that? My interpretation was that he was not out to be impressed by anyone. He had made up his mind what he was going to do – what team he was going to pick and so on – and would not be dissuaded from his set course of action. In fact, much of the training was taken by Jimmy Gordon and this was a bit of a joke, really. He would walk around like a sergeant major, with a brush in his hand that he used as a prop as he barked the instruction: "And . . . stand to attention!" You would have to stop what you were doing and stretch yourself to your tallest to listen to the latest battle plan. Crackers! It was just so daft it was pathetic.'

And Lorimer remembers: 'The Charity Shield was ten days away. To say that, as a squad, we were amazed by events would be an understatement. Usually, when a new manager arrives to take over a club, the priority on the first morning is an introductory meeting in which there is a chat with everybody, the manager reveals his hopes, plans and ambitions, and announces what his first steps will be. Clough didn't do anything. He had sent in ahead of him his physio and fitness trainer, Jimmy Gordon, and his first two player signings for Leeds, John McGovern and John O'Hare. So on Clough's first morning, Jimmy initiated training as he had been doing for the previous few days while we all thought that after 20 minutes or so the gaffer would appear and we would soon be working on tactics, ball skills, set pieces and the like, as is the norm. Not a bit of it. Jimmy kept looking over anxiously to see if the boss was coming over the horizon, but there was no sign. It was a deliberate ploy.

'When he did arrive, we were all sitting down on the grass having completed our routines. There was a bit more training, though nothing specialised, before Clough announced that there would be a five-a-side game in which upon his instruction the next goal would be the winner. We were soon to learn, as this became part of our daily training ritual, just how babyish the man could be. You simply could not get off the training field until his team had got the last goal. If you were on the opposing team to him, you could score five goals and every one would be ruled out by him for some imaginary indiscretion. Then his team would contrive a goal out of handballs, fouls, offsides and skulduggery, and it would be declared the winner. Very childish. Anyway, we soon worked out that the quicker his side got a goal, the sooner we would be home from training, so plans were laid accordingly. But all of this was most strange, not at all what you would expect in a Leeds United set-up.'

It was certainly not Revie's idea of productive management, nor a situation he would have tolerated. For a group of players used to the fatherly presence of their long-time manager, Clough's idiosyncrasies were difficult to embrace. Eddie Gray remembers: 'Every pre-season, the boys would have a get-together at The Mansion at Roundhay. It was a smart do, with all the directors, the players, the staff and their wives and girlfriends, and there would be a lavish dinner with a band playing. It was always 7.30 p.m. for 8 p.m. Cloughie came at 10.30 p.m. in a tracksuit on this night of all nights, the first opportunity for everybody to meet the man. In so doing, I think he was trying to stamp his authority on the club. The message he wanted to impart, I think, was that he was tougher than Don, a man who was such an idol to the players and the fans and the city in general. Such a powerful character. You can understand it in a way. What Cloughie was saying was, "Forget about him. I'm here now."'

'FORGET REVIE'

The business of setting about retaining their league title and embarking on another tension-packed European campaign was due to start any day now. But first, the new manager had something to say . . .

3

CHARACTER ASSASSINATIONS

Players lose you games, not tactics.
There's so much crap talked about tactics by people
who barely know how to win at dominoes.

Brian Clough

Friday, 2 August, the players' lounge, Elland Road. Clough has gathered together the full squad. He wants to make an address. And Peter Lorimer, all these years later, still cannot believe its tone. 'After about seven days, Clough did what had been expected on day one and he called a meeting,' says Lorimer. 'The oratory went thus: "You might have wondered why I haven't done this earlier but I wanted to have a look at everything that was going on here, what happens and to form my own opinions. I did not want to be influenced by the opinions of others. I wanted to make up my own mind." You thought that was fair, that what he was saying was sensible and measured.

'However, he then ventured, in those sort of semi-sentences in which he spoke, "But. There's something I've got to tell you. You lot. Before I start working with you, I've got to tell you that you may have won everything – league titles, cup competitions, big European games – but in my book you have never won any one of those things fairly." And then he went through everyone individually, starting with the goalkeepers, through the defenders, midfielders and forwards, basically hurling gratuitous criticisms man for man. In my own case, he repeated what he had said at that awards dinner: that I was a good player but I had this habit of going down too easily, which got people into trouble. He classed this as cheating.

'Last in line was Eddie Gray, who, unfortunately, had had more than his share of injuries in the game. He had major problems with a thigh strain – a nightmare injury, actually – and Clough's compassionate view on this was: "And you . . . if you had been a racehorse, they'd have put you down years ago. You're always injured." Very unsympathetic. And quite insulting. Nobody who saw Eddie Gray play would tell you anything other than he was a quite brilliant winger who teased and tormented defenders, was an excellent crosser of a ball and scored his share of goals, some of them breathtaking in their quality.

'Throughout this series of character assassinations, we remained silent, affording the new boss the respect he deserved as he delivered his opening address. At the end, to our complete amazement, the first player to put his hand up to speak was Paul Madeley, who, generally in life, never said anything to anybody. Paul said, "We have listened to what you have had to say, and I for one have found it a total insult. I don't agree with anything you have said. Nothing was constructive. It was a demolition job." We were starting the new season in a matter of days.'

Gray observes: 'Because we had won the league, the first big game of the new season – and Cloughie's first in charge – was the Charity Shield. If Brian had come in and just thought, "I know I'm a bit of a character and I've got this reputation, but I'll just play it cool and let them get on with it and slowly stamp my authority," he would probably have been fine. Instead, he went about things in the wrong way. He came in like a bull in a china shop. Saying things like, "You can throw your medals in the bin," brought a response from people like Bremner and Giles of, "What the hell are you on about?" And quite rightly.

It was insulting. We had just won the league on the back of going the first 29 games unbeaten.

'I later became a manager myself and the first golden rule is that you have to get the players onside. You can be hard with them and, if you're Sir Alex Ferguson, you can be harsh with them, but you need them to be playing for you. If the players are not allies of yours, then you have got nothing. You also want the directors and the supporters on your side. I remember taking over as manager of Rochdale and the old chairman, Mr Kilpatrick, saying to me, "We've got a good nucleus of support here."

'"How many's that?" I asked.

'"Oh, about a thousand."

'Fair enough. That was the size of the task. Cloughie should have come into Leeds and thought about the quality of the players already there, the crowds of 40,000 to 45,000, the great financial stability of the club, the standing of the club both at home and abroad. Instead, he wades in with, "You, you should be shot. You, you're a cheat. You lot, medals in the bin."

'Players are in football to train and play, play and train. That's all they are there for. Everything else is politics. I suffered badly with injuries throughout the 1973–74 season and barely played. Indeed, when Cloughie came I was waiting to hear from the Football League insurers about packing the game in. There's the famous story about him telling me that I would have been shot if I were a horse, but in truth there were times when I felt I could have saved someone the trouble and shot myself!

'I remember that famous first meeting with Clough in the players' lounge as though it were yesterday. Our boys were disgusted. And after he came out with that immortal line to me, I said, "Thinking about the way your own career finished, I would have thought you'd have had a bit more sympathy." Clough had been a prolific goal-scorer in his playing career. I'd read his book in which he spoke of his feelings when a bad injury brought an abrupt end to his playing days, and I added, "It's a funny thing to say that to a player who's struggling with injury in the way that you did. Remember?" He seemed a little taken aback by that, and there was something of a climbdown when he said that he had only been joking. "Well, it didn't come across like that," I insisted. He went a bit sheepish.

'I don't know if the way his career finished made him bitter. Maybe it did. He went on, though, to adopt an even more arrogant air, and I think this was because the lads were not slow in taking him to task with questions like "What are you on about?" and "What do you mean by that?"'

Says Peter Hampton: 'I first became aware that Clough was about to take over from Revie at Leeds – everyone had been away on their summer holidays – through a rumour sweeping the camp that Clough had invited Billy Bremner over to Majorca to join his family on holiday and that Billy had thrown a custard pie by refusing to do so.

'The time to report for pre-season training duly comes, and we're all waiting for the Big Arrival. He marches in, but he hasn't got Peter Taylor with him, he's got Jimmy Gordon. Straight away, he's on the front foot. I think he thought he had to be after all he had said about the club and its players in the past. Like a whirlwind, he goes round the squad and is not very complimentary to people. One of his first gambits is to give the evil eye to one of the young pros sitting just along the bench from me – I think it was Gary Liddell – and tell him to bugger off home, have a shave and come back when he's clean-shaven.

'It was an aggressive stance, and I'm sure it was born out of fear. It was very tense. Some of the Scottish lads had just come back from the World Cup, and he started an open forum about them in terms of who he planned to let go and who he planned to retain, when such matters, surely, would have been better discussed in the confines of an office. He was saying, "You're going . . . you're on your way," and this was to international footballers. I am sure that, as brassy as he came over, he had his insecurities like everybody else. But he just got stuck in. Rule by fear is the way some people operate, and he appeared to have adopted this as his stance from day one. But it was a big mistake. The worst thing he could have done. You could have cut the atmosphere with a knife, and it's not hard to imagine what it was like when he left that room. It was almost with one voice that people were saying, "Who does he think he is?" and "Cheeky bastard!" There was no attempt to get people onside and therefore battle lines had been drawn.'

Midfield stalwart Terry Yorath has his own recollections. 'I was met with an immediate problem when Don Revie vacated Elland Road for the England job in that my contract was expiring,' says Yorath. 'I was on £125 a week and Don had promised to double this to £250 a week, but I suppose that would be the last thing on his mind when he collected his things and headed for FA headquarters. So I didn't know what to expect when Brian Clough walked in. All I knew was that I had been an integral part of the team that had just won the championship, I was still young – 24 years old – and had, I hoped, plenty to offer Leeds for years to come. But I had no contract. This was a pressing problem, and I thought that maybe a good way of approaching the issue was to go through Maurice Lindley, who had been Don's assistant and was something of a fixture at the club.

'I duly knocked on Maurice's door and got as far as saying that I had been hoping to speak to Brian Clough when a booming voice from an unseen source rasped, "Boss to you!" I hadn't realised Clough was in the room, but there he was, behind the door. "What's the problem?" he asked. I explained that just before he had left, Don Revie had promised that he would double my wages, but there hadn't been time to do the paperwork and I was, in fact, out of contract. "How much is involved?" asked Clough. I told him that I had been on £125 a week and I was sure clearance had been given for this to be raised to £250 a week. He looked at me with utter contempt all over his face and said, "You? £250 a week? What makes you think you're deserving of that kind of money?" I said that the previous season I had played 35 matches in a championship-winning team, and this seemed to mellow his mood a little. "Does the chairman know about this?" he asked, in a much more reasonable tone. I assured him that he did.

'Ten days passed with no response, so I thought it was about time the subject was brought up again. "The chairman knows nothing about it," he said. My heart had begun to sink when he added, "But I think the chairman is a liar. You've got your money."

'There were lots of strands to that little episode. Firstly, the man has been at a new club for no time at all and already he's calling the chairman a liar. Next, if you wanted to undermine the confidence of a young player, then delaying such an important issue so long is probably the right way to go about it. And further, more positively, it showed he could be persuaded to do the right thing.'

David Harvey had no doubt from the outset about the folly of the decision to bring Clough to Leeds. 'My first reaction to the appointment – and it holds good to this day – was to question how the directors could have been stupid enough to give the job of managing one of the most successful club teams in Britain and Europe to a man who so openly and so viciously criticised the club, its previous manager and the players at every conceivable opportunity, and how such an embittered man with such a vendetta against this club could even contemplate becoming its manager. It simply did not add up and, as an arrangement, was always surely destined to be very temporary.

'To my mind, the chairman and directors had a responsibility to the club, its players and its fans to get the very best possible man for the job in place, and if they had needed time to sort that out they could always have appointed a caretaker manager to hold the fort until the best became available or could be persuaded to join Leeds. Instead, they rushed into things and could not have made a worse choice if they'd tried. Anybody, anybody at all, would have been better than Clough. No one could have treated the Leeds players in the way that he did and expect to get results. Like chalk and cheese, Leeds and Clough simply did not go together.

'Having said that, we, as a bunch of players, gave him every chance. We worked hard, giving just as much effort in training as we had done under Don Revie, and did nothing at all that could be construed as undermining him or attempting to destabilise him. In the event, he did a pretty good job of that himself. The thing about Clough was that he achieved all his success with players who were just embarking on their careers, youngsters he could mould into his ways. At Leeds, he was inheriting a squad full of highly experienced players who were household names and most of whom were internationals. I think that freaked him out a bit. Players who have been there, seen it and done it and got the shirt will invariably listen to a new manager and be open-minded about his views, opinions and modus operandi, but when all you're getting is a verbal onslaught, life becomes very difficult.

'Clough's first duty was to attend the pre-season party, which was a fixture in the club's social calendar. Wives and girlfriends were invited, and it was always a thoroughly enjoyable occasion, at which the highlight was the presentation of awards. I had won the Players' Player of the Year award and was eagerly looking forward to the handover by the new boss of this prestigious piece of crystal. The evening was thrown into disarray because Clough took it upon himself to arrive two hours late. However, upon his arrival he was soon taking to the stage and his observation upon handing over my trophy was: "How the fuck you've won this, I will never know." Thanks a bunch, pal. How rude.

'It was interesting to get an insight from conversations with the ex-Derby players who had joined Leeds, like John O'Hare and John McGovern, into how much Clough had been liked at Derby, because as far as I could see there was not much to like. I felt a little bit sorry for his trainer, Jimmy Gordon, who, in his role as middleman, would leap to Clough's defence with asides like "His bark is worse than his bite", "Don't get upset with him, he doesn't mean what he says" and so on. But it certainly came over as heartfelt when Clough delivered his infamous "You can throw your medals away" speech in his first proper meeting with the players.

'I have to say, I wasn't really surprised by the outburst. Nothing he came out with was surprising. Everybody had seen and heard Clough in his television and radio interviews, and his tendency to lean towards the controversial and the outrageous was so well documented that you just thought you were never going to get anything sensible or well thought out from him. If you expected the unexpected with Clough, then you were not going to go far wrong.

'Our training pitch in those days was the area right next to the ground behind the West Stand, now known as the Fullerton car park. It was usual for 20 or 30 fans to turn up to watch us being put through our paces, but when Clough arrived there were suddenly 2,000 or 3,000. It was manic. The police had to be drafted in to control the traffic on Elland Road.

'His first training session brought my first direct contact with Clough. I was in what we called the bottom goal, and my first feel of the ball was a short goalkick to Paul Reaney, who, in an instant, had Joe Jordan bearing down on him. Joe took the ball off him and blasted in a shot that went only narrowly wide, and the next I knew, Clough, who was at the other end of the pitch, stopped the game. Dressed in the squash gear that he was often photographed in – the green top, shorts and rolled-down socks – he folded his arms as he walked ever so slowly over the halfway line and headed in my direction. He carried right on until our noses were nearly touching and boomed, "If you ever do anything as stupid as that again, you will never get into a team of mine."

'In front of the other lads, this was a real humiliation, and I could feel my hackles rising. "Mr Clough," I said, "if you ever again try to make me look a prat, I'll squeeze your balls even harder than I'm squeezing them now." There was the kind of stare between us that you see at the weigh-ins in heavyweight boxing until, probably much quicker than he would have liked, he completely bottled it and walked away, restarting the game as if nothing had happened. I was sure I was going to get reprimanded or fined, but that was the last bit of trouble I had with him.'

If flexing his muscles was an attempt by Clough to win friends and influence people, it was doomed to spectacular failure. His preconceptions about Revie's Leeds – the cheating, the fouling, the diving and the gamesmanship – had clouded his tenure before it began.

4

DIRTY LEEDS?

If a player is not interfering with play,
then he shouldn't be on the pitch.

Brian Clough

It has been referred to by such great players as Teddy Sheringham and John Terry as 'the biggest personal award you can get in the game' and 'the ultimate accolade to be voted for by your fellow professionals whom you play against week in and week out'. Kevin Keegan, Kenny Dalglish, Gary Lineker and, more recently, Steven Gerrard and Cristiano Ronaldo (twice) have been recipients. The Professional Footballers Association Players' Player of the Year award is universally regarded by the players themselves as a great honour. Every spring, each member of the association casts two votes for fellow players. The names of the nominees shortlisted for the award are published and the winner is announced at a gala event held in London every April.

The inaugural Player of the Year award, recognising achievements in the 1973–74 season, went to a defender who had such a reputation for tough, aggressive, uncompromising play that he had acquired the nickname 'Bites Yer Legs'. It was more an affectionate than a derogatory soubriquet, but still, it was generally accepted that you did not mess with Leeds United's

Norman Hunter. It had been a vintage season for members of a Leeds side awash with recognition, honours, prestige and medals, so to be confronted by accusations of cheating from their new manager must have been difficult to countenance. In 2004, Hunter told the *Huddersfield Examiner*'s Ed Reed:

> They [opponents] were frightened of us but a lot of the time I never hurt anybody – not really . . . We deserved all the titles we got because we were aggressive. That was in the personality of the majority of the players. They were very, very competitive. That will to win was absolutely extraordinary and it was different in different people but, yes, we also deserved the reputation . . . You think now [looking back on Leeds' success], "By God, that must have been something special." At the time you didn't think anything of it. It was a great team. We should have gone down as one of the best teams this country has ever produced but we didn't win enough silverware. I was in ten finals and won four. We should have been in ten finals and won seven – and that's without the League.

Clough would not have been convinced by that overview. Where Revie saw sheer human spirit, a will to win and a desire for success, Clough saw only cheats and thugs. His opinion was not universally shared. Hugh McIlmoyle was in awe of Don Revie's team and appreciative of the qualities that made them champions. 'Leeds were not a well-liked team,' he says, 'but setting about quick change was the wrong thing for Clough to do. Leeds had some very strong personalities who were well used to a manager in Don Revie whom they liked and trusted. Don mixed with the players where Cloughie would not. Also, the new man was dealing with some big egos, and rightly so because they were all international players.

'I played against Leeds a few times down the years, going back, even, to when the legendary John Charles made his brief return to the club from Juventus, and through the times when Revie moulded a team from the youngsters he had on board like Peter Lorimer, Eddie Gray and Frank Gray. They were always an aggressive team, very hard to beat. You could tackle from behind among lots of other things you could do in those days that you can't do now, and Leeds were well practised in these areas. For instance, they were the first team to station a player, usually Jack Charlton, right in front of the goalkeeper when they had a corner, and then later it would be two or three players hindering the keeper.

'The thing was, it was all within the laws of the game, but there was the general feeling that Leeds pushed these laws to their very limit. They were also the first to jump on the referee as a team, baying at him to change his mind over decisions given against them or pleading for a penalty or a free kick, having been instructed by Revie that refs were generally weak and could be cajoled. Their tactics sometimes riled opposing teams and certainly infuriated rival fans, but they had some great, great players. I think if they had been more measured, concentrating more on their playing abilities and less on the snappy, aggressive stuff, they would have won a lot more trophies than they did, although there is the counter-argument that if you had taken the aggression out of them, they would not have been the team they were.

'I never enjoyed any success against them, but then there are a lot of members in that particular club. Not many players can say they had a beanfeast against that Leeds side. To have had a team of such quality – Reaney and Cooper at full-back, Bremner, Charlton and Hunter as half-backs and a forward line of Lorimer, Giles, Jones, Clarke and Gray – gave them a great chance every game they played. In the '60s and '70s, that half-back trio alone would virtually guarantee victory, and that wing pairing was devastating for opponents. It was the contrast in them that was so marked. Lorimer was so direct and Gray, when he was running at players, could just ghost by them in the way that George Best was to do later. He was fantastic. Leeds didn't buy in many players, but the one I thought was an excellent signing was Mick Jones. I could appreciate him as a striker because he was just so in your face, with the right amount of tempered aggression in his play. Giles was a gem of a player and you had the same kind of contrast between him and Bremner in midfield as you did with Lorimer and Gray on the wing. Bremner was all action and pumped up with aggression, whereas Giles, who nonetheless could look after himself, was more the architect and playmaker. Class.'

One player more than any other epitomised the knife-edge balance between aggression and skill described by McIlmoyle as characteristic of Revie's Leeds. To witness Billy Bremner in action was to see combat, tenacity, confrontation, pragmatism, determination, dexterity, flair, ability, athleticism and leadership all rolled into a diminutive frame that once gave birth to a headline 'Ten Stone of Barbed Wire'. As a footballer, Bremner was quite simply brilliant.

Never in the game's history can a run of matches have conspired to make such demands on the reserves of the human body as the programme undertaken by Leeds in the spring of 1970. They were challenging on three fronts, for the league, the FA Cup and the European Cup, and the fixture pile-up that was created was brutal. There were nine matches in the month of March alone, and when April breezed in there were three games in the first four days of the month and eight in all. This totalled 17 matches in 56 days, with none of them meaningless, all of them counting for something and the stakes high throughout. There was no taking the foot off the pedal even for a moment. In the end, they won nothing, but this was not for want of supreme effort in a squad led throughout by a red-headed firebrand whose name is immortal.

I first saw Bremner live in action in a game that held the country spellbound during that epic run of matches: the FA Cup semi-final second replay against Manchester United at Bolton Wanderers' Burnden Park. The first attempt to settle this tie, on 14 March at Hillsborough, saw two impregnable defences hold firm in a goalless draw; the replay, at Villa Park on 23 March, also ended in stalemate, even after extra time. Three days later, these two famous clubs were at each other's throats again, the prize a Wembley final against Chelsea, who had walloped Watford 5–1 at the first time of asking in the other semi-final at White Hart Lane. This had become personal for Bremner, who emerged into the Lancashire night air a man possessed. There were just nine minutes on the clock when he contrived a net-busting shot and proceeded to give such an authoritative demonstration of the meaning of the expression 'running the show' that it has remained clear in my memory to this day. The whole Leeds team performed wonderfully that night, but Bremner, with his non-stop probing, constant bustling and inarguable instruction, was outstanding. Poetry in motion. I had, of course, seen miles of television footage of Bremner and this fabulous Leeds side, but to be there to witness such artistry provided a golden memory.

More than a quarter of a century later, seeking an informed opinion on a forthcoming Euro 96 clash between England and Scotland, I was privileged to meet the great man. One school of thought maintains that you should never meet your heroes lest you be disappointed. It's wrong. Or at least it was wrong in this case, because Bremner was entertaining, great fun, warm, friendly and welcoming. Here is what, as sports editor of the *Daily Star* at the time, I wrote:

> I did not know quite what to expect from Billy Bremner. A kick in the goolies was probably routine from the man who, I always feared when watching him as a young fan, would cripple you first then ask questions later. Along with Liverpool's Tommy Smith, he was my football hero. What we all had in common was a number 4 shirt. I tried to model myself upon them. Although I was always going to be markedly less successful, my thirst for seeing them in action was unquenchable. Now the unthinkable was happening. Walking through the gates of a pristine cottage in the South Yorkshire hamlet of Clifton, I was

about to come face to face with the feisty Scot. He was charming. Completely disarming. He went to make a cup of tea in the neat kitchen and carried out the chore beneath an ornamental sign which confesses: 'I can't do anything right until I've had a cup of cigarette and smoked a coffee.' All a far cry from the pocket Hercules who, in his prime, thought man-marking was a set of stud abrasions up and down an opponent's leg. Staying so close to your opposite number that the game might end with a marriage proposal was something that happened abroad. The British game was freeflow in Billy's day but the subject of man-to-man arises as we contemplate this afternoon's titanic Wembley battle.

The feature of the game promises to be the shadowing job Billy believes will be carried out by Stuart McCall on his Rangers teammate Paul Gascoigne. 'I can't imagine that Gazza will be allowed to roam free,' says Billy, 'because he is the most potent threat. Keep him quiet. That's the key. McCall is a great wee competitor. People think he is just a destroyer but he's there to protect John Collins and Gary McAllister when they go on the break. He does it better than anyone. The players appreciate him, but I'm not sure the fans always do.'

Billy then recalls how he himself once had to do a man-marking job. On Pelé. He was told to stick tight to the Brazilian legend in a World Cup warm-up at Hampden in 1965. 'Every time he got the ball he would back into me and there he was – gone! Early in the game he kept looking at me and smiling. The message coming over in those smiles was that the first chance he got he was going to do me. We'd been playing an hour when we both went up for a ball and, in one blinding movement, he got his head to it first and wheeled round with an elbow that caught me full in the eye. It came up like a tennis ball within seconds. My Leeds colleague Willie Bell – he's a holy man in America now – said

after the game how disgusted he was. He told me, "Pelé
– I'll never have any respect for that man after what
he did to you." I'd just kicked seven bells of shit out
of Pelé for an hour and he'd got his own back in style
and Willie was crying about it! Willie never swore. His
wife used to send him with cake and sandwiches she'd
made specially if we were playing abroad. And tight?
One player took a dab of his aftershave one day and
Willie told him, "Hey, that's not water, you know." I'm
sure the horror of Pelé's elbow in my eye figures in his
sermons to this day.'

Back to Wembley and today's Battle of Britain. What
result did Billy predict? 'I can't see anything other than
a draw,' he insists. 'England will have the greatest
difficulty in breaking down the Scots and I can see us
catching them on the break and nicking one. Make no
mistake, this is war. Nobody will need any motivation
for this one. Can we score? That's the million-dollar
question. McAllister is another key player. He's not
as fiery as I was, but probably it's better that way. I
used to let my heart rule my head when I played for
Scotland, particularly in games against England. He's
more composed. But the guys are on a real high. You
look at the Dutch and the English, who are not a bad
side, and nine times out of ten you'd back the Dutch to
win. That's why the result today is so important. And
the fans are so critical a factor. Against the Dutch they
were like having an extra man on the park. They were
fantastic. They went along to enjoy it, found a good
comradeship with the opposing fans and the whole
atmosphere was electric. Scottish fans are the best in the
world. It must have been so intimidating for any team
going up to play in front of 110,000 at Hampden in the
old days. Wembley still has a bit of magic, though. The
man who led England to the World Cup, Alf Ramsey,
didn't like the Scots. He would simply tell his players

to go out and beat the Jocks. But throughout history the players have had a friendly animosity towards each other. Personally, I was always all right as long as they didn't start throwing punches at me.'

Punches? At Billy Bremner? Well, there have been a couple of celebrated incidents, but you would have had to have had a death wish to start mixing it with the man who made the number 4 shirt his own in 19 years at Leeds and whose 54 international caps included 9 against England. He might be small, and those fiery red shocks of wavy hair may now be grey and receding, but when his ice-blue eyes fix you with a stare you can sense the discomfort, as you squirm in your chair, that opposing players must have gone through. 'I'll tell you why it will be a battlefield out there,' he resumes. 'I've seen it so many times. Training sessions at Elland Road used to involve five-a-side matches and I don't know whether it was the governor's sense of humour or what but he would make it England versus the Scots. At one time there was me, Eddie Gray, Frank Gray, Joe Jordan, Gordon McQueen, Peter Lorimer and David Harvey and it was war against the likes of Allan Clarke and his Sassenach softies. Guerrilla warfare. That Lorimer was something. We were playing Red Star Belgrade one day and we got a free kick 40 yards out. He whispered to me that he fancied shooting and I said, "You're out of your head." But he let this thing go and the keeper never moved. Whoosh! Do you know what? He can still do it. There's an ex-players' team in Leeds who turn out most Sundays and Peter's shot is as lethal today as it was back then.' Lorimer, it will be remembered, was once scientifically measured as having the hardest shot in British football.

Bremner has never been screened as a diplomat. 'England does nothing for its football heroes,' he says. 'Three years ago Bobby Moore, Nobby Stiles, Denis Law and I were invited to a dinner in Aberdeen, none of us knowing what it was in aid of. It was only when the cheese was being passed round that we learned it was the 25th anniversary of Scotland being the first team to beat England since they won the World Cup! Moore said "What? We've never had a dinner for winning the World Cup!" Scotland would still be having three dinners a year! Mind you, that was some game in 1967. A lot of Scots would be hard put to name the team that day. Jim McCalliog and Bobby Lennox weren't regulars but they both scored in a match that lives on in my memory. The one I'd like to erase, but never can, is when England won 5–0 at Hampden. It was just shit. It was a night match in February and the pitch was like a road. It should never have been played. They must have done it for the money or something.'

Bremner, having acquired more than 50 caps, is in the Scottish Football Hall of Fame, a privileged bunch who receive a gold medal, commissioned self-portrait, tickets for international matches and the inevitable annual dinner. 'I've had my time, but I'll be envying those boys at Wembley. When I was a laddie watching at Hampden I used to wonder what they were doing in the dressing-room. Then the ballboys would run out, the teams would emerge and this most colossal roar filled the air. Ah, the passion. The fervour. I always dreamed that maybe one day it would happen to me and it did. I was a proud man. Now it's their time and I hope they come out with the right result. My other hope is for a sensible referee. If he's the type to give out cards willy-nilly we could have a procession. As schoolboys in Scotland you are indoctrinated with how the English came up and pillaged the place and all the other nasty things they did to us throughout history. I wouldn't even mind the historical tables being turned a bit.'

The Scots could do worse, Bremner ventures, than to look back on an old icon, Jim Baxter, for inspiration. 'There was nobody like him when he was at his cocky best,' Bremner recalls. 'He actually liked humiliating people. We were set to play Italy in a World Cup qualifier and somebody mentioned he would be marked by their hero, Rivera. "Fucking Rivera? I'm a different class to him," he said. "If I don't get six nutmegs on him it's drinks all round." In front of a packed Hampden he put the ball through Rivera's legs after five minutes, turned to me and shouted, "That's one!" He stopped the count after six, but it could have been twenty-six!'

Just as his instincts were always pin sharp out on the pitch, Bremner's pre-game analysis of the epic Euro 96 clash that followed was incredibly accurate – a demonstration of how well he understood his art, how accurately he could read the game of football and, above all, the passionate and intelligent character who stood at the heart of the squad Clough saw fit to deride.

Stirling-born Bremner has been voted Leeds United's greatest player of all time and is a member of both the Scottish Football Hall of Fame and the English Football Hall of Fame. Having been rejected by Arsenal and Chelsea because of his diminutive stature, he was brought south by Leeds in 1959, signing for the club the day after he turned 17. He appeared for the first team in 1960 and was rarely left off Revie's team sheet thereafter. His goal-scoring was quite prolific for a midfielder and that goal I witnessed against Manchester United was just one of four winners he came up with in major semi-finals. Bremner was at the heart of Leeds' renewal in the early 1960s. As the decade wore on, the team became more and more successful, with Bremner an inspirational leader.

A heart attack claimed Bremner's life, aged 54, in early December 1997. On the tenth anniversary of his death, Ron Yeats, who captained Liverpool to two championships and an

FA Cup final victory over Leeds in the 1960s, recalled:

> I'll never forget a picture of the two of us tossing
> up before a big game at Anfield. I was 6 ft 3 in. and
> Billy was about 5 ft 3 in. We looked like Little and
> Large. But although he was only a wee man, he was a
> heavyweight player. He had the heart of a lion and he
> was a tremendous leader. He never gave up. He was
> an inspiration and he led by example. He expected the
> whole team to follow and they did.

Like most of Revie's players, Bremner gave his soul to Leeds
United and to a coach who needed every fighter he could find
when he jumped into the hot seat at Elland Road. The same
was true of Norman Hunter, as *The Independent*'s Brian Viner
reported in a 2004 profile:

> In Revie's first full season as player-manager, 1961–62,
> his task was not so much to get Leeds out of the old
> Second Division into the First, but to prevent the drop
> into the Third. The notion of not only gaining promotion
> but building a side that would win European trophies,
> and come within a goal of winning the Double, must
> have seemed ludicrously remote . . . But Revie did just
> that, thanks not least to the promise he saw in a skinny
> Geordie, on whom he forced a daily glass of sherry with
> a raw egg mixed into it. And not just any old sherry,
> but Harvey's Bristol Cream. 'But there were still times
> when it made me throw up,' says Hunter . . .
>
> The Hunters live in a nice detached house in a genteel
> northern suburb of Leeds. His playing style, of course,
> was neither detached nor genteel. I ask whether it ever
> bothered him that his reputation was that of a hard
> man with an uncompromising tackle? After all, he was
> the inaugural Players' Player of the Year in 1974, so he
> certainly had the respect of his peers.

Yet among the fans, he was cast as little more than a highly effective bruiser. When I interviewed the old Liverpool enforcer Tommy Smith, he grumbled that he was never given the credit he deserved for his ability to play. But Hunter claims to have suffered no such frustrations.

'I was never concerned about anyone outside the Elland Road dressing-room,' he says, 'except maybe for Alf Ramsey.' Even inside the dressing-room, Revie would only half-jokingly cast him as a one-dimensional footballer, reminding him that his job was to secure the ball and distribute it to the play-makers. 'And he was right. Win it and give it to [Johnny] Giles or [Billy] Bremner. That's what I did.'

Nonetheless, Hunter finds it remarkable that his name is synonymous even now with the turbo-charged tackle.

'It's quite amazing, really, why all those reputations should stick around from our era. The famous football hard men, even now, are Nobby Stiles, Tommy Smith, Chopper Harris and Norman Hunter, and I wonder why.

'Even youngsters seem to know about us. There have been plenty of hard men since, harder men than me, but that period just seems to stick in people's minds.'

I ask Hunter whether he ever intimidated an op- posing player in the tunnel before a match, as Smith did. With a few choice words, two of which invariably were 'effing' and 'hospital', Smith was able, on occasion, to put the wind up an opponent to the extent that he was unable to concentrate on the game.

'No, I never did that. But Don Revie always used to tell us to go in hard with the first tackle, because the referee would never book you for the first one. We used to call it the freebie. I'd go in hard, pick 'em up, say sorry to the referee, and sometimes you hardly saw the player again. Jimmy Greaves was one who didn't like it, although having said that, he scored against me almost every time we played, did Jimmy. That was a brilliant era for forward play, and most of them hunted in pairs: [Alan] Gilzean and Greaves, Jeff Astle and Tony Brown, Denis Law and Georgie Best. I used to love playing against all those guys. I was never the quickest, and always had to give myself a start against a fast lad, but I could read situations.'

However, he got the script badly wrong in England's infamous World Cup qualifier against Poland, in 1973. It is often forgotten that Hunter was part of England's 1966 World Cup squad, and by 1973 he was still very much on the international scene. But he it was who lost the ball on Wembley's halfway line, whereupon Poland cancelled out Allan Clarke's opening goal. A dazzling performance by the Polish goalkeeper, Jan Tomacewski, ensured that England, world champions only seven years earlier, were denied a place in the following year's World Cup finals in West Germany, which in turn caused Big Ben to stop chiming, and Admiral Nelson to fall off his column in Trafalgar Square. At any rate, a shocked nation mourned.

Not, of course, that Hunter needs any reminding of the implications of that unhappy 1–1 draw. 'It's funny,' he says, with admirable lack of rancour, 'I played over 700 games for Leeds, 120-odd games for Bristol City, and I'm remembered for three things: Norman bites yer legs [famously emblazoned on a Leeds United banner at the 1968 League Cup final], the punch-up with Francis Lee, and that goal against Poland. I was never even given a chance to forget about it, because every fourth year, when we tried to qualify for the World Cup, who did we draw in our group? Bloody Poland. And so the television clip of me missing the ball on the halfway line, Barry

Davies commentating, them scoring, kept being shown again and again. Unbelievable.'

He proclaims it unbelievable, too, that his mentor, Revie, might ever have been involved in match-rigging. But he is aware of the rumours, which surfaced again recently when Bob Stokoe died. Stokoe loathed Revie, largely because he insisted that the Leeds manager had tried to bribe him, when he was manager at Bury.

'I'll defend Don Revie to the hilt,' Hunter says. 'My father died before I was born, I went there when I was 15, and he was a father figure to me. I got on extremely well with him, about as well as a player and manager could. He may have bent the rules a bit, and I noticed certain things myself, but I still think he was the best manager I've ever seen.'

Hunter's praise for Revie is hardly unexpected; not so the implication that the great man may indeed have been corrupt. What does he mean by saying that he 'noticed certain things' himself? 'Well, I heard those things that Bob Stokoe said, and there's no smoke without fire,' he says, disingenuously.

'But he was a fantastic manager. Nobody paid more attention to detail than him and Alf Ramsey. He had all his famous dossiers on the opposition, and his methods were before their time. When he was England manager he tried to get Admiral to sponsor the kit, and got hammered for it. Look at sponsorship now! He also used to tell us to take the ball into the corner if we were winning with a couple of minutes to go. That was unheard of at the time. Everyone just played until the 90 minutes were up. But not Don Revie.'

The players at Elland Road in 1974 understood Revie's management implicitly, in a way they never would Clough's. The feeling was mutual, and Clough was adamant that changes at Leeds were necessary.

Peter Hampton says: 'What became evident over Clough's career was his total abhorrence of cheating in the game. I well remember playing against his Nottingham Forest side for Stoke, at Stoke, and the ball going out for a throw-in right by where he was standing. Probably 99 out of 100 managers in the game would pick it up and hold onto it until he was sure his own players had taken up their marking positions or kick it several yards down the track, but not Cloughie. As quick as a flash he threw the ball to me, an opposition player, so that I could take the throw. I was genuinely surprised by that, but in one gesture he had made something of a statement. He appeared to have got it into his mind before he joined Leeds that he did not like them for what might be termed their professionalism and I think that cleaning up their image was number one on his list of priorities.'

Hugh McIlmoyle adds: 'He was a stickler for fair play. When I had finished playing football, I went to Forest to watch them play Arsenal and the home crowd, for some reason, were right on the back of the Gunners forward Charlie Nicholas. It was aggressive, brutal stuff and Cloughie came out of his dugout, turned to the fans, put his index finger to his lips and pushed down his hands in a hushing gesture. They suddenly went as quiet as mice.

'That was the degree of Clough's authority. On this occasion, he was a one-man crowd controller, and we all remember his cuffing of a couple of fans who ran onto the pitch after a cup tie and his subsequent apology. He was a truly remarkable man and the certainty is, in these days of political correctness, with the high-powered business world that football has become and with behavioural standards constantly under the microscope, we shall never see his like again.

'I'm only guessing, but where he went wrong at Leeds was to have gone in there with the attitude "I'm going to show these bastards". All he had to do was nurture what he had inherited.'

5

SIGN HERE

*I'd ask him how he thinks it should be done, have a chat about it
for 20 minutes and then decide I was right.*

Brian Clough on
disagreements with players

With the inevitability of night following day, an incoming
manager will bring changes to the club at which he is newly
in charge, and Clough wasted little time before trying to stamp
his mark on Leeds. He splashed out £240,000 on striker Duncan
McKenzie from Nottingham Forest, £50,000 on Derby County
centre-forward John O'Hare and £75,000 on Derby midfielder
John McGovern, prompting local journalist John Wray to note:
'Brian Clough has spent half as much inside a week as Don
Revie paid out in 13 years as Leeds United's manager.'

In another life, McKenzie could have made a highly successful
career as a stand-up comedian, an actor or a circus performer.
Born in Grimsby in the summer of 1950, the man who could
mimic people so well, jump over a Mini car and throw a golf
ball the length of a football pitch instead chose to be a footballer,
and he was pretty good at that too. So good, in fact, that those
who were privileged to see him in action still marvel at his silky
skills. Having been hauled into Elland Road, McKenzie would
be the only one of Clough's signings to subsequently flourish

at the club. Once he was a fixture in the Leeds side he soon became a high-profile member of the team, though it wasn't until the 1975–76 season that he established himself as Allan Clarke's striking partner and scored 16 goals in 39 matches. McKenzie was a hugely talented individual who could make mugs of the best defenders.

However, despite his skills, he could be an immensely frustrating player to play with. While he reserved his finest moments for big games, he was often anonymous against lesser opposition, and it was this inconsistency that caused him to be sold to Belgian side Anderlecht at the end of the 1975–76 season.

McKenzie believes that it was an FA Cup tie against Manchester City in January 1974 that earned him the lucrative move to Leeds. He played the starring role and scored as Forest inflicted a 4–1 defeat on the visitors in front of more than 40,000 fans. He says: 'No one had really heard of me until one particular game, but then I had some luck. It was when there was a power strike, and Forest were playing an early game on a Sunday. It was the only game that was on, and all the number-one sportswriters were there to see it. It was one of those matches where I could have played well with my eyes shut, with everything going right. But I felt I deserved it because I had laboured long and hard without getting a break, often under conservative management. Knowing Cloughie, he would have probably been there watching that match.'

McKenzie, who spends much of his time these days as a very entertaining after-dinner speaker, elaborates: 'I have a slightly different perspective on Cloughie's time at Leeds in that, unlike the vast majority of the players there, who were part of the furniture and had grown up under Don Revie, Brian bought me. He paid Nottingham Forest £240,000 for my services, and his opening gambit once I had arrived was that he wanted me to mark his card about what was being said in the dressing-room and to be on the lookout on his behalf for any conspiracies or rebellious rumblings. I told him this was an unfair request and there was absolutely no way I was going to get involved in tittle-tattle or being his snitch. In some ways, I was the man in the middle, wanting to repay the faith the boss had in me with good performances out there on the pitch while also nurturing good relations with my new colleagues, most of whom disliked him.

'It was a very delicate time all round for everyone at Elland Road. Don Revie had expressed a desire for Johnny Giles to succeed him in the hot seat, which was common knowledge, while Billy Bremner had wanted the job equally badly, which was less well known. Neither got it and Brian Clough did, and while there wasn't exactly a division in the dressing-room, the overpowering feeling was that you had better be very careful what you said to whom both inside the club and beyond its environs. These were Yorkshire folk, suspicious of newcomers and interlopers and possessed to an extent by a sort of private members' club mentality.

'One of Cloughie's signings, John O'Hare, was known to the Scottish contingent, such as Lorimer, Gray and Bremner, through their Scotland international involvement and was anyway a good lad who would have no trouble in fitting in. But they didn't know me or John McGovern, Brian's other signing. I was a joker both on and off the pitch and could usually raise the kind of laugh that would lighten the atmosphere and spark friendships. I think this was something they had never really experienced before at Leeds. I quickly made pals of all the players and many of us remain friends to this day.

'I was in the least biased position of anybody at Elland Road, but I walked in there with something puzzling me. I could not fathom what Brian Clough had been doing with his life recently and could only conclude that he had become involved in a series of mistakes, of which managing Leeds was just the latest. What he was doing taking the job in the first place, I simply had no idea, but prior to this he had walked out on Derby County having won the championship with them, which was surely a misjudgement, and then accepted the job at Brighton. Getting

Brighton out of the Third Division would have been beyond the powers of Houdini. Another error. I can only think that with Leeds he would have thought, with tongue planted firmly in cheek, "Yes, I'll have this. We can have a bit of fun here."

'The backroom staff, particularly Syd Owen, despised Clough. During team talks, Syd would express his displeasure at Clough's presence by deriding almost everything he said. In mocking tones, he would say, "Yeah, yeah, yeah," and, "Blah, blah, blah," then tut-tut or give a groan, and it was both distracting and disrespectful. It was clear that he was anti-me, anti-O'Hare, anti-McGovern and anti anything else that was no longer Don Revie. Maurice Lindley, by contrast, was more easy-going and happy to go along with whatever was happening. But it was difficult to get away from the fact that here was Don Revie's flock, into which a few of us had strayed. The Leeds situation consumed the football world at the time with questions such as why Revie had left, why Clough had taken over from him and how deep the hatred they had for each other ran.

'Within a very short time of my arrival at Leeds, I did think, "This – Clough managing Leeds and Leeds being managed by Clough – isn't going to last very long." I was only 24 and a bit wet behind the ears, but I wasn't so naive as to be unable to work out that they were not made nor meant for each other. The players didn't like him. They didn't like his traits of being very arrogant and hugely self-opinionated, nor his threats of how he was going to sort them out. They took umbrage, and I have to say that I could understand and had some sympathy for them when I looked at things from their points of view.

'But I liked Clough. I loved the banter with him. He said to me one day at Leeds, "Oi, Smokey Joe! Pack those fags in or go and get yourself another club." I came back with, "Fine, boss. I'll have 5 per cent. Where am I going?" He laughed and I laughed, and that, I found, was the key to him. Interaction. As difficult as it was for Revie's Leeds players, you wonder how differently things might have shaken out had they been able or willing to engage with him on that kind of basis.

'Diplomacy was never Clough's strong point. At Leeds, he would have been absolutely correct in his vision for the club and how he would go about achieving his aims. But then the squad wakes up one day to newspaper reports saying that he wants Peter Shilton as his next signing, and what are the goalkeepers on the books, and indeed the rest of the players, going to make of that? If you were a sports journalist or a television football correspondent, he was absolutely brilliant, manna from heaven, but that is nightmare stuff for footballers.

'So too was his labelling of some of the Leeds players as the Over-30s Club. A footballer does not want to be reminded that he is coming towards the end of his career and that his best days are behind him, but for Cloughie hitting a tender spot would be part of the strategy. He wasn't the kind of character to bring things about tactfully. He would wade straight in where angels fear to tread. There is a misconception that his rule was by fear. It was not. It was more of an authority through plain speaking. And if he got it back, it would usually end up humorously.

'I'll never forget signing for Brian from Forest. His first words were, "Am I wasting my time, young man, or are you going to sign for me at Leeds United?" He ordered me to meet him at the Victoria Hotel in Sheffield within the hour. My wife was seven months pregnant and came with me. Brian advised her to take cod liver oil tablets and was so persuasive about me going to Leeds, I signed three blank contracts there and then. The details were filled in later!'

Scottish international O'Hare had begun his career at Sunderland in 1963, scoring 14 goals in 51 appearances before joining Derby County in 1967 for £22,000. He scored 65 goals in 248 outings spanning 7 years, and won a league championship medal in 1972. Despite his abilities, when Clough took him to Elland Road he had a tough time gaining popularity with the fans; he was seen as the new manager's man and therefore viewed with suspicion.

John McGovern's sporting life might easily have taken a

different course. As a youngster, he was just as adept at rugby as he was at football, and indeed at school in Hartlepool, playing at fly-half, he captained the 1st XV. But the persuasive powers of Brian Clough ensured that it was in football that he made his career. The reward for McGovern was that he was in Hartlepool's first team by the age of 16. He became a Clough favourite, following him to Derby County and playing a big part in the successes enjoyed by the Rams. When Clough moved on, however, his successor, Dave Mackay, felt that McGovern was surplus to requirements.

Clough, however, had no hesitation in making McGovern a part of the Leeds United set-up when the opportunity arose, particularly in view of the ongoing suspension of Billy Bremner. Two things worked against McGovern. First, he was viewed by the fans as a Clough man when Clough himself was unpopular; and second, McGovern was filling the boots of their hero and was judged by them to be an inferior player. Accordingly, he was never taken into the supporters' affections, and indeed some on the terraces treated him with disdain.

Joe Jordan recalls the stir caused by the new arrivals: 'What happened with me under Clough at Leeds was that I had had this long run of being in top form and for some reason – probably the after-effects of the World Cup – I was a bit below my best and didn't play particularly well in my first couple of matches. The next thing I know is that he's signed two goal-scoring forwards in John O'Hare and Duncan McKenzie and an attacking midfielder in John McGovern. It was, of course, his prerogative and I have no criticism of that. He possibly thought, having seen me in action, that that was one area of the pitch in which he could make improvements, and he had every right to go and get the players he thought capable of bringing those about. Throughout my career, I always accepted competition for places as being part and parcel of the job anyway, so I had no complaints. The plus side was that as a young player I was keeping my place in the Scotland team, so my overall form can't have been too bad.'

If goals are football's currency and those who score them in abundance valuable commodities, then Clough was denied the riches he ought to have inherited when he took over at Leeds. In Allan Clarke and Mick Jones, he should have had a strike force that would put fear into the hearts of opposition defences, just as they had done for years before his arrival in Yorkshire. The deadly duo had most famously demonstrated their combined lethality in a glorious day for Leeds at Wembley – the centenary FA Cup final of 1972. Jones delivered a beautiful cross on the turn from the byline for his partner to plant a glorious diving header past a helpless Geoff Barnett in the Arsenal goal for a priceless single-goal victory. Now, though, just when Clough most needed every ally he could muster, golden-haired Jones was in the knacker's yard.

The toil, strain and exertion of making an immense contribution to Leeds' 1973–74 championship-winning season had taken a heavy toll on the Worksop-born idol, and the summer of 1974 was spent undergoing extensive physiotherapy on a serious knee problem that was to require surgery and prematurely end his career. Jones' Leeds record stood at 111 goals in 312 appearances. He had become, in the summer of 1967, the first player to go to Leeds for a six-figure fee when he was snapped up from South Yorkshire rivals Sheffield United, where his partnership with Alan Birchenall had been prodigious. Jones was top scorer in his first season at Elland Road, and went on to inspire Leeds to their first top-flight title in the 1968–69 season. Then, when Clarke joined the following season in a £165,000 move from Leicester City, a great partnership was formed. They had contrasting styles. Where Jones, the more physical of the pair, was the battering ram, Clarke relied heavily on a well-honed predatory instinct both on the ground and in the air. 'Allan and I developed a tremendous understanding,' Jones once commented. 'I took the knocks and he finished it all off.'

Clarke had begun his career at Walsall, scoring 41 goals in 72 outings having made his debut as a 16 year old. He then moved to Fulham and was equally free-scoring, netting 45 times in 86 appearances. This kind of form prompted Leicester to pay £150,000 for his services and his stay at Filbert Street, while short-lived, brought an FA Cup final appearance, although Leicester lost 1–0 to Manchester City. Just weeks later, Clarke was on his way to Leeds, where he made an instant impact. He scored 26 goals in his first season, 1969–70. Everybody sat up and took notice of Clarke, and he was brought into the international fray by Sir Alf Ramsey for the 1970 World Cup in Mexico. He had a dream debut, too, scoring the only goal, a penalty, in England's first-round defeat of Czechoslovakia.

When Clough arrived at Leeds, however, Clarke was set to begin United's league season by serving a two-match ban. The start of that campaign was drawing close, yet striker Peter Lorimer could not see a coherent strategy coming together. In general, the players felt vulnerable and uncertain, at a loss to understand Clough's plans. Lorimer says: 'When you listen to other guys who played for him, the overwhelming consensus is that his managerial style was to bully people. At Leeds, I think he thought, "These are too big. I'm not going to be able to bully these. So if I go in big and brash and bold and strong they'll think, 'Hell, he's a Herculean character.'" This was probably OK in theory, but he didn't deliver his oratories in a strong way. They were risible really. He'd say something and you'd come away thinking, "Well that's just pathetic." He made no attempt to endear himself to us. He always came over as meaning, "You're a set of tossers," and an even more sinister side to this was being left with the distinct feeling that you'd be replaced as a player as soon as the opportunity presented itself. So there was an overriding feeling on our part of "Who does this guy think he is?"

'Whichever way you shake this mix, it doesn't work. And of course there were consequences. As a team, players must first and foremost play for their manager. Secondly, you've got to play for your club. Thirdly, you've got to play for each other. So if you're not playing for your manager, you're not playing for your club, because one is dependent upon the other. As far as the third strand of that argument goes, certainly in the case of Clough and Leeds, we just went out there to play the game and get the game out of the way because we thought, "This guy doesn't rate us. He's going to piss us all off and get rid of us all so let's just get on with things in that context." Jack Charlton was getting on a bit, Billy Bremner and Johnny Giles were in their early 30s, and Norman Hunter, Terry Cooper and Paul Reaney were at the older end. So you thought Clough would maybe get rid of them. I was two or three years younger, so was Eddie Gray and we had lads like Gordon McQueen and Joe Jordan who were younger than us, so there was enough youth in the squad for there to be no cause to feel vulnerable. Yet everyone did. And in fostering that insecurity, Clough ripped the heart out of the club.'

It wasn't only among the playing staff that the Leeds boat was rocking, as explained in this contemporary article from the Bradford *Telegraph & Argus* by John Wray:

I STAY AT LEEDS SAYS SYD OWEN

Leeds United's chief coach Syd Owen today crushed strong rumours that he is preparing to quit the club following behind-the-scenes rows with new manager Brian Clough. His future became uncertain when Clough recruited trainer-coach Jimmy Gordon from Derby to succeed Les Cocker. The rumours snowballed when Clough decided to send Gordon to Switzerland next Sunday to run the rule over FC Zurich, the team Leeds meet in the first round of the European Cup. Owen is recognised as the Leeds 'master spy', having travelled thousands of miles with assistant manager Maurice Lindley during United's nine years of European competition.

A somewhat marginalised Owen was to remain at Leeds a while longer but things were just not the same at the club, as explained by Lorimer: 'There were a few significant telltale signs about his inner feelings towards Leeds in Clough's behaviour at the club. For instance, he wouldn't sit on the chair that Revie had sat upon; he wouldn't have the desk that Revie had used in his administration of the club; he wouldn't have the settee that had been a part of Revie's office furniture. He had everything removed. But rather than just getting on with those things and doing it he had to let everybody know that he was doing it. "I don't want anything that Revie had. I'm not going to be tainted by Revie's presence here" was his mantra. To put this into context, it has to be realised that there was a long history at Leeds of a tremendous bonding between the players and the manager.'

Now, after all the drama of recent days, Leeds were down to the real business. It was all about to kick off.

6

UNCHARITABLE

Get in there – that's what I pay you for!

Brian Clough

Saturday, 10 August 1974. There is so much that is new and unfamiliar about this year's FA Charity Shield. It is the traditional curtain-raiser to the English domestic football season, but much has changed.

When the first Charity Shield match was played in 1908 between Manchester United, the reigning Football League champions, and Queens Park Rangers, the Southern League champions, it was professionals versus amateurs. This format was continued for many years, and the match often featured teams that were assembled on a one-off basis. Back then, the games were fairly informal and played at the end of the season, at a neutral venue or at the home ground of one of the teams involved. In 1930, the league champions versus FA Cup holders format was introduced and in 1959 the Charity Shield (known today as the Community Shield) was moved to coincide with the start of the new season. Until 1974, it was a less prestigious fixture, and the match continued to be played at various club grounds.

Then, in 1974, FA secretary Ted Croker proposed that the FA Charity Shield should be played at Wembley. Instantly, its profile was raised. The fixture was to be played at the venue where only eight years previously England had won the World Cup, and it drew the attention of television executives who deemed the Leeds United versus Liverpool fixture attractive enough for the event to be screened for the first time.

There were good reasons for the cameras to be there. Not only did the match concern two teams who were the deadliest rivals of the time, but there was added interest in the fact that it was to be the swansong of Bill Shankly, the man who started the Liverpool revolution. He had shocked the football world with his decision that enough was enough after 15 years in charge at Anfield. What was more, it was also to be the first game in charge of Leeds for Brian Clough. Wembley that day was a paradise for voyeurs. A crowd of 67,000 was attracted and they, in common with the watching millions, had an almost morbid interest in issues such as how emotional an occasion it would be for Shankly and what public face would be shown by Clough, the enemy sniper turned commander-in-chief of the Leeds battalion. If Clough looked sheepish, then that would be understandable; if he appeared comfortable in what might be deemed excruciating circumstances, it would be entirely in character.

In terms of club service and loyalty it would have been difficult to imagine two men further apart. Shankly had guided Liverpool out of the Second Division and won the Football League championship in 1964, 1966 and 1973, the UEFA Cup in 1973 and the FA Cup in 1974. He had stunned the adoring fans when he announced his retirement, five weeks after he'd told his directors, who'd spent every minute trying to get him to change his mind before the news went public. Insisting he wanted to spend more time with his family, Shankly had said, 'The pressures have built up so much during my 40 years in the game that I felt it was time to have a rest.' Clough, on the other hand, had nothing at all in common with Leeds other than that he was their new manager. There was no camaraderie between Clough and Shankly. Leeds' manager was simply ignored by the elder statesman when he attempted to initiate some light-hearted conversation.

He and Shankly were two men with very different things on their minds as they led out their respective teams on a day that was to disgrace the game of football. As Eddie Gray admits: 'The Charity Shield did Clough no favours.' The match had an extraordinary prelude, as later explained by Clough in his book *Clough: The Autobiography*:

> The television pictures from Wembley, for the traditional curtain-raiser of the Charity Shield, should have been different. They showed dear old Bill Shankly leading out his magnificent Liverpool side and alongside him, followed by the Leeds team with the glummest faces ever seen at such an occasion, there was me. Much as I admired Shanks, and I loved the man, I didn't want to march from the tunnel at the head of the Leeds United side that day. I asked Don Revie to lead them out, instead.
>
> Yes, I was prepared and eager to relinquish the honour of that managerial march onto the Wembley turf which was, and still is, the dream and ambition of everyone who enters the profession. I had not won the title with Leeds – Revie had. I phoned Revie on the day of the match. 'This is your team,' I told him, 'you lead them out at Wembley.' Apart from anything else, I thought it was a decent thing to do, a nice gesture towards a man who had just won the League title – the toughest test of management anywhere in the world. But he was not to be tempted.
>
> 'Pardon?' he said, obviously taken aback by my offer. 'You've got the job now, Brian. I'm not coming down to lead them out. It is your privilege.'
>
> There should be a feeling of pride and immense satisfaction when you make that walk from the tunnel to the touchline at what is still the most famous old

stadium in the world. There always was on the umpteen occasions I did it with my Nottingham Forest team. I wonder how many managers have taken their teams to Wembley as often as I did? Not many.

I was proud – and, to use Revie's word, privileged – to walk out alongside Shankly. In fact, I remember turning towards him and clapping him as we walked. But there was no sense of togetherness with those who walked behind me.

This set the tone for a fiery afternoon.

Match of the Day commentator Barry Davies' observation that this was a 'sunshine start to the season' was ironically undercut when, in the opening exchanges, Tommy Smith clattered into Allan Clarke and went straight into the referee's notebook. Then Norman Hunter clipped Steve Heighway, but these two stern challenges did not prevent some good football developing. Then in the 19th minute, out of nothing, Keegan brought a fine save from Harvey only for Phil Boersma to bundle home the rebound from close quarters, with the Leeds defence appealing for handball. The goal appeared to deflate Leeds, with Liverpool assuming the ascendancy, A wild challenge in midfield just before the interval brought Johnny Giles a stern rebuke from the referee before the teams marched off, with Liverpool deserving their narrow lead.

Leeds began the second half with renewed vigour, but then the game took an ugly turn. Keegan held his face after an incident described by Davies as 'looking like a right hook from Johnny Giles' and earning the Leeds man a booking. Then Bremner and Keegan, two of the biggest names in football, began throwing punches at each other. The referee was called over after the intervention of a linesman. A clearly incandescent Keegan, who moments earlier had appeared to be sympathising with Giles, was sent off and immediately removed his shirt. On the long walk back to the dressing-room, he threw it down in disgust. Bremner, meanwhile, had received his own marching orders and he too took off his shirt. 'This is just what English football did not want to see,' remarked Davies. 'Surely, we have got to get away from this. What do the players think they are doing? To dismiss the referee's authority in such a manner cannot be good for the game. We are seeing the unacceptable face of English football.'

Thankfully, football once again became the order of the day, and on 70 minutes, Lorimer's well-measured cross into the box was met by Trevor Cherry, who headed sweetly past Clemence to bring Leeds level. It was to end all square, requiring a penalty shootout, with the Reds coming out on top. Now the inquests were to begin.

In the wake of the incident, some commentators went so far as to suggest that both clubs should be demoted from the First Division. The article by Geoffrey Green that appeared in *The Times* condemning the display of violence was representative of the general view:

> That [the brawl], in itself, would have been enough to disgust. But both men compounded the felony as they began the long walk to the dressing-rooms by shamelessly stripping off the shirts they should have been proud to wear, Bremner, indeed, throwing his petulantly to the ground, where it lay crumpled like a shot seagull until cleared away by a linesman. It was a disgusting scene, the volcanic climax of three earlier affrays which had seen Smith and Giles booked.
>
> Sadly, Keegan could have been the man of the match. Leeds patently realised this by half-time and seemed intent on eliminating him by fair means or foul. They chose the unfair method, finally goading the little Liverpool man into hot-headed retaliation with all the dire consequences for those who consider themselves above the law.
>
> Never before had Wembley witnessed such a disgrace as two British players for the first time were dismissed

from the stadium. It made child's play of the Rattin affair in the World Cup of 1966.

Argentine central midfielder Antonio Rattín was dismissed against England in the quarter-final at Wembley for repeatedly protesting to German referee Rudolf Kreitlein over decisions given for his teammates' misdemeanours. England manager Sir Alf Ramsey famously labelled the Argentinians 'animals' and Rattín's sending-off was the incident that sparked the introduction of yellow and red cards.

Green concluded:

> If clubs are held responsible for the behaviour of their supporters, so should they be for their players. The final responsibility and remedy rest with all directors and managers and they also should share the penalty. The harder they are hit where it hurts most, the better – either through their pockets, with heavy fines, or by deducting points from a club's league total. That might make everybody think twice.
>
> One way or another, a solution has to be found if the game is to survive as a respectable spectacle. The final sanction may be for all reasonable people simply to stay away and let ritual violence destroy itself.

The fallout from this debacle was immense. Bremner and Keegan were each fined £500, with Bremner being suspended for eight games and Keegan for three. It would be October before Bremner played again. The FA must have been disappointed that their new Wembley showcase had been ruined, and the chairman of their disciplinary committee, Vernon Stokes, confirmed that the harshness of the punishments had been influenced by the fact that the match had been televised.

It was certainly a baptism of fire for Clough, who was to comment in *Clough: The Autobiography*:

Billy Bremner's behaviour was scandalous, producing one of the most notorious incidents in Wembley history. It was as if the players were offering grounds for all my criticism that they had resented so much.

Bremner seemed intent on making Kevin Keegan's afternoon an absolute misery. He kicked him just about everywhere – up the arse, in the balls – until it became only a matter of time before a confrontation exploded. There is only so much any man can take. Eventually, inevitably, Keegan snapped – and they were both sent off, Keegan whipping off his shirt and flinging it to the ground as he went. It was a stupid gesture, but I could understand the man's anger and frustration. It was the action of a player who felt he had been wronged, not only by an opponent but by a referee who had failed to stamp out intimidation before it reached the stage of retaliation. Keegan will have regretted his touchline tantrum immediately. A Liverpool shirt was not something to be thrown away.

Keegan was a victim, not a culprit, that day at Wembley. The double dismissal was all down to Bremner. Keegan was an innocent party who had been pushed beyond the limit by an opponent who appeared determined to eliminate him from the match, one way or another. I told Bremner afterwards that he had been responsible for the confrontation. He should have been made to pay compensation for the lengthy period Keegan was suspended.

Long-serving Reds defender Tommy Smith, talking to the *Sunday Times* in 2008, remembered feeling that the match had the potential to be explosive:

We had players who could look after themselves, and so did Leeds. We went at each other hammer and tongs. Nobody was going to shy away, and there was no complaining or whining on the field that day. As for the sendings-off, Leeds had been getting at Kevin all day, Johnny Giles in particular. It was at a corner, and Giles came up behind Keegan and whacked him. Kevin whirled round but Giles had disappeared and Billy was the nearest Leeds player so Kevin went for him. OK, so Billy ended up throwing punches too, but it should have been Giles who got Kevin's attention.

Despite the dismissals, there were only two other bookings: me, for a foul on Allan Clarke, and Giles. The disciplinary committee tried to throw the book at us too, accusing us of starting the ill-feeling. But Matt Busby [the former Manchester United manager] was on the panel and he soon put a stop to that and we both got off without even a fine.

As a rule, Giles made no apology for his or United's combative approach to football, which he claimed was both legitimate and necessary. Looking back on his career in an interview with the Irish *Evening Herald*, he said:

It's a physical battle. You have to go through the battle. It was my living, not my sport and if I didn't respond in the way I should respond, I was going to be out of this game, so I became as big an assassin as there was and as dangerous in my own way. You keep your head, you do it coldly, you do it clinically, but you let everybody know in the game that there are no liberties taken here. I was given the choice of becoming a lion or a lamb and I was determined not to become a lamb.

Liverpool's Glaswegian midfielder Brian Hall was in no doubt beforehand that the match would be bruising. Also talking to the *Sunday Times*, he recalled:

Manchester United were in decline at that time, so our big games then were against Leeds and Everton. There was always something about playing Leeds. They were tough matches and I had to learn fast. I remember lining up in the tunnel to face Leeds for the first time when Tommy Smith nudged me and said, 'Hey, Brian, that fucking degree won't do you any good against this lot.' He was right, too. My background was different from most of my teammates. Like Steve Heighway, I'd come to Liverpool late, having played amateur football after leaving university. The difference was that I was more of a passer while Steve liked to run with the ball at his feet. Before that first game, Shanks told me that Big Jack [Charlton] and Norman Hunter in the Leeds defence were not quick and that I should run at them when I got the chance. Well, Norman kicked me all over the pitch. I was counting my bruises in the bar afterwards when this big arm wrapped around my neck and Norman leaned over and said, 'Sorry about that, Brian, I thought you were Steve Heighway.'

Of the notorious match, Peter Lorimer says: 'The Charity Shield was always a huge occasion and no matter how antagonistic our feelings towards Clough were, there was no way we were going to underperform. Firstly, this was at football's Mecca, with the eyes of the world upon us, and secondly we were up against opponents who were our arch-rivals and enemies of the time. It was a big day for Mr Clough, too, having come up from the relative obscurity of Brighton. This did not need stoking up as a contest. For a decade, we had traded blows with Liverpool as the best two teams in the land and pride was very much at stake. This was the game, of course, in which Billy Bremner and Kevin Keegan wound each other up so much that they both ended up rolling round the pitch a few times like fighting dogs, for which they both got their marching orders.

'There had been no specific pre-match instructions from the new manager, who was content to tell us that we'd all been in this kind of situation before and therefore knew what we were doing. In a way, that was a refreshing change for me personally, because I had come to loathe Don Revie's dossiers on the opposition. Such was the detail in his analysis of players we were up against that he could make Hartlepool United sound like Real Madrid. It was all very tedious and you could be forgiven for wondering why, for example, Hartlepool, as our cup opponents, were two or three divisions below us, and we were the champions of England, when, according to Don's dossier, they were such fabulous players.

'By and large you wouldn't be nervous when you sat down to listen to him, but by the time he'd finished you'd be on the verge of collapse with fear. He'd make the full-back marking me sound like the world's best defender, but five minutes into the game you'd discover he was the tosser you always thought he was before Don planted his seeds of doubt. He'd be saying, "He's got a great left foot, he really gets stuck in, he's up and down the line for 90 minutes," and so on, and in the third minute you've nutmegged him, he's fallen over and you've got an unmissable chance from three yards. Pretty soon, Don's dossier was going in one ear and out of the other, but that suited me anyway. That's how I was about football – laid-back and very relaxed. Really, it was just Don's way. He felt you had to know everything and that if you didn't he hadn't done his job.

'Cloughie, on the other hand, was very basic. "Get out there" was about the sum total of it, and to be honest that suited me. My idea of playing football was just getting out there and playing football. I know what I'm doing, I know what I'm good at, I know why I'm in the team, I know what's expected of me. So let's get on with it.'

With a fractious Charity Shield defeat behind Clough and Leeds, that was exactly what they were going to have to do. The English league season was about to begin.

7

RAIN ON OUR PARADE

*What I tell my players about defending a lead is this:
'If you have the ball and you are in their half,
they cannot score.'*

Brian Clough

Some venues are considered bogey grounds by clubs who struggle to achieve victory on their travels to certain stadia, and for Leeds United, Stoke City's old Victoria Ground came very much into that category. If Brian Clough had not already had a difficult enough start at Leeds, then the fixture list would ensure that life was not going to get any easier. The opening-day fixtures of the 1974–75 season put Leeds on the road to the Potteries. Peter Lorimer recalls: 'There was some consternation in the camp, given our introductory meeting, about what the match-day build-up would be like and the tone and contents of the manager's pre-match team talk. As usual with Clough, it was amazing. We were staying at a hotel not far from the ground and a couple of hours before kick-off he said, "Come on, we're going for a walk."

'Bizarrely, he took us to the central reservation of a dual carriageway, and as we followed, looking at each other and shrugging our shoulders, he ordered us to sit down. We did as we were told, and right there and then he embarked upon his team talk. He wasn't far into it – I think he got as far as "Things are going to be different . . ." – when the heavens opened and within seconds, dressed only in casual shirts and trousers, we were drenched. We thought we'd better find shelter indoors fast, so we all got to our feet with the intention of heading back to the hotel. "Oi, you lot," he bellowed. "Where do you think you're going? Sit back down. You'll get back up when I tell you to get back up." That was him again, wanting to belittle us – you'll sit in the rain and listen to me. Well, of course, the reaction was a derisory guffaw and "You can please yourself. We're not sitting here in the pissing rain."

'So off we went to the match venue. We lost 3–0 and I think that was no surprise to anybody in the Leeds camp. At half-time, he had a rant about this and a rave about that, but nobody was listening. We just thought of this individual who held us to be thieves and thugs, "You can go and fuck yourself." None of us needed to be boastful. You could ask many of the big-name players who played against us at the time – the great Arsenal centre-half Frank McLintock springs readily to mind as one of them – and they would be of the opinion that Leeds were unquestionably the best team in England and just possibly one of the best teams that the country ever produced. And Clough was treating us with disdain and contempt. It was unacceptable.'

* * *

SATURDAY, 17 AUGUST 1974
STOKE CITY 3, LEEDS UNITED 0

'We played enough football to have won three matches. In the first half we could have been three up. I am sorry for the lads, they wanted to win this one very much.'

That is the new manager Brian Clough's verdict on Leeds United's shock 3–0 defeat by a lively and skilful Stoke City side at the Victoria Ground.

At first glance this defeat does nothing for the morale of United players or their supporters, but there was something in what Clough said. Analysed more closely, defeat does not seem depressing.

United will play far worse and win and will create fewer openings in a match and score goals.

At Stoke, United's main problem was their inability to make the chances they created in front of goal count. There were several times when they could have scored had the finishing been a little sharper or more accurate.

I could not help wondering if the story might have had a happier ending had Clough been able to call upon suspended striker Allan Clarke, or the injured Mick Jones and had not new signing Duncan McKenzie been at a disadvantage through his comparative lack of pre-season preparation.

Clough's dilemma up front forced him into thrusting McKenzie into the demanding arena of First Division football with little or no pre-season training behind him.

Because he had been in dispute with his previous club, Nottingham Forest, McKenzie trained with amateur teams in the Derby area and with the best will in the world this, as Clough says, is no substitute for the preparation he would have received had he been at Elland Road for the full pre-season build-up.

United's best chance fell to McKenzie at a crucial period. They were trailing by only a goal – a 50th minute 30-yarder from Welsh international John Mahoney – when Peter Lorimer, United's most industrious player, found him with a low right-wing pass, standing some two or three yards from goal.

Somehow the ball stuck between McKenzie's feet and when he recovered his poise he shot weakly into the grounded Stoke goalkeeper John Farmer.

Had that gone in Stoke might not have been basking today in the glory of such a resounding triumph at the expense of the league champions.

Paul Madeley had two close-range efforts – a header and a shot – blocked by Farmer, the second more by good luck than good management, Lorimer shot narrowly wide and so did Johnny Giles, who also brought a fine save from Farmer with a well-taken free kick.

Jimmy Greenhoff got the goal that sickened his former teammates four minutes from the end, his 18 yards shot deflecting off Trevor Cherry and wrong-footing David Harvey.

When John Ritchie fired in the third with two minutes left it hardly mattered, United were already beaten.

Though it might have been different had United taken their chances and had that bit of luck when it mattered, there was no doubting Stoke's right, in the end, to victory.

They won because Alan Hudson, one-time Chelsea rebel who has settled down surprisingly well in the austere surroundings of the Potteries, gave them the edge in midfield, with a display that would have earned him the man-of the-match award had there been one.

Stoke are no longer the pushovers they once were. They are an entertaining team – strong in defence, imaginative in midfield and powerful up front.

It would come as no surprise to me if Stoke chairman Albert Henshall's belief that this season could be his club's greatest came true.

A 3–0 victory over the league champions, which has made Stoke 12/1 to win the championship compared to 28/1 before the game, is good enough for starters . . .

Stoke City: Farmer, Marsh, Pejic, Dodd, Smith, Mahoney, Haslegrave, Greenhoff, Ritchie, Hudson, Salmons.

Leeds United: Harvey, Reaney, Cooper, Bremner,

McQueen, Cherry, Lorimer, Madeley, Jordan, Giles, McKenzie.

Referee: Mr Ken Burns.

Don Warters, *Yorkshire Evening Post*

* * *

Eddie Gray was beginning to fear the worst. 'It just wasn't working,' he says. 'Clough was no inspiration with his team talks, and his treatment of the players was shoddy. He showed nothing. There was no mutual respect, and in the end the players treated him with disdain. I felt sorry for little Jimmy Gordon. I don't know whether Clough planned these things or not, but when it came to training Jimmy would be jogging us round and round, and Cloughie would be messing about shooting at one of the goals, completely ignoring us, as much as to say, "I'll show you. I'll come out when I'm good and ready, not when you think I should be ready."

'I think Brian without his right-hand man Peter Taylor – and I don't know the ins and outs of what happened to effect a split in their professional relationship – wasn't the same Brian Clough who had done such extraordinary things with Derby. They had known and trusted each other for so long, and had their partnership survived and Peter accompanied him to Elland Road rather than going solo at Brighton, where together they had had a bit of a nightmare, things might have been different. Peter would maybe have been able to calm him down and say to him, "Now come on. They've got some good players here. Let's just slowly do what we want." But Peter decided against accompanying Clough to Leeds. Maybe he thought, "I know what Cloughie's like. He doesn't like Revie. He doesn't like Leeds. It has all the ingredients of one big mess." He would have been right.'

* * *

WEDNESDAY, 21 AUGUST 1974
LEEDS UNITED 0, QPR 1

'Don't jump to gloomy conclusions.' These were the words of comfort offered to Leeds United supporters by Queens Park Rangers' manager Gordon Jago.

Speaking immediately after his lively Rangers side had sent United toppling 1–0 to their second defeat in five days, Jago told me: 'Leeds are still a great side and they will be there or thereabouts in the chase for honours – make no mistake about that.

'They were lacking several top players, and we expected them to be a bit desperate following their defeat at Stoke and because they would be wanting to please their new manager.

'That desperation showed as the game went on. They threw plenty at us, but we dealt with it well.'

Despite the fact that several Leeds first-teamers were unavailable through suspension, illness or injury, Jago was highly delighted with his side's 1–0 victory even though they received help on the way to that success from a most unlikely source – goalkeeper David Harvey.

Normally one of the soundest keepers in the business, Harvey allowed a 30-yard shot from Rangers striker Gerry Francis, which he appeared to have well covered, slip from his grasp for the ball to go into the net.

Disappointed Harvey said afterwards: 'I feel terrible about it, especially as it cost the lads the match. The ball must have "kicked" right at the last minute.

'Mick Bates said it definitely swerved to the right very late, but I should have got my body behind it. It's the worst mistake in my career.'

There was some comfort however for Harvey from manager Brian Clough. 'My sympathies went out to David Harvey. I felt sorry for him. It is essential however, that he forgets it,' he said.

Although that one error brought the only goal of the game, Harvey should not be made to shoulder the entire blame for this setback.

United did not play as well as they can do. This was one inescapable fact. They lacked the rhythm and confidence that led them to becoming worthy champions last season.

And Harvey redeemed himself later with some splendid work, notably when he raced out to save bravely as Givens rushed onto a poor back pass from Paul Reaney.

Then a fine diving save to stop a shot from the same Rangers player further helped to make up for that first-half blunder.

Though United are not at their best yet, there was a greatly encouraging display from Terry Cooper, who showed several glimpses of his skilful left-wing raiding, which helped make him the best attacking left-back in the country before he broke his leg.

Also on the credit side was a sound display from defenders Gordon McQueen and Paul Reaney.

Duncan McKenzie looked fitter than he did when he made his league debut on Saturday, and he went close on a couple of occasions to scoring that elusive first goal for Leeds.

Clough named John O'Hare as substitute, but he gave Bremner's vacant midfield role to Mick Bates in preference to his other Derby signing John McGovern.

Bates worked hard, but again United lacked luck in front of goal, especially in the final 20 minutes when they launched a hectic assault on the Rangers goal.

Attendance 31,497

Leeds United: Harvey, Reaney, Cooper, Bates, McQueen, Cherry, Lorimer, Madeley, Jordan, Giles, McKenzie.

QPR: Parkes, Clement, Gillard, Venables, Mancini (Busby), Webb, Thomas, Francis, Abbott, Back, Givens.
Referee: Ralph Lee (Cheadle).

Don Warters, *Yorkshire Evening Post*

* * *

John Wray says: 'The immediate thought when Leeds got beaten 3–0 at Stoke in the first league game of the season was: "Are the players playing for him or aren't they?" There was that sneaking suspicion that they might not be, although I cannot go entirely along with that because those players were proud men and proud of their own performances and abilities. They would not want to let themselves down. But there is such a thing as going the extra yard and there is the question of where those players would have gone, and did go, the extra yard for Don, were they prepared to do that for Cloughie? Don't forget the lead-balloon stuff of orders to throw their medals away and the accusation of them being cheats. The second league match was a 1–0 home defeat by Queens Park Rangers in a match missed through suspension by Bremner, Clarke and Hunter. My match notes include: "Harvey let Francis's shot slip through his hands for a soft winner."'

8

PERSPECTIVES

Don't send me flowers when I'm dead.
If you like me, send them while I'm alive.

Brian Clough

One of the perspectives I wanted to include in this book was on the value of a good relationship between the manager and the players, and between the manager and the board, at a football club. That, or the lack of it, was patently a crucial factor in the short time that Brian Clough survived as Leeds United's manager. Further, I wanted to illustrate how that relationship might have changed between the 1970s and the 2000s. Peter Reid is the perfect authority on such matters.

He was signing his first professional playing contract at the same time as Clough was taking over Leeds. By April 1998, he had been boss at Sunderland for three years and chairman Bob Murray was offering him a ringing endorsement, backing him as the club's manager for the new millennium. He told the Newcastle *Journal*'s Ian Murtagh, 'I think he is the new Brian Clough.' Murtagh's piece ran:

> On the eve of tonight's do-or-die showdown against Ipswich at Portman Road, [Murray] compared Reid to the legendary Brian Clough, one of the most successful

managers in footballing history. Reid's contract at the Stadium of Light has 12 months to run, and once Sunderland's destiny this term is decided, the board are ready to negotiate an extension to his current deal, which would make him the club's longest-serving manager since Alan Brown in the '60s.

Murray said: 'There are so few talented English managers in the game but Peter is definitely one of them. In some ways, I think he is the new Brian Clough. He can go all the way and I'd like to think it is with Sunderland. I believe the relationship between him and me is to be treasured and valued. Something awful must have gone wrong at Manchester City for them to sack him. I certainly haven't seen it in his management here. He is in football for life and his commitment is total. We rarely talk about anything else than the game and he never takes holidays. He will do what he wants because he's his own man but he loves this club and has an affinity with the people and the region.'

In fact, Reid's tenure at Sunderland lasted until October 2002. When he departed he had completed almost eight years' service – a lifetime in modern-day football – and had etched his name forever on football in the north-east of England.

That affinity with the people and the region mentioned by Bob Murray was something Reid shared with Clough, whose Middlesbrough contract was taken over by Sunderland in July 1961 and who was a great success in the North-east. At Boro, he scored 204 goals in 222 games, and he was equally prolific for his new club until, on Boxing Day 1962, he suffered a career-ending cruciate ligament injury.

The coincidence of Clough's and Reid's involvement with Sunderland was to be repeated with Leeds. After departing Sunderland, Reid was out of work until March 2003, when he was appointed interim manager at Elland Road following the dismissal of Terry Venables. It was against all the odds that he kept Leeds in the Premier League, and he was rewarded with the offer of the job on a permanent basis. Leeds, however, were struggling financially, and Reid was forced to sell Harry Kewell to Liverpool and bring in cheaper players to take his place. Leeds were soon fighting to avoid relegation once more, and before the year ended Reid had been sacked after a 6–1 loss to recently promoted Portsmouth.

As a player, Reid had few peers as a midfield enforcer. He joined Bolton Wanderers in 1974, gaining promotion to the top flight with them four years later, although they lasted only two seasons in the First Division. Reid, suffering from injuries and therefore commanding a fee of only £60,000, left for Everton in 1982. There, he was a member of the side that won the 1984 FA Cup, the league championship and European Cup-Winners' Cup in 1985 (they came close to making it a treble but were defeated 1–0 by Manchester United in the FA Cup) and the championship again in 1987.

Reid, who was voted PFA Footballer of the Year in 1985, won 13 caps for England and was outstanding in the 1986 World Cup in Mexico. In 1989, he went to QPR on a free transfer before travelling to Manchester City the next season. When he arrived, City were managed by Howard Kendall. When in November 1990 Kendall left to return to Everton, Reid was given his first managerial role, being appointed City's player-manager. In his first season in charge, the Blues came fifth in the league, beating rivals Manchester United. They finished in the same position the following season, but in 1992–93, they dropped to ninth. Reid was sacked at the beginning of the next season.

Then, in a surprise move, Reid joined Southampton as a player. The team had been defeated in all but one of their first nine games of 1993–94. Despite playing only eight games, Reid was significant to the team's revitalisation, and Saints made a partial recovery. When, after a defeat at the Dell at the hands of Norwich, their beleaguered manager Ian Branfoot was sacked, it was suggested that Reid might take the job. He maintained, however, that as Branfoot had brought him to Southampton, he felt that he too ought to move on. He played for Notts County and Bury, but soon retired for good.

It was then that he restarted his management career at Sunderland. The team were struggling to stay in Division One, but Reid succeeded in keeping them there. Next season, 1995–96, they topped the division and were promoted to the Premier League. Reid had won the affection of the fans and that year a group of supporters had a minor hit under the name Simply Red and White with 'Cheer Up, Peter Reid', sung to the tune of 'Daydream Believer' by the Monkees. Unfortunately, Sunderland were back in the First Division for the next season, which meant, disappointingly, that their new 42,000-seat Stadium of Light, built to replace Roker Park, would initially be a second-tier stadium rather than one hosting Premier League football.

In 1997–98, Sunderland lost out on automatic promotion by one place and drew 4–4 with Charlton Athletic in a thrilling play-off final at Wembley. Reid's side were finally beaten 7–6 in a penalty shoot-out, only to come back the next season with a record-breaking 105-point First Division victory. In 1999–2000, Sunderland narrowly missed out on a place in Europe. They made it to seventh in the league, one of the best results ever achieved by a newly promoted Premier League team.

Reid, who had briefly managed the national Under-21 team at the turn of the millennium, took the team to second in the top flight for a time, raising hopes for Champions League qualification, but gradually they dropped back down the league and ended up once more in seventh place.

Having left Sunderland for Leeds, Reid had a brief spell in charge of Coventry City in 2004. Then, in 2008, when he had been out of the game for four years, he was appointed manager of the Thailand national team, aiming to qualify for the 2014 World Cup in Brazil.

Reid says: 'You were very aware as an apprentice professional not only of what was going on at your own club but throughout English football – after all, it was your lifestyle and livelihood – and Don Revie's appointment as England manager and the arrival of Brian Clough as his replacement at Leeds was certainly very big news at the time. Even bigger news was Clough's departure after only 44 days. What could Clough have achieved in that time? You rarely know the ins and outs of such high-profile events. The reasons for the sackings of football managers down the decades have been many and varied, and have made laughable that cliché of an explanation 'mutual consent'. As I discovered most recently through what happened to my good friend Sam Allardyce at Newcastle, if a club wants you out, it will have you out.

'Leeds had such great players . . . Giles, Hunter, Lorimer, Gray, Bremner – you could go on and on – but clubs are not necessarily successful through having good players alone. For big things to be achieved, the players have got to have respect for the manager and, in turn, the manager must respect his players. As manager, it's your job to get the best out of your players and to give yourself a chance of doing that you have got to treat them right. If a player has done something to warrant a bollocking, then he must be given a bollocking but, by and large, I think players like discipline. They like to know where they stand. They're human beings and, being human beings, if they're allowed to take an inch, they'll take another inch and then another. They have got to know where the cut-off point is. And it's the manager who puts that marker in the sand who will gain the players' respect.

'They do this in different ways. Howard Kendall, for instance, was a terrific manager who got some great results through tactical awareness, although he had to earn the respect of the players and he got it in the end. The modern-day perception is that you can't be too much of a disciplinarian with players, but Ferguson, Mourinho and Wenger have given the lie to that.

'The '70s was a golden era for character managers, Clough among them. Joe Mercer, Malcolm Allison, my own manager at Bolton Wanderers Ian Greaves, who was one of the Busby Babes, Ron Greenwood, Tommy Docherty, Bertie Mee – it was a generation of absolutely outstanding managers. Nowadays, the chairmen, chief executives, directors of football – all the hierarchical figures – are well known, but then it was just the manager at the forefront of affairs.

'In my days at Manchester City, you'd just have the one local radio station coming down for a pre-match interview, but now a manager's office, or the media centre, is like one huge recording studio, with microphones everywhere. You've got to be media savvy. Having said that, even back then Clough, Bill Shankly and Matt Busby were masters of it. There was an honesty about them in front of a television camera or a radio microphone that was somehow disarming. Clough, particularly, was brilliant. You don't handle players like he did without having a certain amount of intelligence. These days, they put an emphasis on sports psychology; he ordered his players to have a pint, or a glass of wine if they preferred, just before a European Cup final. He made them do it. They had to have one. That's genius. Clough's generation didn't have degrees, but they knew how to handle people. And that's a gift. When Clough lost it and clipped a fan round his earhole, we were seeing his passion. Today, he'd have been in front of the Court of Human Rights, but then I think most people related to what he was doing and why.

'I managed against him and played against teams managed by him, and it was invariably a pleasure because Clough's teams played in the right way. He was always a laugh, as well. I remember being injured in one game, and by the time the final whistle had gone I was already changed. I had this blue check suit on. It was a bit loud. He came into the dressing-room and said to me, "Young man, you look like a clown. You should be in the circus." I said, "You should borrow it. You'd make an even better clown because you've got the red nose to go with it!"

'I always got the impression with Clough that he would say something controversial or provocative to his own players to test them, to see what they would come back with. And if they retorted with something amusing or witty, I think he liked them from that moment on. I never played for him, but that was always the impression I got when I was in his company. A big, big personality. With Peter Taylor, I think there were differences of opinion that led to a falling-out. Peter was a big character as well, and maybe, in the end, it was a clash of personalities. Peter would spot the players he knew could be moulded into his and Brian's ways, and they had a great partnership together. I find it sad that they were never reconciled. Life's too short for that.

'Under Revie, Leeds had a very decent European pedigree, and they did well on the Continent again during the David O'Leary reign at the turn of the millennium. Some say Leeds have underachieved down the years, but I don't go along with that opinion. They have had very good sides, but the truly great sides, the ones who win league championships, the domestic cups and the European trophies, invariably have great goalkeepers. This may sound harsh, and I don't mean any disrespect to them, but I would not class Leeds' Gary Sprake, David Harvey or David Stewart as being in the same league as people like Peter Shilton or Peter Schmeichel or Petr Cech. I believe that with a great, world-class goalkeeper in their ranks the Leeds of old would have won more than they did.

'There are some rude things said about Don Revie sometimes, but there is no denying that he built a fantastic football side. There was genuine affection among the Leeds players for both Don and Les Cocker, who had brought most of them through from being boys into giants of the game. Just like Sir Alex Ferguson has been a father figure at Old Trafford over two decades, so Don was Daddy at Elland Road. I got into the England Under-21 side under Don and so acquired first-hand knowledge of the family atmosphere he was able to create, with his quizzes and card games and the like. The trouble with Clough at Leeds was that he tried to build Rome in a day. He was a man in too much of a hurry.'

By the third game of the 1974–75 season, and with two league defeats on the board, Clough had every reason to feel a growing sense of urgency.

* * *

SATURDAY, 24 AUGUST 1974
LEEDS UNITED 1, BIRMINGHAM CITY 0

There was an air of anxiety over Leeds United for much of their game against Birmingham City at Elland Road, but their 1–0 victory took them a step along the road to recovery.

United began in a way which suggested they might swamp the Blues with powerful attacking play, similar to that in the first half of last season, when they went 29 League games without defeat.

Yet, when that much-needed early goal failed to materialise, United lapsed into a state of near nervous tension.

Birmingham had not only been able to deal competently with United's early intentions but succeeded in making time and space to show off their own attacking ability.

They succeeded in giving as good as they got, but half-time came with the scoresheet blank and 60 minutes had gone before the stalemate was broken.

United's England striker Allan Clarke, playing his first game of the season after a two-match suspension, was the man to score and one could sense the huge sigh of relief around the ground as the ball sped low into the net.

It had taken 240 minutes to bring United their first goal of the new season. It was a goal which, said manager Brian Clough afterwards, could only have been scored by Clarke.

United were attacking when Joe Gallagher moved to tackle home 'new boy' John O'Hare. The ball spun away, struck Wrexham referee John Williams on the shin and bounced forward.

Even then Birmingham should have cleared, but Clarke's ability to pounce on opportunities like this got him the better of defender Dick Sbragia and before City knew what was happening the ball was in the net.

'No one in England could have scored that goal better than Allan Clarke. It was a touch of class above all others,' a happy Clough remarked.

The way Clarke took his chance posed the question as to how much his lightning speed in and around the penalty area and his lethal finishing have been missed in United's two opening matches, when plenty of chances were created without being turned into goals.

Clarke told me before the game that he was keen to get back into action and it certainly showed in his play.

He along with defender Norman Hunter were two in the United side not affected by the tension which grew in the first half.

While Clarke was eager for the ball, Hunter marshalled United's defence in great style and was helped by another sterling display from Paul Reaney, and one from Trevor Cherry who switched to full-back again.

But there was another performance to take the eye – that of O'Hare. The former Derby striker remained calm and showed touches of his class in a debut which was almost crowned with a goal near the end, his 20-yard shot swerving away from the far post at the last second.

Said Clough: 'It took Clarke just a few minutes to read O'Hare. The crowd took to O'Hare but more important to me was the fact that the players accepted him.'

United's other newcomer from Derby, John McGovern, had a quiet game in midfield. He made plenty of space for himself but saw little of the ball. I have seen him much more involved in a game for Derby in the past.

United still have some way to go before they are back to the peak form of last season. But they are on their way.

This victory, narrow though it was, has lifted the gloom and set the stage for more accustomed results to follow.

Leeds United: Harvey, Reaney, Cherry, McGovern, McQueen, Hunter, Lorimer, Clarke, O'Hare, Giles, Madeley (Jordan).

Birmingham City: Latchford, Page, Styles, Kendall, Gallagher, Sbragia, Campbell, Francis, Burns, Hatton, Taylor.

Referee: John Williams (Wrexham).

Don Warters, Yorkshire Evening Post

* * *

Hugh McIlmoyle shares Peter Reid's view on the quality of coaches who plied their trade around the time of Clough's reign at Leeds. 'Football was blessed with some very talented managers in the 1960s and '70s,' he says. 'The game is the poorer for the passing of Clough and Bill Shankly, between whom I always make comparisons. I cannot bring to mind one without the other, because they were alike in many ways. Both were truly charismatic, though where one was very outspoken the other, while also able to amuse, was more measured and less aggressive in his profound pronouncements and proclamations. Both loved the game deeply. Both were winners. Both were loved by their players. Except, of course, Clough was not loved by the Leeds players, and that could only have been down to a clash of personalities.

'The thing with players is that they can generally see through a manager. As a breed, they are notorious for mickey-taking, and if they spot a flaw in the boss, it will become the subject of much banter. They'll pick holes in him. Clough and Shankly, masters of their craft, were generally above that, and in all my years in the game I never heard a bad word said about either of them. Players, like any group of people in all walks of life, have different temperaments and need handling in various ways. Some need a bollocking, perhaps every other game, and respond well to that; others need an arm round them and will be all the better for it. Football is an emotion-charged sport. Man-management is the key, and I think Clough was probably brilliant at that most of the time.

'With him, you could expect the unexpected. His teams could have a stinker, and where the normal reaction to that would be the manager screaming on the top note about how rubbish they had just performed and a summons to an extra training session at 10 a.m. on the Sunday to be thrashed round the running track, Clough would say, "See you Thursday, lads." My guess is that he instinctively knew how deeply the players would be hurting and deemed it pointless to rub more salt into their wounds.

'He sometimes took it upon himself to take the players away for a change of scene, say to Blackpool for a couple of days, and before such excursions he would send each of the wives and girlfriends a bunch of flowers and a box of chocolates. These gestures would endear him to the players, and from his perspective the reciprocal gift from the players would be that they would determine to play out of their skins on his behalf. Shanks' strategy would be to go on television after some fine performance and declare his players the best XI in the world. For them, it was all about making their players feel good about themselves.'

Further insight into what makes a successful player–manager relationship was given by the then Sunderland supremo Roy Keane in an interview with Rob Stewart for the *Daily Telegraph* ahead of his side's Carling Cup clash with Nottingham Forest at the City Ground in August 2008. Insisting that the man who managed him at Forest would still have what it takes to thrive in the Premier League, Keane described Clough as 'the best manager I played under, without a shadow of doubt'. While recognising that Clough's maverick methods might not go down too well with today's multimillionaire footballers, in answer to the question 'Would he survive today?', Keane concluded:

Most definitely. He'd stand up to the challenges, although he might have been reluctant to move with the times in terms of the scientific side of things. And I bet Sir Alex Ferguson would tell you the same.

I'm pretty sure Cloughie wouldn't like what's going on in the game now, with fitness coaches taking over, ProZones, weights, dieticians, pasta and bananas. But he would be a success, because he was a football genius.

Cloughie would have survived. He'd have adapted and made his mark at whatever club he was at, because he knew his football. The stuff he used to come up with at Forest was so simple, and I try to take that into what we do here.

Stewart noted, however, that, despite his respect for Clough's abilities, Keane seemed less than likely to take on board his more unusual methods. Keane, who today is in charge of Ipswich Town, recalled:

Before I made my debut, I ended up at his house in Derby on the way to Anfield. He gave me a pint of milk. I said, 'I don't like milk.' He said, 'You'd better drink it because I'm putting the bottles out.' Trust me, I drank it.

The day after the game he asked me my name, gave me a pair of his shoes and told me to polish them. If I brought my shoes in for one of the players to polish, I'm sure they'd throw them back at me. But modern-day players would put up with him if he was still around. They'd love playing for him, because he was different.

Once he made the whole Forest first team squash into a five-a-side goal, for no reason. But it was brilliant, just like a big game of Twister.

If someone did that today, you'd be thinking, 'How has this lad got his A or Pro Licence?' You all say, 'Why does he do that?' and that's the beauty of that. I don't know.

Once he made me go to a charity night with him and at the end he gave me a £50 note – I'd never seen one of those before. He was a kind gentleman and did loads of stuff for charity. He was a great man.

* * *

TUESDAY, 27 AUGUST 1974
QPR 1, LEEDS UNITED 1

Fears that Leeds United's crown is slipping were dispelled by the champions in an exhilarating display against a first-class Queens Park Rangers side in London.

Playing with zest and confidence, two qualities lacking in their previous games under new management, United were full value for their 1–1 draw in an action-packed thriller which was a splendid advertisement for English soccer.

Rangers, famed for their flying starts, set a scorching pace in the first quarter of an hour in the warm evening sunshine before a 24,965 crowd and threatened to annihilate United.

But United's defenders, notably Gordon McQueen, who scarcely put a foot wrong or misjudged a header in the 90 minutes, and the ever reliable Norman Hunter, stuck manfully to their tasks.

The artistry of Stan Bowles, the ball-playing brilliance of Gerry Francis and the speed and directness of Don Givens made for compulsive viewing, but although bubbling with flair and urgency, the Rangers attack foundered time and again on a formidable defence, which looked like the Leeds of old.

Francis, Rangers' man-of-the-match in their 1–0 win at Elland Road a week ago, made one sinuous dribble past three lunging defenders only to see Hunter block his shot, but generally was impotent thanks to the effective shadowing of Terry Yorath, playing his first match of the season and the 100th of his United career.

The tough Welshman, drafted into midfield in the absence of his suspended skipper Billy Bremner and the injured Paul Madeley, effectively carried out his orders not to leave Francis's side.

So the usually troublesome QPR striker spent a very unhappy evening trying to shake off his escorts, while Yorath, thriving on work, found himself with time to knock in the game's first goal with a cool lob from just outside the penalty area in the 21st minute.

All credit to Yorath for spotting keeper Parkes off his line, but new signing John O'Hare deserves praise for his brave challenge.

The Scot hurled himself at the ball, which by rights belonged to the keeper, and his persistence threw Parkes and fellow defender Mancini into confusion and the ball rolled out to the lurking Yorath.

United, their early season anxieties forgotten, were now in charge.

With acting skipper Johnny Giles providing midfield inspiration with as energetic and skilful a performance as I have seen from him for some time and a revitalised Allan Clarke sharpened and unselfish, United looked dangerous for long spells, particularly when making full use of Peter Lorimer and the overlapping of that splendid attacking full-back Paul Reaney on the flanks.

Rangers, too, effectively employed touchline raiders and their equaliser resulted from their switching the ball to the opposite wing.

Givens, their most dangerous attacker, snapped up a long ball from Mancini and slipped past Reaney and McQueen before hitting a magnificent left-foot shot past Harvey from 20 yards.

This goal in the 47th minute triggered off a hectic series of raids by the fast-moving Rangers forwards and two minutes later Givens struck the foot of the post with a fine header.

But United, displaying their traditional coolness and security when lesser sides would have lost their nerve, weathered the storm and might have clinched victory when Clarke was denied the goal he deserved, Gillard clearing from the line after fine work by Yorath.

To sum up: United recaptured much of the magic of that record-equalling start of last season, quick raids out of defence proving a constant threat to an exciting Rangers side, which tends to live dangerously at the back in their single-minded quest for goals.

But this performance suggests that manager Brian Clough will soon face selection problems. Last night's encouraging result was achieved without Bremner, Madeley and £250,000 striker Duncan McKenzie, and Scotland's World Cup hero Joe Jordan was on the subs' bench.

Keeping a huge first-team squad happy could yet prove Clough's biggest worry, as it was for his predecessor Don Revie. If he finds the answer, success must surely lie at the end of what promises to be an exciting and interesting winter.

The only blot on a reassuring all-round United display was Yorath's 18th-minute booking for a foul tackle on Francis, which was clumsy rather than malicious.

QPR: Parkes, Clement (Busby, 74), Gillard, Venables, Mancini, Webb, Thomas, Francis, Beck, Bowles, Givens.

Leeds United: Harvey, Reaney, Cherry, McGovern, McQueen, Hunter, Lorimer, Clarke, O'Hare, Giles, Yorath.

Mike Casey, *Yorkshire Evening Post*

* * *

Sunderland hotshot Brian Clough has Leeds United goalkeeper Alan Humphreys stretching in a Second Division clash at Roker Park in September 1961. (© Getty Images)

Late for work? Brian Clough arrives at Elland Road to take up his duties as Leeds United manager in August 1974.
(© *Yorkshire Evening Post*)

Clough's Leeds United squad. (© *Yorkshire Evening Post*)

The Leeds United squad celebrates winning the 1973–74
championship with the club's adoring fans.
(© *Yorkshire Evening Post*)

Brian Clough and Bill Shankly lead out their teams for the Charity Shield, with Leeds captain Billy Bremner holding the League Championship trophy and his opposite number Emlyn Hughes the FA Cup. (© Varley Picture Agency)

Clough shares a joke with some of his players, but the mood at Elland Road would soon turn sour. (© Varley Picture Agency)

Clough arrives at FA headquarters in London for a disciplinary hearing following the clash between Billy Bremner and Kevin Keegan. (© Getty Images)

A hole in his bucket? Clough, taking up residence in the Leeds United dugout, had poured cold water on the club's trophy-winning past.
(© Varley Picture Agency)

Eddie Gray, seen here in typical wing wizardry, was absent injured for most of Clough's Leeds United reign. Might things have worked out differently had he been fit? (© *Yorkshire Evening Post*)

Clough with his coach Jimmy Gordon (left) and new signing John McGovern in the Leeds United dugout. (© Varley Picture Agency)

Joe Jordan receives pitch-side instructions from Clough.
(© Varley Picture Agency)

Clough sits alongside Leeds United chairman Manny Cussins.
(© *Yorkshire Evening Post*)

Duncan McKenzie, pictured alongside Arsenal's John Radford, was a Clough signing for Leeds, and in this match in October 1974 he was on the mark as Clough's successor Jimmy Armfield got off to a winning start. (© *Yorkshire Evening Post*)

A winning team . . . but Clough endured his 44 days at Leeds without the assistance of his trusted right-hand man Peter Taylor.
(© *Varley Picture Agency*)

Leeds United pictured before the 1975 European Cup semi-final
against Barcelona. Back row (l–r): Norman Hunter, Peter Lorimer,
Paul Madeley, David Stewart, Gordon McQueen, Joe Jordan; front
row (l–r): Terry Yorath, Allan Clarke, Billy Bremner, Frank Gray,
Trevor Cherry. (© Keystone/Getty Images)

Allan Clarke is tackled by Franz Beckenbauer of Bayern Munich
during the 1975 European Cup final in Paris.
(© Keystone/Getty Images)

The greatness that Keane would later see in Clough had still to show itself at Leeds United as the end of August neared in 1974. On the back of a mediocre start to the season, some were beginning to question whether it ever would.

Reid appreciated Clough's wit and sense of humour, McIlmoyle his man-management and Keane his off-the-wall methods. All three men would no doubt consider their lives richer for having met Old Big 'Ead. David Harvey, United's goalkeeper, has never felt that he missed out. 'They say Cloughie was at Leeds for 44 days, but in reality it was more like 20,' says Harvey, recalling the sporadic training routine that characterised Clough's tenure. 'He was there so rarely that no one really had the chance to get to know him, and, from what I saw of him throughout his career, I'm at least grateful for that small mercy.'

9

HARD TIMES

It only takes a second to score a goal.

Brian Clough

Four games gone and the champions, in defence of their trophy, had picked up only three points. Much was going on in the background, and midfielder Terry Yorath relates: 'It developed into a sort of love–hate relationship between Brian Clough and me, with more hatred on his side than love. We were four games into the season before he gave me a first start, an away fixture at Queens Park Rangers. I scored a lovely chipped goal that earned us a 1–1 draw and was expecting all the plaudits back in the dressing-room, but instead I got a huge bollocking. The way at Leeds was always to try to get the first goal and hang on to the lead, and consequently when at one stage I got the ball on the halfway line, seeing no other immediate options, I passed the ball back to the goalkeeper. Clough went mad at this. From being the goal-scoring hero, I was suddenly the villain of the piece – in his eyes, anyway.

'It was Clough's attitude to training that was a source of great concern to the lads. When Revie was in charge, he'd be there from about 8 a.m. or certainly 8.30 a.m., but Clough never turned up until 9.30 a.m. or 10 a.m., and this would be after a game of squash. He very rarely took a training session, and if he got involved at all, it would be in shooting practice. Don't forget, he was dealing with a lot of seasoned professionals who had been used to and certainly expected better. He had deeply upset the players and the club before ever he arrived on the scene, and from the moment he walked in, I could not understand why he had taken the job.'

* * *

SATURDAY, 31 AUGUST 1974
MANCHESTER CITY 2, LEEDS UNITED 1

For much of the first half of Leeds United's attractive clash with Manchester City at Maine Road the champions looked to be approaching the form which took them to the title last season.

But the early penetration was blunted in the second half by a classic City side, who sent United to their third defeat in five games with a 2–1 win.

United faltered because they allowed themselves to become bogged down in midfield by a City plan aimed at stifling Johnny Giles.

Said City manager Tony Book afterwards: 'Leeds were going a bit in the 20 minutes before half-time so we started putting more pressure on Giles.

'He is the mastermind and we decided to push him back further into his own half. The plan worked.'

Before the game Book studied reports on how the Eire international had played in United's 1–1 draw at QPR and once City succeeded in reducing Giles's contribution they got on top.

Unfortunately for United, with Giles so closely marked, they had no Billy Bremner to fall back on. John McGovern tried hard but I have seen him have much more authoritative games for Derby.

In addition United were without Paul Madeley, who had a calf-muscle injury.

Even so United played a fair part in a game which was thoroughly entertaining and played in a sporting manner, the type designed to win back missing fans.

United began in lively fashion and played some encouraging football even before City took a shock lead in the seventh minute when Mike Summerbee, no longer skipper but still a great competitor, shot his side ahead with a low shot from the edge of the penalty area after he shuffled to the side of Norman Hunter.

United, however, continued to play attractive football and deservedly equalised eight minutes before half-time with a great goal by Allan Clarke.

City were moving into attack when McGovern hit a punted clearance which found Clarke handily placed just inside the home half.

With defenders slow to turn and thinking he might be offside, Clarke raced on and when goalkeeper Keith MacRae challenged, he calmly took the ball round him and slotted it home.

It was a typical Clarke goal – 'a classic' was how United boss Brian Clough described it – and it raised hopes of United's ability to win.

But City's second-half plan to stamp out Giles put paid to United's prospects of their first away win of the season.

Yet despite City's defensive solidarity, built very much around Alan Oates, United found a chance to equalise.

It fell to Gordon McQueen when MacRae could not hold the ball, but the centre-half, some six yards out, lifted his shot over the bar.

Clough said he could not complain about a centre-half missing a chance like that but the 'miss' served to highlight another of United's problems.

Clarke apart they are not lethal enough in their finishing, as three goals from five league matches clearly indicate. For a manager as attack-minded as Clough this will seem a meagre return.

Colin Bell showed how it is done when he slammed home an unstoppable shot in the 57th minute to give City their fourth victory in five games.

But former Sunderland winger Dennis Tueart who frequently troubled United defenders with his skill and tireless running, paved the way for the goal by slipping Hunter's tackle and laying the ball into Bell's path.

Manchester City: MacRae, Barrett, Donachie, Doyle, Booth, Oakes, Summerbee, Bell, Marsh, Hartford, Tueart.

Leeds United: Harvey, Reaney, Cherry, McGovern, McQueen, Hunter, Lorimer, Clarke, O'Hare, Giles, Yorath (Jordan).

Referee: Gordon Hill (Leicester).

Don Warters, *Yorkshire Evening Post*

* * *

Duncan McKenzie, the player whom Clough intended to be his inside man, was getting the impression that United's boss might be starting to crack. McKenzie says: 'I remember my phone going at one o'clock in the morning before a testimonial match at Southampton. I was half asleep, but I recognised the voice barking at me: "Young man, mezzanine, now." When I got there, Clough started giving me a rollicking about being drunk on the journey to Southampton, which was ridiculous because I didn't drink. But it became clear he had called me just to have someone to talk to. He was lonely, and the pressure was getting to him more than he would let on. So we stayed up and talked. He admitted how hard it was for him with Revie's picture on every wall and corridor at Elland Road. Although I was the new boy, I was the only one he seemed able to confide in.'

* * *

SATURDAY, 7 SEPTEMBER 1974
LEEDS UNITED 1, LUTON TOWN 1

If Leeds United manager Brian Clough was shaken by the boos and jeers a large section of the Elland Road crowd aimed at him after the 1–1 draw with Luton Town, he is not showing any reaction.

Few people enjoy being the target of such disapproving actions, not even a man like Clough, who appears to have thrived on being controversial in recent years.

When asked about the crowd's action Clough retorted: 'They were disappointed by the result. We all were, we worked hard to win.'

Clough was upset, however, about the attitude of the crowd to one of his three new signings – John McGovern, from Derby County, who to be frank, had what must have been his worst first-team game.

The 24-year-old midfield man could do little right and quickly became the target for a section of the crowd who voiced their disapproval in the strongest manner.

Said Clough: 'To say the crowd gave him some stick is the understatement of the season. Their attitude to him sickened me. But though he is a boy in stature, he is a man out there on the pitch and he won't allow it to destroy his game.'

The crowd, who at one stage during the game sang out the name of Clough's predecessor – Don Revie – also called for Terry Yorath, who sat on the substitute's bench throughout.

'I would not have brought McGovern off if we were losing 5–1,' Clough said.

'Terry Yorath spoke to McGovern at half-time and told him that when United won the title last year the fans were giving him the "bird". Today they were wanting him – that is how it goes in football,' Clough added.

McGovern had the sympathy, too, of former United

centre-half John Faulkner, who, after playing his part in holding the league champions to a draw, said: 'I felt very sorry for him. Clough brought him here and the team is not doing well so they had to pick on someone.'

Despite only being able to draw with the sort of opposition the United of old would quite conceivably have 'gobbled up' the United boss was not pessimistic.

Clough must have been mindful, too, that one leading firm of bookmakers had seen fit to offer United as a 10–1 bet for relegation – the first time in ten years that United had been quoted in the relegation stakes.

But Clough is a man who sees a way out of the present crisis in which United find themselves.

Four points out of a possible twelve is a disastrous start, but Clough says dogmatically: 'Our performance against Luton was only a yard away from being a superb performance.

'It was a question of confidence and the confidence is down to me. I instil it or destroy it, and I have not been able to instil it as yet. If we had stayed at 1–0 for a time against Luton and then got another one, we would have blossomed,' he added.

As manager it is up to Clough to motivate his team, to give it back the confidence, the flair and general arrogance it had last season when United swept to a record 29 matches without defeat in the league.

As manager it is Clough who has to bear the brunt of the disappointment and frustration the crowd felt at Saturday's display.

Clough is by no means a quitter and he will tackle the problems that face him. There can be no doubt about that.

In some ways Clough has been given a difficult Elland Road 'baptism' because he has been hampered in his team selections initially by injury, illness and suspensions.

Now he is unable to call upon the drive and leadership of the man who means so much to the side – skipper Billy Bremner, who is suspended until the end of the month.

Against Luton, United badly missed his leadership, though Johnny Giles worked well in midfield.

Bright spots for United were the displays of Paul Reaney, Peter Lorimer, who contributed much on United's right flank, and Allan Clarke, who scored United's goal.

Leeds United: Harvey, Reaney, Cherry, McGovern, McQueen, Hunter, Lorimer, Clarke, O'Hare, Giles, Madeley.

Luton: Barber, Shanks, Thomson, Anderson, Faulkner, Ryan (John), Hindson, Husband, Butlin, West, Alston (Jim Ryan).

Referee: John Bunting (Leicester).

Don Warters, *Yorkshire Evening Post*

＊ ＊ ＊

Peter Lorimer says now: 'The boys I felt sorry for were O'Hare and McGovern, because they were smashing lads who had been accepted in the dressing-room and obviously they felt caught up in the middle of it all. It quickly became apparent what was going on, and poor old McGovern was made to bear the brunt of the backlash, with the fans constantly getting on his back. As a fellow pro, you felt sorry for John because the problem was not of his making.

'But McGovern and O'Hare, frankly, were not good enough to get into our team and, further, I think they knew they were not good enough to get into our team. Certainly it was evident to the crowd, who were not getting the entertainment they had been accustomed to only a few short weeks before when we were celebrating winning the title with them.

'It was no surprise to me that after six games we were second bottom in the league. We didn't even look like winning a match.

There was a simple reason: nobody was going to play for Brian Clough.'

But Clough hit back at his critics in a *Yorkshire Evening Post* front-page article, saying, 'Do people really believe I would go out and destroy something for the sake of destroying it?' He insisted, 'I am getting the full support of the players. I have never been so convinced of anything in my life as that.'

Leeds chairman Manny Cussins echoed his manager's comments, saying, 'I know there is no unhappiness among the players.'

However, alarm bells were ringing.

10

HERE TODAY, GONE TOMORROW

If a chairman sacks the manager he initially appointed,
he should go as well.

Brian Clough

'So after these half-dozen games, here we were,' says Lorimer. 'We were the reigning champions, and just as we were about to embark on our European campaign, the whole place was falling apart.

'It was apparent to the directors who had appointed Clough that things were going awry. Manny Cussins and Sam Bolton, a former Leeds United chairman who was still on the board while ensconced in the higher echelons of the Football Association administrative structure, called a players' meeting. It was apparent, they maintained, that a problem existed and what they wanted to know this day was what that problem was. We basically told them exactly what Clough had said and what he had done, and they let it be known that they had already heard Clough's take on matters but he would now be brought into this meeting so that we were all under one roof together.

'"What is this?" asked Clough when he came in. It was put to him by the directors that we, as a group of players, were not responding to him or his managerial techniques and that this was obviously detrimental to the welfare of the club. "Are you sure?" asked Clough. "Who's saying that?" Again, astonishingly, it was Paul Madeley who was first into top gear and he said, "We just don't think you're any good as a manager. What you're doing is simply wrecking the football club." Paul had our full endorsement of this, and, it being our turn now to express an opinion on the capabilities and talents of an individual, we let him know what we thought of him. He wanted to know what he had done wrong and why in our view we were at the bottom of the league, and we told him.

'The following evening brought an away fixture against our lower-league West Yorkshire neighbours Huddersfield Town in the League Cup.'

* * *

TUESDAY, 10 SEPTEMBER 1974
LEAGUE CUP SECOND ROUND:
HUDDERSFIELD TOWN 1, LEEDS UNITED 1

The sight of Brian Clough leaping to his feet with fist clenched in triumphant salute told its own story at Leeds Road, home of Third Division Huddersfield Town.

That was how the Leeds United manager greeted the 89th-minute equaliser Peter Lorimer lashed into Town's goal from a near-impossible angle to give the league champions a 1–1 draw in their League Cup second-round tie.

It mattered little that United had been only 60 seconds away from the embarrassment and encumbrance another defeat would have brought.

It mattered little either that Lorimer's face-saving act had earned a draw against a side currently second from the bottom of the Third Division.

For these are difficult times for United, who are still searching for the light at the end of a dark passage. In circumstances like these any crumb is a comfort.

The relief Clough obviously felt was mirrored in his reaction when Lorimer's shot thundered past Town goalkeeper Terry Poole into the net, and it showed, too, when I talked with him afterwards.

Speaking like a man who had just had a load lifted from his shoulders Clough said: 'It was a goal good enough to win a cup final. After the misses it was going to take something like that to get us one.'

No one, however, was more delighted with the goal than Lorimer, who, as early as the ninth minute, missed a penalty he had to take twice.

Ironically for United, Lorimer's first effort beat Poole and went in, but referee Pat Partridge ordered the kick to be taken again because Allan Clarke had moved into the penalty area while the kick was being taken.

Lorimer sent Poole the wrong way with his second kick but the ball hit the keeper's foot and was diverted to safety.

'That is the sort of thing that happens when a team is going through a bad patch like we are,' Lorimer said. 'The keeper dives the wrong way and still manages to save it.

'It did not worry me really because I thought at that stage we were playing well enough to win. And in any case it would not have helped me in any way if I had let it bother me.'

After yesterday's 'clear-the-air' talks between players, manager and chairman, there was no doubt United were keen to answer their critics on the field.

It showed in their early play when for the first 20 minutes they were the more impressive side – even if they lacked the flair and poise of last season.

Despite this, the honours of the evening must go to

the Town side, who rose to the occasion these 'derby' clashes provide in magnificent fashion.

After that initial period Town matched the champions in every department – in midfield, in defence, up front, in determination and even in skill.

It was the kind of display Town usually reserve for matches against United, and it thrilled and delighted Town's biggest crowd of the season – 15,013.

And it brought a fitting tribute from Clough. 'I have never in my life seen a Third Division side play as well. They never stopped running from 7.30 until the final whistle. It was not just their running that caused us problems – it was their football which was superb.

'It would have been different if that penalty had gone in, but if Huddersfield play that sort of football week after week, they will walk it in the league.'

Both sides contributed much to a gripping game which saw fine displays from goalkeepers Poole and David Harvey.

Poole twice thwarted Allan Clarke and Joe Jordan, and Harvey produced splendid saves to efforts from Alan Gowling and one from Town newcomer Billy McGinley, signed for £8,000 from Elland Road and making his home debut.

In addition there were misses at both ends. Clarke, of all people, missed a sitter in the 69th minute, and Gowling and Bobby Hoy fluffed chances for Town.

Gowling, however, had the satisfaction of giving Town the lead with a good goal in the 78th minute, beating Norman Hunter and Gordon McQueen before hitting a rising shot past the advancing Harvey.

Clough, who replaced John McGovern and John O'Hare with Mick Bates and Jordan, was given a chanted welcome by a section of the United fans on a night when Don Revie chose to watch the side he managed until this season.

The England manager missed United's face-saving equaliser. He left ten minutes before the end!

Don Warters, *Yorkshire Evening Post*

* * *

Lorimer continues: 'My last-minute equaliser took the game back to Leeds for a replay, but as we arrived back at Elland Road on the team bus from Huddersfield, the chairman was heard to say that he wanted a chat with the manager. The next thing we knew, the press were ringing to say that Cloughie had been relieved of his position. It was all very sad really.'

After 44 days, it was all over for Clough. One of the shortest and most volatile reigns in football was ended with Leeds paying up Clough's contract.

Ray Fell, the Leeds United Supporters Club chairman, says: 'It is difficult to analyse the appointment and short reign of Brian Clough at Leeds. Much has been written and said about the period, a good proportion of it fictional, lots of it guesswork. Observers are often biased and can be too quick to apportion blame in accordance with their prejudices.

'Clough's arrival at Elland Road saw him become manager of a club who were current champions and a team that had felt the sting of many of his comments. Not all of the Leeds fans were hostile to Mr Clough, but there were many who remained apprehensive about his appointment.

'I firmly believe that the parting of Clough and Peter Taylor was instrumental in driving Brian's desire to succeed at Leeds, so that he went at it full throttle. His early approach to the job only alienated the players and the fans, who questioned why the board had decided to appoint a manager whose every word and deed appeared to indicate that he resented Don Revie and the Leeds United players.

'Before Clough's arrival at Elland Road he attended a tribute dinner in which Peter Lorimer was to receive an award as Yorkshire Footballer of the Year. To the amazement of the audience when Brian rose, supposedly in tribute, he decided to attack and deride the player who was being honoured. Brian had previously attacked Billy Bremner and other members of the team and, shortly after his arrival at Leeds he castigated a player of the calibre of Eddie Gray. These outbursts were not the actions of a friend knocking on your door.

'The previous criticisms of Leeds United that had come during their early days as a top club had, by 1974, abated, and respect was starting to come, albeit often begrudgingly. The occasional reference to "Super Leeds" showed that their performances in the early 1970s were earning them some cachet. The timing of Clough's ill thought through remarks, coupled with the overall consensus, too simplistic in my view, that "player power" alone removed him, did, I believe, damage Leeds tremendously and gave rise to much of the criticism that we still suffer, often from those who weren't born at the time. Contrary to the popular perception, Leeds were at that time a squad of 14 internationals, and the quality of football that won them the championship still has the media delving into the archives to relive the experience.

'My own encounter with Brian Clough came with his one and only visit to the Supporters Club. His address followed the same pattern as his previous outbursts. He addressed the meeting by outlining the faults of Billy Bremner and teammates, stressing that he was going to change the dressing-room, the attitude of the players and the image of the team. Accompanying Brian Clough on this occasion were the trainer Jimmy Gordon and two players, John McGovern and John O'Hare. These were the players who were to replace icons like Billy Bremner and Johnny Giles and others who were, of course, the reigning champions.

'Having said all that, I think Clough's time at Leeds ended too soon. The board, having made the questionable decision to appoint him, proceeded to fall at the first hurdle. They parted company with him without backing their own judgement or giving him time to prove himself.

'Brian Clough was, I believe, delighted to be offered the

Leeds United post. I think he showed he was happy to have the opportunity to further the success of a big club like Leeds United. The sad thing was his burning desire to show he could equal or better the achievements of Don Revie. Unfortunately, his ego and so-called wit robbed him of the advantages that may have been his reason for accepting the job. He was inheriting a club at the top with tried and trusted players. He lost the chance he had to win them over with the right early appeal and take the club forward to the further success that both he and the fans could have enjoyed together.

'Who can say? Perhaps with Taylor alongside him to calm him down and advise him, he might have tackled the job differently. Suffice to say that when Clough and Taylor were reunited, they went on to great achievements, and Brian duly earned his rewards as a manager. I believe that the success he achieved afterwards owed a little to his experience at Leeds.'

Within an admirably short time of Clough's sacking, Yorkshire Television pulled off a considerable coup by persuading Revie and Clough to go head-to-head in an interview with TV journalist and lifelong Leeds United fan Austin Mitchell, now the long-serving Labour MP for Great Grimsby. The body language of the two former Leeds managers, brought up just streets apart in Middlesbrough, was awkward, akin to two miscreants in front of the local beak, and at times the interview made for excruciating viewing. Why, Revie wanted to know, had Clough taken the job in the first place when he so despised the club? Because, said Clough, it was the best club job in England. They were the champions. 'And I wanted to do it better than you.'

11

THE HACK

*If you think of a killer phrase that sums up your story,
the media will swoop on it like vultures. Keep them fed and
you'll keep them at arm's length, with you in control.*

Brian Clough

Brian Clough's last days at Leeds were charted by wordsmith
John Wray for the Bradford *Telegraph & Argus* as follows:

ONLY ONE WAY TO END THOSE DOUBTS

No one hung out a 'Welcome' banner when Brian
Clough reported for duty as Leeds United's new
manager last month. Predictably, his arrival was
greeted with stony silence by the apprehensive players.
It was the sort of welcome a stepfather might expect
from his newly acquired family. The decision of trainer
Les Cocker to accept an offer to become assistant to
England team manager Don Revie spread still more
gloom in the dressing-room. Lesser mortals than Brian
Clough would have bolted for the door within minutes
of arriving.

LEEDS HOLD MEETING TO CLEAR THE AIR

Leeds United chairman Manny Cussins called a clear-the-air meeting with the players and manager Brian Clough today. Cussins decided to arrange the get-together despite an assurance from the manager that the players were giving him full backing. Clough said: 'I have never been more convinced that I have the full support of every player at Leeds United.'

GILES: LEEDS BOARD DECIDE ON MONDAY

Leeds United will not make a decision until Monday on whether to appoint Johnny Giles as their new manager following last night's sensational sacking of Brian Clough. 'If the terms are right I'll take the job,' said Giles. Now player power has overthrown Clough. 'No club can be successful unless the players and staff are happy,' said Cussins. 'The players were critical of his methods.'

DIRECTOR LASHES CLOUGH SACKING

Leeds United director Mr Bob Roberts – the only member of the board not present when the decision to sack Brian Clough was taken last night – reacted angrily to the news today, saying: 'It's absolutely shocking. Clough hasn't had a chance. He's not been there five minutes.' Speaking from his holiday hotel in Majorca, Mr Roberts said: 'I'm sorry I wasn't there to take part in the discussions, but I have not heard a thing from Leeds. If there was a crisis, they could at least have asked me to return. I still think we got the right man and it is a loss to Leeds United in my opinion.'

IT TOOK COURAGE TO SACK CLOUGH

Don't castigate Leeds United's board of directors for showing Brian Clough the door after only 44 days in the job. They had no alternative! Drastic measures were called for to prevent internal ill feeling from destroying the club. The differences between Clough and his players were too deep-rooted to be solved by moderate methods.

BREMNER HELPS TO PICK TEAM

Suspended Leeds captain Billy Bremner was called in today to help with the selection of the squad for tomorrow's league game at Burnley. The squad of 13 was chosen by assistant manager Maurice Lindley and chief coach Syd Owen, in consultation with Bremner. Significantly there is no place for any of Clough's signings since he took over the job at Elland Road – John O'Hare, John McGovern and Duncan McKenzie.

BREMNER HITS OUT AT CLOUGH REMARKS

Leeds United's suspended captain Billy Bremner lashed back at Brian Clough today after the fired Leeds boss accused him of trying to run the club. Clough, in a recorded interview for the ITV programme *On the Ball*, said: 'When Bremner called me boss it meant nothing. He'd got to call me boss and believe it. What Bremner has to establish is that he is not the manager of Leeds United. I was.' Bremner rapped back: 'Nothing that Brian Clough says or does surprises me. Although I don't want to be drawn into a dispute with him, his remarks make me very annoyed. It is ridiculous to say I tried to manage the club. I have my own opinion of Mr Clough.'

Given the sequence of events Wray describes, it comes as no surprise that the opening chapter in his book about Leeds United is entitled 'When Brian Clough Was Mr Angry'.

Today, explaining how he came to follow the club so closely, Wray says: 'I'd been brought up on rugby league rather than football. I failed my 11-plus miserably – on the maths side, I hasten to add – but fortunately my parents moved house so that I could get into the comprehensive school in Leeds rather than the dead-end of the local secondary modern. I was a late developer in a school that played rugby union, but while I preferred the 13-a-side game, union came a good second. There was football, cross-country and athletics as well, so I did do a bit of sport and ended up getting my school colours. I hadn't a clue what I wanted to do career-wise, even though I always got top marks in English and it should have seemed natural to marry sport and English together. Then a friend of my mother's saw an advert in a local paper, the *Pudsey News*, seeking somebody keen on sport to write for them. I applied and got the job and it turned out to be that of sports editor! I was straight in at the deep end, planning pages and subediting all the submitted reports, and, as you did in those days, I ended up getting a grounding in everything. Paid-for papers covered everything that moved – the town council, all the courts and even funerals and local dramatic society reviews. There were also the obligatory visits to the vicars.

'From a sport point of view, it was great because it meant that I could cover Bramley Rugby League Club. That was a joy. I would travel everywhere with them, and I became really good friends with all the players, who were part-timers. A lot of them didn't have cars and would travel to games on buses. I became particular friends with a player called Dave Horn, a big prop-forward whose job was as a drayman at Tetley's Brewery. He was the players' shop steward. If ever they had a grievance, he would go to the board and argue their case. I would not have liked to have been on that board, because Dave was pretty formidable! He used to score tries with five men on his back – that kind of colossus. They had a social club at Bramley, and I'd go with the team to watch the turns before we'd all pile up to Dave's house in Pudsey and sink a barrel of beer! By the time we'd finished, I'd have enough in my notebook to last a week. I also wrote about the local non-league football team Farsley Celtic. The first time I covered them, I got a team sheet, but, unbeknown to me, between me being given that team sheet and the team taking to the park, there had been several changes. Of course, I got all the goal-scorers wrong and goodness knows what else wrong, and with everybody knowing everybody else in Pudsey, there were lots of angry phone calls to the editor.

'I survived that and around this time, the early 1960s, Leeds United had started to do really well in the Second Division under Don Revie. Having been rugby-mad all my life, it was kicking and screaming that I was dragged by a few school chums along to Elland Road to watch a few matches in the old Scratching Shed, but I thought, "OK, it's not bad this." I liked Jim Storrie, who scored lots and lots of goals for Leeds but who was bow-legged and didn't have a lot of skill. He was, however, always in the right place at the right time and the ball would go in off all parts of his body. He scored some vital goals and the fans loved him. This developed a grain of interest, and after a couple of years at the *Pudsey News*, I thought we should be writing about Leeds, if for no other reason than it would get me into the press-box. To start off with, I did something a bit different, an early version of a form report, consisting of a little write-up and a rating out of ten for each individual player. I can't claim that anyone copied it, although today, of course, it's the norm.

'Also around that time, I got a call from a guy called Victor Railton, the main soccer writer for the now long defunct London *Evening News*, asking if I would cover the London teams when they came up to Leeds. Soon after, when Leeds were doing well in Division One with a team of household names, the *Evening Standard* made the same request, only they wanted coverage of Leeds whenever a story broke. These were my first tastes of freelancing, which I eventually became involved in permanently. I reached the end of my five-year indentures as deputy editor of the *Pudsey News*, and the logical next step was to move to an evening newspaper. I was offered the editorship when the editor left, but I was only in my early 20s, and although it was flattering, I felt I didn't have enough experience. I still don't know if I made the right decision but when I think about all the experience covering Leeds United brought me – the travelling throughout Europe, rubbing shoulders with interesting people and so on – I think I was right to join the Bradford *Telegraph & Argus*, who anyway offered me a couple of pounds more to be a news reporter than the *Pudsey Times* were offering me to become editor.

'I thought my first day with the *T&A* would be just a gentle introduction, but on that particular day there had been a shooting in Farsley. A nightwatchman and a police inspector had been shot dead, and a massive manhunt was on for the killer. It became big national news. I was sent out on the story, and, instead of a nice little nine-to-five, I was on duty for the best part of twenty-four hours, mostly at Pudsey police station after knocking on doors and doing an atmospheric piece. The headline was "Doors Knocked in Village of Fear", and it was on the front page, so I was well chuffed with my first day! This was when papers were papers. You didn't have to wait until the next day to get your story into print; you rushed it through from a payphone.

'The *T&A* had an excellent editor called Peter Harland, who went, I think, to the *Sunday Times* eventually. He decided that although he was editing a Bradford paper, Leeds United were doing so well that they merited coverage. Don Warters was presented with this task, and in 1970, when Phil Brown of the *Yorkshire Evening Post* in Leeds retired, Don moved over there and opened the way for me in Bradford. The first game I covered was a friendly at Doncaster, and the first proper game I covered was against Manchester United at Old Trafford, which was memorable for Mick Jones scoring the winning goal.

'Don Revie was so welcoming. Three of us journalists were allowed to travel to away matches on the team coach, which was great, because we had access to the players. However, anything you overheard that was not supposed to be in the public domain was fully expected to remain on that team coach. You were put on trust, and, of course, that trust was never to be compromised. It was clear that any transgression would result in your being kicked off the bus double quick, never to return. It was an unwritten law, really, that you heard all, saw all and said nothing. I did once get banned for a couple of days over something I'd written. Don had been criticising referees and was in trouble with the FA. After this particular match, I think at Sheffield United, there were questions as to how well his team had played. He bristled at this, saying, "Look, you shouldn't be criticising my players. The man you should be criticising is the man in black." This, of course, was an obvious story because of his brushes with the authorities, and I couldn't ignore it. Had I done so, the editor might have read it elsewhere and would have wanted to know why I had chosen not to mention it.

'The following day, unfortunately, Don was driving through the centre of Leeds and the *T&A* had placed a newsbill just outside the railway station. He saw it. "REVIE SLAMS ANOTHER REF", it screamed, so without even reading the story he rang the editor and told him, "You can tell that John Wray that he will not be welcome at this club any more." My boss called me into his office and said I really should have realised that Don potentially could have been in serious trouble over this and did I not think I should have gone a bit easier on him. I was really surprised at this reaction, though I realise in hindsight that Don could be very forceful and had clearly made his point. The editor asked me to produce my shorthand note of Don's observations, which, thankfully, I was able to provide, and a couple of days later Don rang me and said, "Sorry I had to do that, but I really had to cover my back with the FA and deny what I'd said." Thereafter, there were no problems between us whatsoever.

'Players of the time would tell you that if they had a grievance or were seeking a pay rise and they had to go to see Don, they would knock on his door with trepidation, almost trembling, at what the reaction might be. He could be a fearsome figure at times, but at others he was a charming, caring father figure. This latter side he showed largely to the players, which was how he got such immense loyalty. If, however, he had a grievance with the press, which he often did, more with the national papers than the locals, then they knew about it and would be castigated in no uncertain terms. But by and large, he was terrific to deal with. Many a time if we were in a hotel he'd insist on putting your meal on his room account and if he didn't have a story he would make one up for you, perhaps concerning a player he might be interested in signing or something like that.

'At that time, publicity was expensive if you had to pay for it through advertising, and Don realised that a story in the local paper every night was wonderful free publicity and space you couldn't buy. He made sure we had plenty of stories. Don's big pal over at Liverpool, Bill Shankly, was similarly well inclined towards the local press. You could ring Liverpool and sometimes Bill would be passing by and answer the switchboard phone himself! You always knew you could get hold of him if you needed to. If Leeds were playing Liverpool and you wanted some quotes from him for your match preview, you'd ring between 8.30 and 9 a.m. and be guaranteed a result.

'Another memorable thing about Don was his superstitious nature. One morning he had left his home for the ground and realised he had left his briefcase behind. So he returned and asked Elsie, his wife, to pass the briefcase through the window to him because it was "bad luck" to leave the house twice to make the same journey. Then, of course, there was the lucky blue suit, of which Brian Clough observed, "It must have ponged a bit after all those years and all those matches he'd worn it!" Perhaps most famously, though, he persuaded himself during a run of bad results that a curse had been put upon the Elland Road ground and duly called in a Gypsy woman from Scarborough to lift it. She apparently crouched down and peed on all four corners of the pitch. It must have worked because Leeds went on to great things. Some of the players had superstitions too. Jack Charlton had to be last out of the tunnel, for instance, and others had to tie their left boot before the right or vice versa.

'Happy days. But one of the drawbacks of travelling on the team coach was that Billy Bremner was a chain-smoker with nicotine-stained fingers and every time I got home after partaking in Billy's card school, my wife Helen complained that I stank of cigarette smoke and insisted that my clothes go to the dry cleaner. The cleaning bills were astronomical! It was the same when Billy became manager. He was just the same at cards as he was on the football field – he simply hated to lose. And if you'd played a wrong card two or three tricks back he would know about it and haul you over the coals.

'You got to know the board members too. Manny Cussins was head of John Peters, the furniture company, and even though he was a millionaire, he would go onto the shop floor and sell suites himself. Helen and I would go in looking for something to smarten up the lounge and he would be there. He'd shoo away the salesman, ordering, "Leave this to me!" He couldn't wait to sell you an item. And if Leeds were playing away, he would pay a visit to one of his shops – they were a national chain – to check out his staff. A few weeks into the Brian Clough micro-era, I said to him, "You're not looking very well, Chairman. Are you OK?"

'"No," he replied, "I'm going into hospital to have a couple of Clough ulcers removed!" Only a joke, but the stress must have affected him. He had been very much in favour of bringing Clough in.

'During the period from 1970 to 1974, I was privileged to watch possibly the finest football team this country has ever produced. They were not given the credit they deserved, with so many people focusing on the physical side of their game. They were accused of having kicked their way out of the Second Division, and that detracted from the real issue of how brilliant a team they were – brimful of talent. Giles and Bremner were simply magnificent in midfield, with Giles able, in old money, to land a ball on a sixpence from fifty yards with either foot. Before that, there was Bobby Collins and his banana shot from free kicks. If Leeds got a free kick anywhere near the penalty area, it was a goal, guaranteed. Bobby was one of Don's most inspired signings.

'So many of Don's players grew up together and, with a great sense of loyalty, stayed at the club. Everyone could recite the Leeds team for years. It tripped off the tongue: Sprake, Reaney, Cooper, Bremner, Charlton, Hunter, Lorimer, Clarke, Jones, Giles, Gray. Injuries necessitated the odd change, of course, and then you'd get Madeley or Yorath coming in, but Bremner would have had to have broken his leg to keep him out, and even then he would have volunteered to play. He played when he was black and blue. A lot of players paid for that level of dedication in later life, though. They were given injections to get them through the pain barrier, and there were repercussions health-wise when they stopped playing. Norman Hunter, a neighbour, remains in very good health, and he always puts the fact that he got through so much football without too many injuries down to his mother's broth strengthening his bones! Football today contrasts greatly with the old days, in that players rarely have the same sense of loyalty to a club or to each other. Back then, there were loads of testimonials for players who had spent ten years at one club. How many testimonials do you see today?

'In the build-up to Clough's arrival at Elland Road, there were persistent rumours first of all that Don was going to Everton, and then the England whispers intensified. He was bitter about the fact that the Leeds United board didn't immediately say yes when the FA came knocking. He felt his achievements for Leeds over those 13 years should have been acknowledged by the club saying, "OK, it's a great opportunity for you, Don. Thanks for everything and you go with our blessing." A wrangle ensued and Leeds ended up being paid compensation, but in Don's view this was a far from satisfactory way of going about things with such a prestigious job at stake. A few weeks later, I got a letter of thanks "for all your coverage" from Don on FA headed notepaper – I should have been thanking him really – and that was one of my personal highlights in a summer of 1974 that was very lively.

'There were lots of rumours about who was going to succeed Don, with Johnny Giles mentioned very early in the proceedings, but it emerged that the board were going to go outside the club for their appointment, and Brian Clough turned out to be the man. I think they sensed there might be problems if they were to give the job to Johnny, because Billy Bremner had also wanted it. The situation actually recurred after Clough was fired, with Johnny again looking set to get the job and then Billy applying for it. That presented the board with a dilemma, because they didn't want to upset either party.

'Leeds and Clough were a marriage made in hell, largely because of the criticism he had hurled at the club. Lots of things were wrong. As soon as he was appointed, he went on holiday, so he was late turning up for the job. He was late for training nearly every day he was there, because he still lived in Derby. Occasionally, he stayed over in a hotel, but most of the time he was commuting. He'd sometimes arrive at Elland Road when training was almost over, which did not go down well with the players. Syd Owen, the chief coach, felt snubbed when Clough brought in Jimmy Gordon, and again the players did not like that state of affairs.

'It wasn't easy for the press either. Reporting for an evening paper, I badly needed to speak to him early in the day if I wanted his quotes to make the first edition, but he wasn't arriving at the ground until after 10 a.m., sometimes 11 a.m. We had to adopt the mentality that we would have to get things out of him one day for the following day's publication, and the whole thing became a bit of a nightmare. Sometimes you couldn't get him at all because he was so busy with other things. Of course, he, as a new manager, must have had all sorts of things on his mind, and you hoped that the situation would settle down into a routine that would include us within a few weeks.

'My story about the rumours that Syd Owen was prepared to leave Leeds annoyed Clough, however, and I got a call from him saying, "Get your arse down here as quick as you can, young man. We've got things to discuss." He tore me off a strip despite my protestations that I had actually toned the story down. This didn't wash with him at all. But then, out of the blue and to my total surprise, he proceeded to give me two exclusives. The first concerned his plans for the club and how he intended to operate, and the other was about the three players he was about to sign: McGovern, O'Hare and McKenzie. Those signings created resentment within the squad. They thought there was nothing wrong with the team to start with, and couldn't understand why he felt the need to bring these new players in.

'I think Brian was really good at managing a team that hadn't done a lot and moulding them into a superb side, but with a team like Leeds at that time, who had seen it all and done it all, he was completely lost. That Leeds team was used to Don's methods, and Brian's were different. In a way, those players were at fault, because they were inflexible, unwilling to take new ideas on board. They would be of the mindset that there was no need for new ideas because they already had a successful formula. But there is an argument that they would have been even more successful if Don had let them off the leash and allowed them to express themselves a little bit more rather than being ultra-cautious, which was one of their characteristic traits. The signing of Duncan McKenzie, whom you couldn't coach or control and who was a flair player and a free spirit, was a strong hint that Clough planned to address that aspect of Leeds' game, and who knows where that might have taken them?

'I sensed the Clough sacking coming. There had been so many rumblings behind the scenes, with several players telling the chairman that it just wasn't working and couldn't go on for much longer. From my perspective, there were titbits and snippets from players that could not be used on the record but which were useful as background information, and I began asking myself the question: how much longer can this go on?

'Clough had become a little bit snappy. Don Warters was on holiday when Clough took up the job and by the time he got back Clough had just about got his feet under the table. On his first day back at work, Don called at the ground to introduce himself, and that morning the *Daily Mail* had done a piece saying that seven or eight players were refusing to sign their contracts because they couldn't get on with Cloughie. Don had a copy of the *Mail* and needed to check the story's accuracy, so after the initial introductions and swapping of pleasantries, Don asked Clough about it. He bristled. "Don't ask me questions like that. You insult me with that type of question," he snapped. "If you ask me that fucking question again, I'll kick you over that fucking stand." But Don, like a good journalist, persisted, insisting that he would have to write a story for that day's paper and saying that if this story was wrong, then here was the manager's chance to refute it. Clough said, "Well, it's wrong. In actual fact there are ten or twelve players who aren't signing!" A delighted Don, now with an even better story, said, "Thanks very much," and hurried off.

'Some time after Clough had left Leeds and linked up with Nottingham Forest, Leeds were playing Forest and there was the usual post-match media conference. I was standing right at the back. Clough had answered three or four questions before he suddenly spotted me. "You've no need to stand there, young man," he said. "You did nothing for me while I was at Elland Road, so why should I do anything for you?" It was a really embarrassing put-down and, I thought, well out of order, especially as I had gone out of my way in his time at Leeds to give up a day off to help him to house-hunt.

'I felt it would help cement a relationship if I were to show him round the area, since I knew it very well and he knew it not at all. When I got down to the ground, he was watching cricket on television. England were playing New Zealand, and I knew that he had a love of the game. He was there in his chair, in his tracksuit top and yellow shorts as usual, and I thought, "Is he going to look at houses dressed like this? Surely not."

'"Pour yourself a beer," he said. "We'll watch a few overs." About three hours and several pints later, neither of us was in any fit state to go house-hunting, and at four o'clock he said, "I think we'll call it a day, don't you?" When I got home – by taxi – I told Helen the story and she was furious. "We could have gone shopping," she said. "Wait until I see that Brian Clough!"

You know, maybe at that stage he'd realised there wasn't much point in hunting for a house because he might well be on his bike at any time.

'It was a nightmare at the time for all concerned. The whole episode must have been an awful blow to his personal pride. If the Leeds directors had been more patient, Clough would have got rid of the ageing players and replaced them and built his own side. He might have been impatient in trying to get started with that too quickly. It would probably have worked eventually, but the Leeds board had been used to the club being right up there at the top, and they weren't prepared to risk a fall. When Jimmy Armfield, Clough's successor, was sacked, they hadn't been outside the top ten – but nonetheless he was replaced. That shows how demanding they were. They really did panic about the results under Brian not being good and about most of the players being in revolt. They felt they had to nip the situation in the bud and get rid.

'Nottingham Forest were the beneficiaries of that decision, because what he achieved there was truly extraordinary. He did, however, shoot himself in the foot at Leeds. Maybe once he realised that Peter Taylor wouldn't be joining him and saw the players' attitude towards him, he wanted a get-out and some of his actions were calculated to get him the sack. But who knows what went on in that mind of his?'

12

HE MET ME ONCE

I've missed him. He used to make me laugh.
He was the best defuser of a situation I have
ever known. I hope he's all right.

Brian Clough on Peter Taylor

By the time they reached the crossroads that pointed one way to Brighton and the other to Leeds, Brian Clough and Peter Taylor had been colleagues, friends and bosom buddies for almost 20 years. Through playing days together at Middlesbrough and as a managerial duo at Hartlepools, Derby and, briefly, Brighton, they had built a partnership that appeared as unbreakable as it was remarkable. Why Taylor declined to accompany Clough to Leeds has been the subject of much deliberation and, in retirement, Clough himself, as he revealed in *Cloughie: Walking on Water – My Life*, reflected long and hard upon this, finally concluding that money would have got his ally to Leeds had Manny Cussins dug deep enough. The Brighton chairman Mike Bamber had offered Taylor more money to stay. But there were other reasons, Clough conceded, as well as financial considerations. Clough had helped to get Taylor's daughter a job on the local newspaper and this added to the happiness of the Taylor family, together in a seaside apartment. Taylor, he mused, had always wanted to be beside the seaside anyway, and he had got his wish. Further, he fancied trying his hand at solo management, and the opportunity had arisen at Brighton.

'I'm staying put,' was his categorical response when pushed by Clough for a clear reason for his refusal to accompany him to Leeds, even though Clough suspected that Taylor was not as happy in his work as he might have been. Taylor stayed on at Brighton for two more seasons, steering them to a fourth-place finish in the old Division Three in 1975–76, a season in which they were nearly unbeatable at home but couldn't buy an away win.

As with the most closely guarded and deeply buried real reasons behind a divorce, or the ending of a friendship, the truth remains hidden from the outside world, but if Clough was confused by Taylor's unwillingness to up sticks for Yorkshire, then as a Frank Sinatra fan – 'He met me once' – he need only have examined the frailties of those inhabiting the world of music for further food for thought. Why fully four decades after their mammoth worldwide hit 'A Whiter Shade of Pale' were members of Procol Harum not speaking to each other and at loggerheads over the royalties? Why did the phenomenally successful Simon and Garfunkel go their own ways so often when the constant worldwide demand was for them to unite on stage, as they did all too infrequently? Why did Scott Walker leave his 'Brothers' for a solo career and then disappear into a dark corner for so long?

Clough and Taylor were two very different individuals, one loud, spontaneous, self-assured and unpredictable, and the other quieter, largely understated, patient and reasoned. It would, and did, take a lot of getting to know each other, and if much of Taylor's coexistence with Clough was spent in wonder at his eccentricities and foibles, then that would be understandable. Duncan Hamilton, in his award-winning book *Provided You Don't Kiss Me*, an account of his relationship with Clough, built up over many years as a sports journalist reporting on Nottingham Forest affairs, recalls:

On a Friday he [Clough] had a habit of writing out his team sheet to the accompaniment of a Frank Sinatra record. A 'gramophone player' (he never referred to a 'record' or 'tape deck') sat on the low glass-fronted bookcase in his office. A drawing of Sinatra hung on the wall. He would sometimes spend a long time hunting for his reading glasses before beginning the painstaking process of putting down each name in large capital letters.

'You know,' he said one day, handing me the team sheet, 'I'd love all of us to play football the way Frank Sinatra sings . . . all that richness in the sound, and every word perfect. How gorgeous would that be?'

His face glowed like a fire, and he began to sing along with Sinatra, always a word ahead of him, as if he needed to prove that he knew the lyrics.

'I've got you . . . under my skin . . .' He rose from his chair, still singing, and began to pretend he was dancing with his wife. When the song finished, he laughed until tears ran down his cheeks. He fell back into his chair, arms and legs splayed. The smile looked as if it might stay on his face for ever. 'Oh that was good,' he said. 'Blow me, if only football could be that much fun . . .'

Hamilton provides an insight into how kind and loyal Clough could be, traits which go some way to explaining why he and Taylor were able to build up such a long-lasting partnership in the first place:

On the one hand, Clough was capable of being unforgivably rude, unnecessarily cruel, appallingly bombastic and arrogant, and so downright awkward that I wanted to drop something large and heavy on his big head. On the other hand, he could be extravagantly generous, emollient and warm, ridiculously kind and loyal to whoever he thought warranted it.

I stammered, sometimes badly. One morning, forcing out a question took me longer than usual.

'Young man,' he said impatiently. 'Do you stammer with me, or do you stammer with everyone?' I told him I always stammered.

'What's the cure?' he asked. I said there wasn't one. He pressed on: 'When do you stammer the most?' I said that talking on the phone was always difficult.

'I'll phone you every day for two weeks,' he said. 'We'll crack this.'

He almost kept to his word. My stammer didn't vanish, but it gradually became less severe.

Hamilton offers a poignant portrait of Clough, showing how isolated the manager could seem after he and Taylor had parted ways for good:

A few months before his enforced retirement, I found him in his office.

He had decided not to go to training, he told me. It was an unseasonably mild day for early spring, yet Clough was sitting in his long fleeced coat, zipped up almost to his chin. He was wearing his flat cap and his spectacles sat on the bridge of his nose. A tumbler, half-full with what I presumed was vodka, was at his right hand. His head was bowed over a piece of paper and he was scribbling on it.

He said he was trying to cheer himself up by writing down the best players who had been at the club since he became manager.

'I'm doing it,' he said, 'to remind myself of what life used to be like here, which seems about half a century ago.'

He reached for his glass and took a long swallow then he vanished for a minute or two and returned with his glass refilled.

He began to sing, belting out the words to 'Fly Me to the Moon'. When he reached the line 'Darling, kiss me', his head rocked back and he let it hang there, like a decorator examining the ceiling to see if it needed another coat of paint. The glass was still in his hand.

After a pause he said, 'Football is a terrible game, you know.' . . .

. . . During his last match in charge, Clough stood straight-backed outside the dugout like a captain determined to be on the bridge when the ship went down. After the final whistle, the crowd spilled onto the pitch. In one photograph, Clough, on the verge of tears, appears in the centre of the passionate thousands who were determined not to let him go. Afterwards, he accepted a flower from a young girl, as distraught as a mourner at a funeral. He looked at her, his head on one side, and said tenderly, 'Hey, beauty, no tears today, please.'

'Can I have a word from you, Brian?' asked a television interviewer outside the ground. 'Of course,' said Clough, walking away. 'Goodbye.'

One former Clough player, Peter Shilton, gives an insight into how Clough and Taylor worked together. In his autobiography, he relates:

As part of our preparations for the European Cup final [in 1980] Clough took us to Spain. We did some light training and played small-sided games, but the football pitch where we were staying was similar to a hard tennis court and no good if I wanted to practise shot-stopping without getting injured.

I voiced my concerns to Brian and Peter, explaining there simply wasn't a suitable grassed area on which to practise.

'Well, you haven't looked hard enough, have you?' said Clough in that nasal voice of his. 'Because we know where there is a grassed area that's perfect for you, Peter me lad.'

Clough retired to the hotel and I dutifully followed Peter to the outskirts of the small town we were staying in.

'There you go,' said Peter. 'There's your grassed area.' I couldn't believe what he was pointing at. Clough and Taylor never believed in pampering their players and I certainly wasn't an exception. We were standing in front of a traffic roundabout and on it was a circle of grass. I got the practice essential to my preparation for the European Cup final against a background noise of tooting horns from the passing cars.

Taylor was certainly privy to many of Clough's eccentricities and what he thought about them was probably known only to Mrs Taylor. He was well aware of Clough's capacity to be outlandish, confrontational and provocative, and there remains the unanswered question of how much disquiet and discomfort Taylor foresaw when he turned down the move to Leeds. Taylor might have considered and quickly rejected a scenario in which the new man was going to go into the home of the champions, trash them and all they stood for, attempt to wipe from history the rise and rise under Revie, take the place of his revered predecessor and immediately embark on a demolition and rebuilding job within the playing ranks. Perhaps Taylor just didn't want to be part of that process, no matter how sincere Clough was in asking him to go with him.

Certainly, there was not much joy for Clough in football at Leeds without Taylor, but two years later the old partnership was back up and running at Nottingham Forest, one suspects to their mutual relief and pleasure. Yet despite all their achievements, all the accolades that came their way and all the celebrity status they enjoyed through their domestic and European forays, there was to be a final and permanent parting of the ways. A falling-out. This time there was no mystery about the crossing of swords. In May 1983, Taylor, who had quit the game a year previously only to become manager of Derby six months into his retirement, signed the Forest winger John Robertson without letting Clough know about his plans. The two stopped speaking and Robertson's transfer was contested, with the result that the fee was set by a tribunal. Robertson was injured shortly after he joined Derby and never regained his usual form.

Clough and Taylor never spoke again, although when Taylor died in October 1990, Clough and his family did attend the funeral. It is said that when Ronnie Fenton, the assistant coach at Forest, phoned Clough to inform him of Taylor's death, the manager hung up and began to cry uncontrollably. After Taylor's death, Clough paid public tribute to him several times, dedicating his autobiography to him, speaking warmly of him when he was given the freedom of Nottingham and acknowledging Taylor's part in his successes at the unveiling of a bust of himself at the City Ground.

Football, like music, and probably because of their fame- and ego-driven cultures, has featured many high-profile bust-ups down the years. Saying goodbye to people you've worked closely with – or sometimes taking separate paths without even saying goodbye – is part and parcel of the game, but some splits, particularly between a manager and his players, are more acrimonious than others. Sir Alex Ferguson has had his share of 'good riddance' moments with the likes of Jaap Stam and David Beckham; Newcastle has witnessed fall-outs between Ruud Gullit and Alan Shearer and between Joe Kinnear and Charles N'Zogbia; John Toshack clashed with Davor Suker at Real Madrid; and at Liverpool, Gérard Houllier didn't see eye to eye with Robbie Fowler.

Splits between managers and their assistants are much less common and are usually driven by the ambition of number twos who, seeing their way to the top at their current club blocked, will seek a prime job elsewhere or be enticed into one.

Had he been able to dictate the course of events, Clough would always have been more comfortable with Taylor at his side. In *Walking on Water*, he says:

> A manager needs an assistant, a number two, a right-hand man, you name it. He needs a prop, a support, somebody to lean on in times of uncertainty and doubt, who will also be a sounding board, a source of reassurance or correction. Believe it or not there were times when I needed to be put right. A manager needs a friend and that doesn't mean a yes-man. Peter Taylor provided the best possible combination of qualities, especially for me, such a big-headed sod from the time I scored my first goal. To be able to work with such a friend was ideal.

That shows a vulnerability and a softer side to Clough's nature that those witnessing his high-profile actions from afar would be unaware of. A popular view would be that he came across as an individual who didn't need help, that he was an ultra-confident, self-assured individual, comfortable acting solus. Certainly, he appears to have presented himself in this way at Leeds, giving rise to suspicions that his brashness was merely a cover for the insecurity he felt in his new surroundings without the support, advice and friendship of his staunch ally.

In April 2009, Taylor's daughter Wendy Dickinson gave an interview to BBC Radio Nottingham's John Holmes in which she said that she went to every game of Forest's European Cup campaigns and described the time as 'magical'. She said her dad was constantly being mobbed in the street by fans. However, Wendy argued that Clough's and Taylor's roles were not as clear-cut as some journalists and historians have made out:

> Dad was much more than a talent scout, Brian was much more than the motivator. I don't think it was a question of Dad being the good guy and Brian being the bad

guy. As Martin O'Neill says, you could get a pasting from Peter and Brian would be the one to put his arm around you.

She added:

> I love my dad. He was a great man. I'm not silly enough to believe he got everything right. Signing John Robertson without telling Brian was probably not the greatest decision of his life.

Wendy said she was thrilled when she heard Timothy Spall was playing her father in *The Damned United*, but felt the film didn't get him quite right:

> Timothy Spall is a bit short, a bit rotund and played my dad with a Brummie accent which I did find a bit strange. I think they made my father too nice and they portrayed Brian as a bit of an arrogant, over-emotional nutter! Both men were far more complex than they were portrayed on screen.

Clough once said: 'I'm not equipped to manage successfully without Peter Taylor. I am the shop window and he is the goods.' He was never as successful a manager without his friend, and the overwhelming majority view is that had they paired up at Leeds, the paths taken by the Elland Road club and Nottingham Forest – one on the decline, the other rising meteorically – might have been very different.

13

DO AS I SAY

*When I go, God's going to have to
give up his favourite chair.*

Brian Clough

There were some compulsive double acts in the 1970s, like
Morecambe and Wise, Cannon and Ball, and Newman and
Redford. Then there was Clough and Newbon. Gary Newbon,
who began his career as a sports reporter for the Midlands-based
ATV Today programme in the early 1970s, was to make his name
as a roving reporter for ITV Sport, often obtaining match reactions
from players and managers in the tunnels during European
Cup games. He grew up in Bury St Edmunds, attending the
same school in the same year as his BBC football broadcasting
counterpart John Motson. Today, he works for Sky Sports. He
struck up a great rapport with the unpredictable Clough, and
their on-air jousting became unmissable. Newbon came to know
Clough well and has much to say about Clough's time at Leeds
and his subsequent success at Nottingham Forest:

'In my 40 years in television, I have interviewed many
international sporting greats. There was Muhammad Ali, as
well as several other leading boxers of their time, such as
Ken Norton, Chris Eubank and George Foreman. There have
been Olympic gold medallists too numerous to mention, and

from the world of football there was, most memorably, Pelé (six or seven times), Franz Beckenbauer, Jürgen Klinsmann, Sir Alex Ferguson and Brian Clough. I've interviewed thousands of sportspeople, but if I had to make a list of my favourites through the decades, the top three, in descending order, would be Clough, Ferguson and Eubank. Clough is my number one for many reasons, one of them being the mutual affection built over a long period of time.

'My professional relationship with Clough was built on such a sound footing that, win, lose or draw, he would come out of the dressing-room and do an interview if he had promised to do so beforehand. He always kept his word, but there were a few anxious moments one evening in April 1990 when, in the middle of a dreadful run in the old First Division, Forest went to Everton and lost 4–0. What was significant about this was that they were only a week or two away from a big date in the League Cup final against Oldham at Wembley, and at Goodison, Forest were frankly awful. Understandably, perhaps, Clough spent longer in the dressing-room than usual, in all probability giving a few character readings to his hapless players, and my producer Trevor East, with, as always, a professional eye to the schedules, began to panic that we would not get our Clough interview in time. I kept reassuring Trevor that Cloughie wouldn't let us down, that he would emerge any minute, and there was a collective sigh of relief when he duly did. He was, as usual, worth the wait.'

As Newbon suggests, Clough's TV appearances were usually good value. In the '70s, *The Morecambe and Wise Show*, with its mixture of slapstick and wordplay, would be followed on the BBC by *Match of the Day*, and you hoped against hope that the programme would feature among the thrills and spills of goals and near misses an interview with Brian Clough – with his own brand of slapstick and wordplay. Television seemed to bring Clough even more vividly to life. Whatever you thought of him, whether you loved or loathed him, you certainly could not ignore him.

One interview with Newbon was a case in point. Clough ended it by planting a great big kiss on the presenter's mouth. Of that memorable occasion, Newbon says: 'You always had to bear it in mind with Cloughie that chaos might ensue when he was at the microphone, and there were ominous signs when he began the interview by saying that the only person certain of his place on the team coach to Wembley was Albert. Cue horror moment. I could not for the life of me think of any Forest player called Albert and therefore to whom he might be referring. "And he's the fella who drives the coach," Clough said helpfully as I scratched around for a sensible next line. Then, some slapstick. "They weren't competitive at all tonight," he started. "They didn't want to know." By now, we were running over by a few seconds, and I was just getting instructions from the studio to wrap it up when Clough went on, "My lot are just a bunch of pansies!" and proceeded to plant upon me a huge kiss. As an interview, it was all over the place but it served to illustrate that with Clough if you expected the unexpected, then you wouldn't go far wrong. On this occasion, Fleet Street's finest all called to pose the question of whether he was under the influence of drink, but I didn't want to get involved in that debate and I don't think he was in any case.

'In 2002, I suffered a stroke and it was thought I would have to undergo a triple heart bypass operation. That wasn't the case and I'm fine now, but I remember the first card I received was from Cloughie. It read, "Get well soon. Behave yourself!" It was a very harrowing time for me and my family, and people were very caring. It was thanks to my specialist Adrian McMillan that I survived this health scare. Anybody who has been there will know it is an emotional time. You start contemplating your own mortality and suchlike, and I was reduced to tears when Cloughie's family let it be known that he was very fond of me and really cared about my well-being.

'I thought then about how Cloughie had made Trevor Francis, a lad I had known since he was 15, Britain's first million-pound footballer and how I had done the first interview with the new superstar. I don't know who was the more nervous, Trevor or me, but we have been great mates ever since.

'Back in the 1970s, I initiated an annual Midlands soccer writers' awards bash, which we held in the old Crossroads studio at ATV in Birmingham. I recall a young Jasper Carrott hosting the first one, and it was always a great evening. On one occasion, Cloughie announced Trevor, then with Birmingham City, as the Young Player of the Year and insisted, after telling him, "You are a very talented young man," that he would gladly hand over the trophy if only the youngster would take his hands out of his pockets to receive it! Old Willie Bell, the Birmingham manager, was distinctly unamused by Clough's embarrassing the teenager, and I really thought he was going to hit him! Cloughie didn't mean any harm by it, though. He was a great bloke whose instinct was to look out for youngsters.

'After his liver transplant, I rang to say that I would dearly like to take him and his wife Barbara out to lunch on a hot summer's day to one of his favourite places, the Dovecliff Hall Hotel near Burton upon Trent. There was only one other couple there, and in these quiet surroundings we talked for hours. Brian was by then off the booze completely. It was a quality day and one that I greatly treasure because it was not long after this that he died.

'Cloughie had once been kind to my father, who had been an RAF pilot during the war and died at the age of 62. Derby County embarked on their European campaign in the 1972–73 season, and I was part of the ITV team covering this. My father rarely attended football matches, but he agreed to come along to one of these big games, and I took the opportunity before the match to introduce him to Cloughie. As usual, I had the manager lined up for a post-match interview, but when he emerged from the dressing-room he took one look at me and said, "Never mind you, it's your father I'm after." He escorted Dad into the inner sanctum of the home dressing-room, where he introduced him to all the players, and it was some considerable time before they re-emerged. "I like your father better than I like you," he said to me after I'd waited with ever-decreasing patience for the interview I had gone along for to be given the green light. This, though, illustrated the brilliant style of Clough at a time when most other managers on the scene would never have thought to do something like that.

'One thing that Clough insisted upon throughout his career was that he would say nothing off the record. "If I let a cat out of the bag, or reveal a secret, you'll use it in 10 or 15 years' time," was his argument.

'He was a very careful man in some ways, but Clough made three big mistakes in his career. Top of that list was going to Leeds, second was resigning at Derby, where he got involved in plot, sub-plot, counter-plot and double plot, and third was falling out with Peter Taylor. Football, too, made mistakes with Clough, not least the Football Association's failure to appoint him as England manager. You look at the great long list of failures since 1966 when we won the World Cup and can only conclude that, with a string of errors such as overlooking Clough, England gets what it deserves sometimes. It is difficult to argue with the Leeds board when they concluded, after Don Revie's departure, that Brian Clough was the right man for the job. They would have taken note of the fact that he had so recently won a league title with unfashionable Derby and gone on to take them all the way to a European Cup final and deduced that if he could do that with Derby, then what he could do with Leeds would be unlimited.

'Becoming involved with Leeds United rebounded on him mainly because of the slatings he gave them while he was with Derby County. The Leeds side he inherited had a reputation for being a bit dirty and a bit sly, and these were traits that went against the grain with Clough. So some of the difficulties he had at Leeds were down to a failure to have recognised earlier in life that if you are going to slag people off, then you should be extremely careful, because you just never know where and when they are going to turn up in the future. It's a good bet that those about whom you have been most critical, or those whom you've neglected, will eventually come back onto the radar.

'There's good value in understanding this. When Dave Mackay was managing Derby County, no one in the media would ever talk to the youth-team manager of the day, probably because of a misguided notion that he was insignificant and didn't warrant the time or the effort. But I did and I gave him my telephone numbers, and one day the phone rang and the voice at the other end said that I should prepare for an exclusive interview. The caller would meet me at the studio at five o'clock. All kinds of technical set-ups have to be put in place for such events, and they have to be judged on priority and news value and so on. But when I was asked about the strength of the proposed interview, I was unable to say. I didn't know what it was about and the only information I was able to divulge was that it concerned somebody who at the time was anything but a household name. You can imagine, then, the reluctance to shuffle schedules to accommodate an unknown quantity, but in the end we got our exclusive – that youth-team manager Colin Murphy had taken over from Dave Mackay as Derby manager – and we got the exclusive first interview, which would have been coveted by all the other outlets and might indeed have been theirs had they shown more interest in Colin in the first place.

'Where Sir Alex Ferguson is out on his own as the most successful English club manager in my lifetime, with a simply stunning record, and Bob Paisley was something of an unsung hero at Liverpool, who are more readily associated with success under Bill Shankly, Brian Clough was truly a legend. The success he achieved was with two smaller clubs, in Derby County and Nottingham Forest. I disagree with those who argue that they are in fact big clubs because they are capable of attracting crowds of 30,000 plus. In the Midlands, only Aston Villa and, to a lesser extent, Wolves are big clubs in the sense of their history, tradition and ongoing potential to be real forces in the game. The detractors' argument slightly annoys me, because it belittles what Clough did and has no basis in fact.

'With Clough and Leeds, probably the best illustration of where things went wrong comes from Manchester United, where the board were once under big pressure to relieve Fergie of his duties but held their nerve and duly got their reward. Had the Leeds board been more stoical about the dip in form and less hasty to judge, who knows where it might have taken them as a club?

'More than the events in house after he took up the post, though, it was the build-up to his appointment that made it unlikely ever to work. That said, it wasn't a bad bit of business from Cloughie's point of view – a decent salary and a £90,000 pay-off for 44 days' endeavour made it worth his while. Yet if only he had stayed, I have good reason to believe that he would have been joined sooner rather than later at Elland Road by his ally, friend and mentor Peter Taylor. I am sure that eventually he would have been unable to resist the lure of the bigger fish to fry up north alongside his buddy. They were a great double act in that Taylor was an excellent judge of a player and Clough was unafraid to go out and buy the very best of them, no matter what it took.

'Clough despised agents, by the way, and their role and influence in the modern-day game would not have sat well with him. He would, however, have adapted, and few agents would have got the better of him. He had a fantastic mind, with a brain that was tuned to thinking at 100 mph. He knew players and he knew football. Leeds had great players then, with the likes of Giles, Bremner, Cooper, Madeley, Clarke and Jones particularly outstanding. In hindsight, the Clough thing was never going to work. With established players like that, there was the probability that there would be unease between them and a new manager, resulting in a power struggle, and that the chairman would buckle under the pressure of that state of affairs.

'The trouble with chairmen down the years is that they have demanded success not over a reasonable period of time but instantly, and many managers have paid the price because they have, understandably, been unable to deliver in an unreasonably short time. If you were to nominate a model chairman of modern times, it would have to be Steve Gibson at Middlesbrough, whose patience, understanding, loyalty and commitment have been simply sensational. David Moyes has kept Everton afloat with the backing of a strong chairman. But then you consider the likes of Tottenham and Newcastle, with their constant wholesale changes, you look at where they are now, Premier League also-rans at best, and you deduce that there is nothing in football quite like stability.'

Unfortunately, short-termism is a hazard of the job in football management. The 20-plus years amassed by Sir Alex Ferguson at Manchester United amount to an aeon in the game, and his long stint at one club is a precious and rare occurrence in a business that demands instant success that can rarely be delivered. There have been some spectacularly brief associations, with Bill Lambton's three days in charge of Scunthorpe a record low. Kevin Cullis lasted seven days at Swansea, where Micky Adams later spent thirteen days in charge. Dave Cowling saw out 10 days at Doncaster; Sammy McIlroy did 16 at Bolton; Paul Went was in charge for 20 days at Leyton Orient; Malcolm Crosby stayed for only 27 days at Oxford. Steve Coppell (32 days at Manchester City), Steve Claridge (36 days at Millwall) and Steve Wicks (41 days at Lincoln) are other notables.

In November 1968, that great character Tommy Docherty, now an octogenarian and a celebrated member of the after-dinner-speaking circuit whose favourite line is 'I've had more clubs than Jack Nicklaus', took charge of Queens Park Rangers. Just 28 days later he was gone. The hysteria surrounding Brian Clough's appointment at Leeds and the huge controversy over his sacking were witnessed from 40 miles or so along the M62 by Docherty, who was then in charge of newly relegated Manchester United in Division Two, with a managerial roll-call that had already taken in Chelsea, Rotherham, QPR, Aston Villa, Porto and Scotland.

Like the rest of the football world, Docherty watched the Clough episode unfolding at Leeds with more than a passing interest and says now: 'If you were not aware of Brian Clough when he was joining Leeds, you must have been living on another planet. He was more famous, or perhaps infamous, than the Prime Minister. Our paths first crossed when I was running the Scotland international team in February 1972 and our Under-23s drew 2–2 with England at Derby, where Cloughie was manager and was having a titanic battle with Leeds and Liverpool for the title, which they eventually won. Clough's stock in the game rose sharply with that title, but there would be several reasons why things did not work out between himself and Leeds.

'I speak as someone with knowledge of these things, having lasted 28 days at QPR – Clough was a veteran at Leeds in comparison – and first and foremost, I think, was the fact that the Leeds players had enjoyed a fantastic relationship with Don Revie, who was not only a great mentor to them but was also liked by their wives and girlfriends on account of the flowers and chocolates he sent them when he felt an occasion merited such a gesture. The place had the feel, nurtured by Don, of a family club. Now they were landed with someone who, while he could be great company, was prone to an abrasiveness that was exemplified by his comment to Eddie Gray, a great player, that he would have been shot had he been a horse. For one who, by my reckoning, made his name and his career overall by being a brilliant man-manager, that was a colossal mistake. That humiliation decimated the team spirit.

'He maybe thought one or two of those players were too full of their own importance and could have won more had they been under his guidance. But in the wider football world, the interpretation of where and how things went wrong was that the players made a stance: where they had played their hearts out for Revie, they were not going to do the same for Clough. In their hearts and minds, it seemed, it was Revie and Us versus Clough. To a certain extent, it was like the situation at Old Trafford, where the two men – Wilf McGuinness and Frank

O'Farrell – who succeeded Sir Matt Busby stayed only for very brief spells. Stability at a club is built on a good relationship between a manager and his players over a long period of time, and when a long, happy relationship comes to an end, there is inevitably a fracture or two as a result.

'I think with Clough and Leeds egos on both sides came into the equation, and Clough's stance would be: "Oi, there's only one manager around here and that's me. Don't do as I do, do as I say." Don's way was pretty much to go along with the players' desires, and in that way he got the best out of them. Man-management is a many-faceted skill. Sir Alex Ferguson has demonstrated time and again that if you fall out with him, then you are out of the door. Others would take the view that you owe it to your supporters to keep your best players no matter what, to take the time and have the patience to make a dissenting player see things your way.

'They were all great players, though, in that Leeds team. They were so good that I was able to pick four of them straight away when I became manager of Scotland: Billy Bremner, Eddie Gray, Peter Lorimer and David Harvey in goal. It was thanks to Don Revie and Leeds that I had the foundation of the team almost picking itself.

'It's uncanny, though, how many instances there are of less talented players who go on to make great managers. Clough may have been a prolific goal-scorer, but he was by no means a great football player. Fergie was a crap player and just look what he has done at Old Trafford. Wenger never played for any of the great clubs and has done wonders at Arsenal, and Mourinho couldn't even make the grade as a player at little-known Portuguese clubs like Belenenses and Sesimbra, yet he seems to have the magic touch as a boss. The opposite, that great players struggle to make it in management, is also true and I'd give you as examples Roy Keane, Sir Bobby Charlton, Bryan Robson, John Giles and Nobby Stiles. These were all fantastic players who haven't reached the same heights in management.

'The ability to cut the mustard at any level, never mind the highest level, is a complicated matter, and you cannot underestimate the importance of man-management skills that ensure that you get the best out of each and every member of the squad at your disposal. A good number two is also an important ingredient, and this, I think, was significant with Clough at Leeds in that he did not have Peter Taylor with him. One of the reasons Bill Shankly was so successful at Liverpool was that he had Bob Paisley with him. Sir Matt Busby had Jimmy Murphy at Manchester United; Joe Mercer had Malcolm Allison at Manchester City. Clough and Taylor were a similarly potent partnership and found great success together. No doubt they would have done so at Leeds had things worked out differently. You get people who are an outstanding number two who would struggle to make the grade at number one. The most important thing in a team like that is that the chemistry is right and the two work well together.

'I managed teams against Cloughie many times, and one thing you were always guaranteed was a football match. He liked his sides to keep the ball down, knock it about and play good football, and it was a joy to watch. I liked Cloughie's players and his teams, and I liked Cloughie. He was great for the game. Mourinho is a modern-day equivalent in some ways. He's good, he knows he's good and he doesn't mind telling the world he's good – one difference being that where Cloughie was never in love with himself, Mourinho, if he had been made of chocolate, would have eaten himself!

'Cloughie and I had similarities in that we were partial to the odd one-liner, such as "Good morning . . . but don't quote me!" My own favourite of his was that the ideal football club board would be made up of six directors – three dead and two dying!

'One of the big regrets in the English game must be – and if it isn't, it damn well should be – that Clough never managed his country's international team. Had he done so, I firmly believe that he would have won at least one and possibly two World

Cups. The FA was wary of him and he of them, but had they taken the plunge together, who knows, much of the mediocrity England has been drowning in since 1966 might have been eliminated and the team might have raised their game.'

Following Clough's death, Docherty wrote in his *Manchester Evening News* column:

> I think it's a disgrace Brian Clough was never knighted. I know you can't become a Sir after your death, but Cloughie should have found his way onto the Queen's honours list. He devoted his whole life to the sport he loved, and is one of the most successful English managers ever to have graced football. Alex Ferguson quite rightly became Sir Alex after leading Manchester United to the Treble in 1999, but what dear Brian did was just as impressive. He turned a provincial club into the best in England, not once but twice – first with Derby County and then again with Nottingham Forest.
>
> At Forest, he went even better, conquering Europe twice. And it was harder to win the European Cup in those days, because if you lost one tie, then you were out. In today's game, where money talks, what Cloughie achieved at the City Ground could never happen again. Can you imagine a team like Coventry winning the Premiership and European Cup in the next few years? But Cloughie is one of a number of footballers who should have been knighted. The England team which won the World Cup should all have had the honour. Can you believe Bobby Moore did not receive a knighthood?
>
> I was deeply saddened to hear of Cloughie's death, for we go back a long way. I first had dealings with him when he was manager at Hartlepool, and I was boss at Derby when Clough had just started his job at Forest. He was a true character, the like of which will never be seen again. He would have sorted out the prima donnas we

have in the game now and would have hated the fact so many foreign players have flooded into the Premiership. He will be sorely missed by me, and everyone involved in football.

Newbon shared that sentiment, and if he found Clough a demanding interviewee at times, then he was not alone among the media corps. Duncan McKenzie says: 'I remember many years ago John Motson ringing me in a state of mild panic saying that he imminently had the task of interviewing Brian Clough and asking for some tips and advice on how to handle him. John expressed the fear that this larger-than-life character had within him the capacity to get him sacked from the BBC if he were to belittle, embarrass or chide him, and that belief in itself was something quite remarkable. John, of course, was almost a national treasure through his football broadcasts, and in the normal course of events it would be the interviewee who may have cause to worry over being very careful about what he said and how he conducted himself in front of the cameras. It said a lot about the stature of Cloughie in the game.'

Asked about his overriding feeling about Clough's departure from Elland Road, Newbon answers: 'History has shown us that his sacking by Leeds was Leeds' loss. What, apart from their unlikely league title success under Howard Wilkinson in 1991–92, have they won in the subsequent 35 years? Nothing. I would suggest that that would not have been the case had he remained in place.'

14

A NEW BROOM

If God had wanted us to play football in the sky,
he'd have put grass up there.

Brian Clough

Christmas 1974. The City Varieties Music Hall in Leeds is packed to the rafters with an eager and excited pantomime-loving audience, craning their necks to get a better view of the all-star cast in a quite unique production of *Cinderella*. In the leading role of this Jimmy Armfield-written show, backed by impresario Barney Colehan, is Duncan McKenzie. Norman Hunter is Prince Charming and Gordon McQueen is the Good Fairy. Billy Bremner is Buttons.

Two months previously, Armfield, a legendary one-club player for Blackpool with over 600 appearances, the holder of 43 England caps (15 as captain) and voted the best right-back on earth at the 1962 World Cup in Chile, had been prised from Bolton Wanderers to manage a Leeds United in tatters following the Brian Clough debacle. The club and its players needed some bonhomie, and Armfield made an inspired move: he sent his players to the ball. He recalls now: 'In fact, we put on two pantos, in 1974 and '75. People warned me that there'd be jokes about a pantomime off the pitch and a pantomime on it, but it was that type of thing that removed the sour taste. It needed to be done. Billy Bremner played the best Buttons I've ever seen. He was down the centre aisle giving sweets out to the kids. We filled the place every night – you couldn't get a ticket. It got the players gelled back together, so it worked.'

The feel-good factor had indeed returned to Elland Road. Armfield says: 'When I arrived at Leeds from Bolton in October of 1974, a number of factors had combined to create a tense atmosphere. At any club, everything in the garden is lovely when you are winning. When results are not going in your favour, things are not so good. Leeds lay second from bottom in the table when I took over. Brian had had his 44 days and on top of the bad chemistry between himself and Leeds United Football Club – they were like two pieces of sandpaper being scraped together – they had not been coming up with the results. Leeds had not done very well either in the interim [under temporary manager Maurice Lindley, they lost 2–1 at Burnley, beat Sheffield United 5–1 at home and lost 3–2 at Everton while progressing 5–3 on aggregate against FC Zurich with a home win and an away defeat in the European Cup] and it was clear from their unenviable and surprisingly low position in the table that an uphill task lay ahead.

'A side issue was the persistent newspaper talk at the time that John Giles and Billy Bremner had wanted to manage the club, and you wondered what effect this would have on matters. The team were struggling. They had lost Don Revie in the summer and had gone through a traumatic 44 days with his successor. When I arrived, Billy Bremner was injured and the team was near the bottom with six points from nine matches. One day, I was chatting to Bob English, our kit man, and he said, "Don't worry, you'll see a difference when Billy's back. When Billy plays, they all play." And he was right. We never looked back once Billy was fit again. He was a real firebrand, but people forget what a gifted player he was. Good touch on the ball, very clever, with just about the best reverse pass I ever saw. He was a great competitor, too, with a tremendous amount of pride. He wanted the job after Clough left and I suspect there was a bit of resentment when I arrived. I didn't go out of my way to win him over. I just treated him with the respect he deserved, and we became close.

'Yet another factor at Leeds at the time was that the club was to all intents and purposes still in recovery from the departure of Don Revie, who had been revered, loved and idolised. Instrumental in persuading me to leave Bolton and join Leeds was Sam Bolton, one of their directors whom I knew from dealings with the Football Association, where he also held an important role. One of the positives was that I knew they were in a false position in the league and that I could and would improve this situation. The club itself was in generally good condition, though I was surprised to discover that the finances were not on as sound a footing as I imagined they might be. In fact the club was in the red.

'What was clear straight away was that in his short time at the helm Brian had made too many changes. In signing O'Hare, McGovern and McKenzie, the balance of the squad had suddenly shifted. Yes, he had inherited an ageing squad that was on the verge of break-up, but I was rather hopeful that I could get another 12 months out of a bunch of players who were, after all, reigning champions. My first task, I felt, was to bring a calming effect to the place. The first time I spoke to the players, I asked what on earth they were doing in such a lowly position in the league and confessed to them that I could not believe it. It was up to them, I told them, to get whatever was troubling them out of their systems, and together we would try to improve matters.

'I think one of Brian's problems had been that he was dealing with players who were household names, individuals who were more famous than himself. I knew him from playing alongside him for Young England, and it would be fair to say, I think, that he was a slightly complicated character. I needed to relax these players, so there was nothing complicated or fraught about the build-up to my first match in charge, a home game against Arsenal. Duncan McKenzie scored both goals in a 2–0 win that took our points tally for the season from six to eight, and we were on our way. We finished seventh in the league, and I think everyone associated with the club was willing to settle for seventh given the unfortunate start to the season.

'The team I inherited at Leeds was of such stature that I was not worried about the players. They were good players in a good team at a good club. It was a solid unit made up of individuals who all had talent. What I set out to do and what I achieved, I think, was to mould them all together. They did well for me. I just wish that I had had them two years earlier.'

Clough, meanwhile, was making hay with Nottingham Forest. He had been out of work for less than four months when, on 6 January 1975, he replaced Allan Brown as manager of Forest, who at the time were in 13th place in Division Two. His first game in charge was a third-round FA Cup replay against Tottenham Hotspur, and a 1–0 victory was eked out thanks to a goal by Scottish centre-forward Neil Martin. Clough's brand of football was to make for some rousing entertainment through to the end of the season, which featured an extraordinary quintuplet of meetings in cup and league with Fulham in the space of 30 days and a final-day 2–1 defeat of West Bromwich Albion which saw them comfortably stave off relegation, which had been feared at the time of the managerial change.

In the beginning, Clough's options were limited by budgetary constraints. Despite his unhappy experience at Leeds, he stayed loyal to those he had brought to Elland Road, installing Jimmy Gordon as first-team coach (although the players at Leeds hadn't taken to him, he became a well-liked and respected figure at the City Ground) and buying John O'Hare and John McGovern. Both John Robertson and Martin O'Neill had made transfer requests before his arrival, and he succeeded in persuading them to stay. Towards the end of his first season, he was able to bring in defender Frank Clark from Newcastle on a free transfer.

While Clough was getting his feet under the table at Forest, Leeds were fully recovered from the trauma of early-season events. Even much-improved league form was put in the shade by their achievement in reaching the European Cup final courtesy of further victories over Újpesti Dózsa, Anderlecht and Barcelona, though if one dark cloud had been cast over the club by the Clough episode then another was to form over them at the Parc des Princes, Paris. The final, against Bayern Munich, was memorable for some questionable decisions by referee Michel Kitabdjian. The Frenchman denied Leeds what seemed a clear-cut penalty in the first half when Bayern's legendary captain Franz Beckenbauer hauled down Allan Clarke. And midway through the second half, with Leeds holding the upper hand but the match still goalless, Kitabdjian disallowed a brilliant volleyed goal from Peter Lorimer. Initially, the referee seemed to be happy with the goal, and his linesman saw no infringement, running back to the centre line with his flag held down. Kitabdjian, too, seemed to be heading back to the centre circle, apparently satisfied that the goal was good. However, as he passed Beckenbauer the German player appeared to point something out to him, and he turned back, indicating a free kick to Bayern. It was difficult to see why the goal had been disallowed. It was possible that Bremner had been forced offside, but if so, the linesman hadn't picked up on it, and in any case he was far to the left of the goal and could not have been considered to have been interfering with play. What was more, the free kick was taken from the centre of the penalty area, some distance from Bremner's position.

Leeds, their spirit broken, lost 2–0, and the game ended with all the see-sawing emotions of a nerve-shredding season reflected in rioting at the Leeds end of the stadium. As a result, the club was barred from European competition for two years, a punishment that the club, going through a time of great change, would struggle to recover from.

In a 2008 interview with Armfield, the *Yorkshire Evening Post*'s Phil Hay offered a trenchant analysis of his time in charge:

Armfield was the man charged with redressing the disorderly regime of Brian Clough at Leeds United . . . and for that alone he deserved a medal . . . Armfield, as history shows, did not receive a medal at Leeds. A contentious defeat in the 1975 European Cup final saw to that. In so nearly becoming the first English manager to win the continental trophy, however, he displayed the traits of a man who liked to see what life could offer him.

While a member of the squad at Blackpool, the only league club he would play for, Armfield would regularly undertake shifts at his local newspaper, the *Evening Gazette*, to train him for a future career in journalism. When Leeds United dispensed with him in 1978 after four years as their manager, he did not look for another managerial position but instead accepted a job with the *Daily Express*.

It was a sabbatical from which he never returned and next year will begin his third decade in radio, an industry which currently employs the 72-year-old as one of BBC Radio 5 Live's matchday summarisers. 'I'm what you'd call a busy person,' Armfield said. 'There was always something on the go. Back in the 1960s, while I was still playing, I took my FA coaching badges at a time when they weren't really in vogue. I would also spend three evenings a week at the *Evening Gazette* because in my mind I imagined that once I finished playing I'd become a journalist. That was the plan.

'But Bolton Wanderers asked me to be their manager in 1971, and a short while later I took the job at Leeds. I'd turned down a different offer to manage Everton. It's a long time ago now, and a different part of my life, but I look back on it fondly. I've got a soft spot for Leeds as a club and I liked the city; the people were very good to me. And in the main I thought I did well.'

Armfield was United's antidote to the poison spread through Leeds by the most ill-conceived managerial appointment ever seen at Elland Road. Clough presided over the club for 44 torrid days, working in the shadow of Revie for as long as he could stand it. For all his precocious talent, the idiosyncrasies of Clough were not compatible with Elland Road and Armfield was appointed in October 1974 with Leeds submerged near the bottom of the First Division. To his eternal credit, United finished the 1974–75 season eight points behind the league winners, Derby County, and navigated their way to the European Cup final by disposing of Anderlecht and Barcelona in earlier rounds.

Armfield has discussed United's 2–0 defeat to Bayern Munich in the final too many times to relive it again but the city of Leeds, and more besides, believed the club had been critically hindered by the ineptitude of the match referee. Supporters at the Parc des Princes in Paris ripped out seats from the terraces, and United were subsequently banned from European competitions for two years. Armfield would have been the first Englishman to manage a European Cup-winning team, an honour which fell instead to Clough with Nottingham Forest four years later. By then, the mess Clough had left behind at Elland Road was a more faded memory.

'The first job for me was to get the Leeds team back on its feet,' said Armfield. 'That didn't actually take a great deal of doing. The players were very experienced, and they knew their way around England and Europe. I'd won a number of England caps and I had more international experience than some of them, but when it came to European experience, they all had more than me. I was working with a squad that should have been doing much better than they were under Brian. We got to the European Cup final, and I've always felt we were robbed on the night. What should have been a great day wasn't such a great day in the end.

'I then had the difficult job of breaking up the great team that Don Revie had built. I brought in guys like Tony Currie from Sheffield United and Brian Flynn from Burnley, and I also signed John Hawley from Hull City. John's a player who sticks out in my mind because I never actually saw him play for Leeds. He came to us in 1978, and the board decided to let my contract run out later that summer. Personally I felt that we were going along nicely, but the club thought differently. I remember after one defeat, when we'd dropped to around seventh in the division, the chairman called a board meeting for the Monday morning. The gist of the discussion was him asking me what on earth was going on and whether the team had had it. I was slightly amazed, to say the least, and I said, "You do lose in football, you know." After four years there, my contract wasn't extended.'

Remarkably, United's selection for Armfield's successor was to prove as great a misjudgement as that which brought Clough to Leeds in 1974. Jock Stein, like Clough, seduced the board at Leeds with his impeccable history and his successful association with Celtic in Glasgow, and a deal was brokered in August of 1978. Two months later, and after a reign which ran for just a day longer than Clough's, Stein uprooted abruptly and accepted an offer to become Scotland's manager.

'The Leeds job wasn't for Jock,' said Armfield. 'I thought that when he took it, but at that point he didn't have a job. He phoned me to ask me about Leeds and I basically told him that the club was ready for him to walk into. There was nothing to do except pick the team up and carry on. I suppose the biggest task for me had been to get rid of the sour feeling that existed at Leeds when Brian left.'

15

UPS AND DOWNS

*They [the Football Association] thought I was going to change it
lock, stock and barrel. They were shrewd,
because that's exactly what I would have done.*

Brian Clough

While Jimmy Armfield steadied the ship at Leeds United and
Brian Clough rejoined the managerial circuit with Nottingham
Forest, Don Revie was continuing to turn his hand to the job
that had lured him away from Yorkshire and instigated so
much change at Elland Road. In succeeding Sir Alf Ramsey on
a five-year contract worth £25,000 a year (several times what
Ramsey had received, in part an indication of the esteem in
which he was held by the FA), Revie, who had won six England
caps and scored four goals in a landmark twelve months from
October 1954, provided something of a contrast in personalities
to Ramsey. Where his predecessor was viewed as cold, aloof
and secretive, the new incumbent adopted a more friendly and
open attitude.

Bringing in Les Cocker from Leeds United as his assistant,
and with Bill Taylor as his trainer, Revie got off to a flyer in
the qualifying campaign for the 1976 European Championships
on 30 October 1974, with a 3–0 win against Czechoslovakia at
Wembley, and followed up three weeks later with a 0–0 draw,

also at Wembley, against Portugal. A successful first season as England manager saw the team undefeated after nine internationals but when, early in the 1975–76 season, England were eliminated, Revie's stock was already on the slide.

The nine wins included a convincing victory over West Germany, the World Cup holders, and a 5–1 trouncing of Scotland. However, the England team became more and more inconsistent, perhaps reflecting a lack of confidence in Revie on the part of the players. The former Leeds manager, whose first team had been set practically in stone at Elland Road, changed the team sheet constantly, leaving the squad unsettled. To give just one example, Alan Ball of Arsenal captained the team for six games in 1974–75 only to be suddenly and controversially dropped and never picked again. Revie's discarding of both Ball and Alan Hudson was seen as a critical error of judgement, and when losses to Czechoslovakia and Portugal put England out of the championship, Revie's critics had gathered ammunition.

***

It took some time, but in July 1976, two years after they had last worked together, Clough was rejoined at Nottingham Forest by Peter Taylor. Together, they transformed Forest's fortunes within a few seasons. In 1976–77, they were placed third in the Second Division, winning promotion. They were to take Division One by storm, being crowned champions in 1978, seven points ahead of Liverpool, whom they also beat to lift the League Cup. This was a tremendous achievement for Forest, but also a personal landmark and a vindication of sorts for Clough, as he became the first manager since Herbert Chapman (Huddersfield and Arsenal in the 1930s) to have won the league championship with two different clubs.

Ironically, long ago in history, Chapman had had his own controversial spell at Elland Road. In the 1912 close season, he was offered the chance to manage Second Division Leeds City, who had finished 19th in the previous season and were forced to apply for re-election to the league. Chapman was a central figure in their successful campaign for readmission. He engineered a sixth-place finish in 1912–13 with attendances at their Elland Road home rising from 8,500 to 13,000 in appreciation of a rejuvenated side who were playing attacking football and netted 70 goals in that season alone. Chapman strengthened the side's defence and City did even better the next season, reaching fourth place. The club looked certain to win promotion in 1914–15. However, larger forces put paid to these hopes with the declaration of war. Attendances were down as men enlisted in the forces, and Chapman lost his confident touch, struggling to pick a first team that he was satisfied with. City finished the season in a disappointing 15th place, and league football was suspended for the rest of the war.

Leeds City continued to play in regional competitions, but many of the pre-war squad were serving their country or had left as a result of the drop in salaries accompanying the suspension of the league. Chapman left in 1916 to manage a munitions factory, coming back to the club only when the war was over. He resigned suddenly and without explanation in December 1918, and during the 1919–20 season, an ex-Leeds City player made allegations against his former club, claiming that during the war there had been financial skulduggery involving payments to guest players. Leeds were thrown out of the Football League in October 1919, and Chapman, along with four other officials, was banned from football for life. The club was dissolved and their ground, Elland Road, taken over by the recently formed Leeds United. Chapman managed to have his ban overturned within a few years and went on to success at Huddersfield and Arsenal.

Unencumbered by such constraints as players going off to war, Clough was about to take a leaf out of Jimmy Armfield's book of fairy tales and animate the stage with sweet romance, swashbuckling adventure and pure fantasy.

Forest's assault on the football world, and the senses, was ignited by the arrival of Peter Taylor. A year after his return to Clough's side, the club gave the pair a vote of confidence when it extended their original four-year contracts by another year, and together they set about building a squad that was to embark on the most dramatic of voyages. They signed Kenny Burns, Larry Lloyd and Peter Shilton, and it looked as if Forest were really going places.

Clough and Taylor thought they saw potential for a great centre-half pairing in Lloyd from Liverpool and Burns from Birmingham, and they were right, which was particularly impressive given that both players had struggled to make it into the first team at their respective clubs. Shilton was signed in 1977, after Forest had gained their place in the top flight, but even so, he was an expensive choice. The deal cost Forest £270,000, but Taylor argued, rightly, as it turned out, that: 'Shilton wins you matches.' Forest conceded remarkably few goals in 1977–78 and Shilton was a key figure in their league success. Another two vital signings were Garry Birtles, a bargain from non-league Long Eaton, and, by contrast, Trevor Francis, in Britain's first-ever million-pound transfer.

The new English champions were now aiming even higher – at the 1978–79 European Cup. The first fixture, however, was not, on paper, encouraging. They were to meet Liverpool, who were the holders and widely tipped to retain the cup. Many wrote Nottingham off, but, their confidence bolstered by Clough, who assured them they could win, they defied expectations winning the home leg 2–0. Before the trip to Liverpool, Clough went further, offering each player a £3,000 bonus for a place in the next round. They drew at Anfield, with Shilton conceding nothing.

The second round saw Forest travelling to Greece, gaining a 7–2 aggregate win over AEK Athens before beating Zurich's Grasshopper 5–2 for a semi-final place. They were to meet German champions FC Köln. They drew the home leg before heading to Cologne to attempt what seemed a near impossible task. However, Forest did their manager proud. Peter Shilton made some outstanding saves, while Tony Bowyer succeeded in getting the ball past Harald Schumacher and into the back of the net.

Before the final against Malmö, Clough made the surprise decision to drop Martin O'Neill and Archie Gemmill, bringing in recent signing Francis. Malmö, not able to play their ideal team due to injuries, played defensively and the match was less than thrilling, at least until Robertson beat two defenders and crossed to Francis, who headed in the match's only goal. 'It wasn't a great game,' commented a triumphant Clough, 'but they were a boring team, Malmö. In fact, the Swedes are quite a boring nation. But we still won, so who cares?'

If winning the European Cup once was a dream for a small-city club like Nottingham Forest, then retaining the glittering prize surely belonged in the land of fantasy. But Clough, Taylor and their merry men had got a taste for it now, and there was to be no stopping them. Early successes against Öster of Sweden and Arges Pitesti of Romania were followed by a quarter-final defeat of Dynamo Berlin and a semi-final conquest of Ajax en route to a final date at Real Madrid's Bernabéu Stadium with a Hamburg side featuring Kevin Keegan. John Robertson's squeezed-home 21st-minute shot was enough to land the spoils and hand Forest back-to-back European Cup final victories.

* * *

The tables had turned. While Clough was triumphing at the City Ground, Revie was struggling at the FA. England's next big target after failing to qualify for the European Championships was the World Cup in Argentina in 1978. They were competing against Italy for qualification, and from the start it looked bad; Revie's side lost to the Italians by two goals in November 1976. The former Leeds manager still struggled with team selection, yearning, perhaps, for players in the mould of Bremner and Giles to run the midfield engine room.

Given the deteriorating relationship between the manager and the FA, it seemed that Revie and England were destined not to enjoy the tournament together in any case. Revie had particular difficulty with Alan Hardaker, the Football League secretary. Hardaker would not bow to Revie's request that First Division matches scheduled for the Saturday before an England international be postponed. This was very frustrating for Revie, who was adamant that the squad needed to spend as much time together as possible, that this was a vital part of big-match preparation.

Furthermore, his relationship with the FA's chairman Sir Harold Thompson, an autocratic former Oxford don, was unsalvageable. When Revie asked the chairman to desist from referring to him by his surname, he replied, 'When I get to know you better, Revie, I shall call you Don,' to which Revie retorted, 'When I get to know you better, Thompson, I shall call you Sir Harold.'

If his dealings with the other officials were problematic, his relations with the players were barely less strained. The detailed dossiers on the opposition that Peter Lorimer had come to hate at Leeds United were ridiculed and his faith in non-footballing bonding activities such as bingo and indoor bowls and golf to foster team spirit was not appreciated either.

In February 1977, a Johan Cruyff-inspired 2–0 friendly defeat to Holland at Wembley – England were so comprehensively outclassed that journalists compared it with the infamous 6–3 defeat by Hungary, captained by Puskás, in 1953 – was the turning point. Revie struggled on for a few months, but in July, convinced he was about to be replaced by Bobby Robson, then manager of Ipswich, he announced, via a story in the *Daily Mail*, that he was leaving the post, stating that he couldn't continue feeling that 'nearly everyone in the country seems to want me out'. Being England manager, he said, had caused him and his family too much pain. But the day after it announced his resignation, the *Mail* revealed that Revie had signed a lucrative deal to manage the national team of the United Arab Emirates. However, the circumstances surrounding his defection gave rise to allegations of financial misdealings, and Revie was charged with bringing the game into disrepute. At a disciplinary hearing, he was suspended by the FA for a decade, and although he succeeded in having the ban overturned at the High Court, the judge had harsh words for him. He was replaced by Ron Greenwood.

UPS AND DOWNS

In 1983, when Revie left the Middle East, where he lived in Dubai and apparently enjoyed the sunshine and the golf, he was only in his mid-50s, yet he never worked in English football again. Meanwhile, Clough, for all the chaos of his reign of Leeds, was once more situated at its epicentre.

16

FALLEN EMPIRES

I can't even spell spaghetti never mind talk Italian. How could I tell an Italian to get the ball? He might grab mine.

Brian Clough

It is remarkable what damage the passage of time can do to a football club, and the once-great clubs managed by Clough have had their share of troubles in recent years. From winning, under Brian Clough, the league title in 1978, back-to-back European Cups in 1979 and 1980 and the League Cup four times between 1978 and 1990, Nottingham Forest went into a tailspin. So awful was the 1992–93 season, when they won just 10 of 42 matches, that they finished wooden spoonists and found themselves in the second tier, right back where Clough had started with them 18 long years previously. As far as football was concerned, this was Clough: The End.

The beginning had been eye-catching. Clough and Taylor had reunited to lead what was a relatively small club to those early victories in the Football League and in Europe. The pair built a strong team, with great names including Peter Shilton, Viv Anderson – the first black player to appear in a full international for England – Martin O'Neill, Trevor Francis, John Robertson, Archie Gemmill and Kenny Burns at its centre. Typically of Clough, his side won its spurs more through soul-bearing, honest endeavour than swashbuckling showmanship.

In 1983–84, with the split from Peter Taylor fresh in Clough's mind and no doubt weighing heavily upon him, Forest made it to the last four in the UEFA Cup but were beaten by Anderlecht in controversial circumstances. A goal was disallowed and years later it was revealed that the referee had been bribed. Clough and Forest would have to wait until 1989 before getting their hands on another major piece of silverware. During the 1988–89 season, Forest looked set to win the Treble. In the end, though they finished third in the league and were knocked out of the FA Cup in the semi-final, originally to have been played at Hillsborough. Forest did, however, beat Luton to lift the League Cup. And all this excitement was in spite of Clough having to manage affairs from the stands in the latter half of the season, when he was serving a touchline ban after hitting supporters who had invaded the pitch at the end of a cup match against QPR.

Forest kept hold of the League Cup in 1990 and hopes were raised that they might win an even more prestigious prize the following year. They made it to the FA Cup final, the only one Clough ever steered them to. At Wembley, they took on a Tottenham Hotspur side that included Gazza, who sustained a serious injury as a result of a wild tackle on Gary Charles minutes into the game. Stuart Pearce scored a tremendous goal from the resulting free kick, but Forest lost 2–1 as a result of an extra-time own goal. Although Nottingham made it to the League Cup final yet again the following season, their league form was starting to dip.

In fact, the 1992–93 season, Clough's 18th with Forest, was to be his last. As one of the 22 clubs in the newly created Premier League, they failed to raise a gallop and were bottom of the table virtually throughout the season. Clough's announcement of his retirement came just before a 2–0 defeat against Sheffield United confirmed the club's relegation after 16 years in the top flight. One of the most colourful passages in English football history was at an end.

Who was to replace Cloughie? This gigantic task befell Frank Clark, one of Clough's first signings and a member of the European Cup-winning team in 1979, who returned to the City Ground, having managed Leyton Orient. He took the Reds straight back into the Premier League, gaining promotion from a second-place finish in 1993–94. Forest made an immediate impact on their return to the top flight, reaching third place and qualifying for the UEFA Cup, making it to the quarter-finals, where they were knocked out by Bayern Munich. In 1996–97, however, with the club heading for relegation, Clark was sacked and captain Stuart Pearce stepped up to become caretaker player-manager.

'Psycho' was an inspirational figure at the City Ground, and Forest's results improved under him. Despite this, he was not offered the job on a permanent basis; instead, Dave Bassett was brought in from Crystal Palace. Forest ended the 1996–97 season in last place and were relegated once more. Again, they made it back into the Premiership at the first time of asking, topping the First Division. At the beginning of 1999, Bassett was sacked after a bad start to the season and 'Big Ron' Atkinson was appointed. A brief spell at Sheffield Wednesday had seen him save them from relegation, but if the board had hoped he could do the same for Forest, they were to be disappointed. At the end of the 1998–99 season, which featured an 8–1 thrashing at the hands of Manchester United, it was back down to the First Division for the Reds. His successor, David Platt, spent millions on players but couldn't take the team back to the Premiership, and resigned in 2001, with the club struggling financially.

Paul Hart took over immediately, but Forest were battling debt and finished 2001–02 in the bottom half of the second tier. He brought them up into the play-off zone the next year, but they missed out on a place in the top flight. Next season, the Reds slid back down the table again and Hart was replaced by Joe Kinnear. It was a brief spell at the City Ground for the Irishman, and before the end of the year, with Forest struggling against relegation, he resigned. Following another short-lived occupation of the hot seat by caretaker Mick Harford, Gary Megson was brought in. He had helped West Brom to achieve promotion to the Premier League, but he failed to pull off the same trick for Forest, and indeed the club was relegated from the new Coca-Cola Championship to League One at the end of the 2004–05 season.

It was a new low. Forest hadn't found themselves in the third tier for more than half a century. Megson went and joint caretaker managers Frank Barlow and Ian McParland were appointed from within to fill his place. They achieved some very good results but even a run of ten games unbeaten couldn't lift the team higher than seventh place.

The stability that the club had achieved under Clough looked to be lost forever. In 2006, Colin Calderwood became the 12th managerial appointment at the City Ground since Clough's departure 13 years before. His first season began promisingly, with Forest heading the division in November. Their lead fell away, but they rallied again and made it into the play-offs. They lost to Yeovil, but it was a good start for the new manager. In the 2007–08 campaign, Forest were favourites for automatic promotion. The club got off to a bad start, but their hard work paid off and in a nail-biting final match of the season they beat Yeovil 3–2 at home, securing second place and automatic promotion to the Championship. Despite this success, Calderwood was soon sacked after Forest lost 4–2 to bottom-of-the-table Doncaster on Boxing Day 2008. Billy Davies, former manager of Preston North End and Derby County, replaced him on the first day of the New Year.

Derby, too, endured a roller-coaster ride that plummeted them from the heights of league titles under Clough in 1971–72 and the mercurial Dave Mackay three years later to English football's third tier in 1984.

It was back in 1967, when England found psychedelia with *Sgt Pepper's Lonely Hearts Club Band* and US activities in Vietnam were attracting global condemnation, that Clough took up the reins and set Derby County on the path to glory. Clough's persistence in capturing Dave Mackay, whose heart had been set on the assistant manager's job at Edinburgh club Hearts, was to be rewarded when the tough, uncompromising Scot played a leading role in Derby's promotion to the First Division in 1969. A year later, his huge influence ensured that, far from disgracing themselves at a higher level, Derby would be a surprise package to many, and they really made their presence felt, finishing a highly creditable fourth.

Derby were now well and truly in the big time, and in 1972 had established themselves so firmly that they were to plunder their first ever First Division title and, with it, a ticket to the European Cup. On this big stage, with its wider audience, yet more people were surprised by the ability and strength of this team from a relatively small corner of England, and they marched into a semi-final showdown with Italian giants Juventus. Clough was incensed by the manner of their defeat in a match that was to become notorious for allegations of bribery of the officials. 'Cheating bastards,' was Clough's terse summary.

Few on Clough's radar, especially Football Association officials, were exempt from withering criticisms when he felt it necessary, and one too many of these for the liking of the Derby County board was to lead to a parting of the ways in 1973.

Derby's tilt at the top was unfettered, however, and they were to land another title in 1974–75, this time under Mackay, whose managerial ambitions had been fulfilled beyond his wildest dreams. This run of success could not be maintained, though, and when they were relegated to the Second Division in 1980, the writing had been on the wall for some time. Four years later, they had deteriorated to the extent that they were scrambling about in the third tier.

These were the bottoming-out days. Derby escaped the clutches of the third tier at the second attempt and won the Second Division in 1986–87. Their second season back in the top flight brought a fifth-place finish, but they were to finish wooden spoonists in 1990–91 and missed out on being among the founder members of the Premier League. They were back in the big league for the 1996–97 season, but by that time the Big Four of Arsenal, Chelsea, Liverpool and Manchester United were tightening their stranglehold, leaving only UEFA Cup places and the mid-table safety net to play for. Consecutive finishes of 12th, 9th, 8th, 16th and 17th were followed by relegation in 2001–02, and despite narrowly avoiding further relegation in 2004, they rose again to the Premier League for one entirely forgettable season in 2007–08, when they became the whipping boys and won just a single one of their 38 matches, scoring a mere 20 goals, conceding 89 and going down with a record low points total of 11.

It was an embarrassing start for new chairman Adam Pearson, formerly commercial director of Leeds United and more recently owner of Hull City. Pearson had replaced manager Billy Davies with Paul Jewell early in his tenure, but Jewell required 27 attempts to engineer his first victory. A poor start to life back in the second tier created a huge dilemma for the ambitious Pearson. It was announced on 29 December 2008 that Jewell had resigned as manager, and the identity of his replacement, introduced a week later as the club's 26th permanent manager, had the football romantics purring.

Some 37 years after his father had led the Rams to the old Division One title, the 42-year-old Nigel Clough ended his 10-year 'apprenticeship' at non-league Burton Albion with the aim of putting the pride back into Pride Park. The former Nottingham Forest player and owner of 14 England caps left Burton with a 13-point lead at the top of the Blue Square Premier and observed:

> This is a fantastic opportunity for me and one that I relish. I know the club inside out. It has always had a special place in my and my family's heart, and I know that this is one of the most exciting jobs in football. Derby County has everything – tremendous support, a first-class stadium, magnificent training facilities and

an ambitious ownership group looking to grow the club even further. Also, we have a terrific squad of players already here and I can't wait to start working with them.

He also commented

I am not shying away from what my dad did. It is something to embrace. I looked at all the photos here, but I've got them all at home, so it will be no different. What dad achieved at Derby is a nice thing, not a negative. It might be 35 years ago but supporters talk about it as though it was yesterday. Many of them are affiliated with the club because of those days. And I don't think people will ever think of me as something other than Dad's son. In some ways, I hope they don't, because that would mean they have forgotten about him.

Pearson told reporters:

We are delighted to have Nigel on board. He is the right man for this club at this time, he has created a fine legacy at Burton and wants to do exactly the same at Derby. He sees it very much as a long-term project.

There was no sentiment or romance involved in the appointment. You can't have that in football. He's tough enough to take the club forward in his own style.

Burton chairman Ben Robinson said that he'd always known the former England striker would eventually join a bigger outfit, adding, 'We can never repay him for what he's done for the club.'

Marking the new appointment in an article for the *Sunday Times*, Duncan Hamilton, the author of *Provided You Don't Kiss Me*, recalled:

Nigel Clough leant against the door frame of the chairman's room at Nottingham Forest. He fiddled with his car keys, impatiently tossing them in the air and catching them. His father, Brian, was lolling across a leather sofa. He'd rolled his tracksuit bottoms as high as his knees. He looked like a holiday-maker about to paddle in the sea.

For more than an hour, Nigel had been waiting to drive him home. At least half a dozen times, his father had told him: 'Give me five minutes.' Now Nigel was visibly impatient. He had an appointment to keep. 'Ring your mother and tell her we'll be a wee bit late,' said Brian. 'I might have a bath and get changed.'

Nigel grimaced, let out a deep sigh and gripped the keys tightly in his fist. As he stomped away, Brian yelled after him: 'Don't lose your rag, busy bollocks. I'm coming.' He climbed off the sofa, rubbing the stiffness out of his knee joints. 'I think I've upset the chauffeur,' he said, promptly vanishing with a quick 'ta-ra'.

I got to know Brian Clough well, through good times and bad, during the 20 years I covered Forest for the *Nottingham Evening Post*. For me, this short, inconsequential scene illustrated the fundamental contrast in character between father and son. Last week Nigel left Burton Albion to become the 15th manager to follow Brian into Derby County. As he begins the job his father abandoned in a fit of pique in 1973, a season after winning the league title – and prepares for a televised FA Cup tie against Forest on 23 January – those personality differences will become more obvious than ever. The name is the same; the style and temperament are not. Nigel brings his father's Baseball Ground principles to Pride Park: discipline, clean sheets and neat passing. He doesn't bring his father's chameleon tendencies.

Brian veered from pyrotechnical flashiness to blissful charm. He was frequently rude and could be exasperating for the sake of it. And he never wore a wrist watch. He lived in his own idiosyncratic time zone, which the rest of us worked around. To be late was his prerogative. Nigel was humbly apologetic if he delayed you for five minutes. As well as being punctual, he was also modest, polite, tolerant and well mannered.

Those traits will shape the quiet way in which he tries to lift Derby out of relegation trouble and dispose of his and his father's former club in the Cup. This early test is critical. The Derby–Forest rivalry isn't just about geography or a century-long feud over bragging rights. A jealous squabble persists over which end of the A52 – the Brian Clough Way – Brian's heart truly lies. When Nottingham unveiled with fuss and flummery their £60,000 statue of Brian eight weeks ago, a glorious piece of one-upmanship, there were anxious squeals in Derby for an identical honour, as if Nottingham were trying to steal Brian from them.

Given Nigel's availability and the cult of Clough, it seems odd that Forest didn't approach him after abruptly sacking Colin Calderwood last month. The former Derby boss Billy Davies stepped in instead. Derby's hiring of Nigel has given the black-and-whites of the East Midlands the justification to boast that Brian Clough – and now his son – truly belongs to them. Forest have missed a trick, a fact that the Cup might yet endorse.

I suspect Brian would be chuffed at how things have worked out. He'd also be nervous on Nigel's behalf. Irrespective of how much he achieved at Forest, the hurt and bitter regret of resigning from Derby never left him. He had an emotional attachment to Derby that Forest, despite 18 years and two European Cups, could never quite match.

He would have viewed Nigel's appointment both as a continuation of that intimate bond and partly as family atonement for his mistake in leaving. Shortly before his death in 2004, Brian admitted some of his heart was always with Derby: 'I wish I'd never left.' With Nigel back, he'll seem to be there still.

As a player, Nigel was that rare thing: a cerebral footballer. He read Graham Greene novels, soaked up Shakespeare's plays. 'He's really more like his mother, Barbara,' Brian frequently pointed out. 'She likes the theatre and the ballet, things that bore the arse off me.' He would say it with stoic acceptance, rather than regret, before adding: 'But then our business together is football.'

At Derby, Nigel practised shooting with title winners such as Dave Mackay, Alan Hinton and John O'Hare. At Brighton, he sat in the dugout.

At Forest, he made his League debut on Boxing Day 1984, aged 18. I've always believed Brian, more than anybody else, struggled to handle his son's emergence as a goal-scorer. He had more difficulty than Nigel's coaches, the other players and Nigel himself. Brian fretted over claims of nepotism. He worried that Nigel would be deliberately hacked down and injured (which is why he played under a pseudonym for Forest's youth team). He was concerned the crowds might bait him purely because he was his son. 'The sins of fathers,' he said, 'shouldn't be heaped on the shoulders of the sons . . . but he'll get a fair amount of that in any case, no matter what I say.' Privately, he was 'our Nige' and Brian talked of him at length not only as a boss but also as an exceptionally proud father. 'He's brave . . . and he thinks, which is an asset 'cos brainy footballers are better than thick ones.'

Publicly, Brian wouldn't call Nigel by his Christian name. He was either 'the number nine' or 'the centre-forward'. Small things bothered him. Headline writers frequently aired the phrase: 'The Son Also Rises'. Brian thought it was being used to the point of meaninglessness. He once asked in a bad temper: 'It's the same old crap. Isn't there any imagination in newspaper offices?'

If Brian were alive today, he'd reveal parental protectiveness for Nigel all over again, but only because of the high expectations others are already placing on him. He'd be confident his boy could handle it. I once made the mistake of casually asking Brian: 'When did you realise that Nigel had talent?' He dropped his chin to his chest and gave me a hard stare, as if peering over a pair of horn-rimmed glasses. He wagged his finger in rebuke. 'As soon as he was born, of course,' he said sharply. 'He's my son – he was bound to have talent.'

There was a touch of magic about Clough Jr's introduction to the Derby crowd. It came just before the kick-off in a Carling Cup semi-final first leg against the mighty Manchester United, with the new manager not officially due to start his job until the next day. The reception he received was predictably warm and enthusiastic, with the added excitement of Derby all set to make their first appearance in a major cup semi-final since 1976 and their first in the last four of the League Cup since 1968. The script was written and Kris Commons' goal on the half-hour was enough for a dominant Derby to take a one-goal lead to Old Trafford for the return leg, but a spirited performance there saw them lose 4–3 on aggregate.

Then, as if some magical, mystical fixture fixer were at work, their visitors in the FA Cup fourth round just three nights later were local rivals and bitter enemies Nottingham Forest. Sometimes you just couldn't make it up. A 1–1 draw meant a further meeting with the old foe, and a City Ground humdinger ensued, Derby coming back from 2–0 down at half-time to win 3–2.

The home crowd that had once adored Nigel Clough as a player and his father as a manager booed him as he sprinted for the sanctuary of the dressing-room at the final whistle, and the man who spoiled the party left the media matters to right-hand man Gary Crosby, who explained: 'Nigel does not look for glory. He is very pleased with the victory, but nothing more than that. He does not want to be seen to be taking any personal glory from it. It is just fantastic to win a cup tie after being 2–0 down.'

It was the first victory Derby had tasted at Forest since they were managed by a certain Clough Sr back in 1971. Soon afterwards, Derby were to fulfil an FA Cup fifth-round tie against Manchester United, meaning that in his first two months in charge Clough had faced the European champions three times and his old club Nottingham Forest twice. All this after Derby had beaten in the FA Cup third round Forest Green, whose name, ever so slightly spookily, makes one think of Brian Clough's trademark squash jersey.

There were good signs in the league for Clough Jr. A 3–0 victory over Plymouth – Derby's third win in eight days – provided the club's biggest away victory for seven years, and daylight was opening between themselves and the Coca-Cola Championship relegation zone. Clough observed:

> Apart from the QPR game, we have been able to take positives from all our performances so far. But there is still a long way to go, I have got to keep stressing that. There are three months of the season left and we are only five points above the bottom three, so we will need a lot more performances like the one at Plymouth. But we feel that the players are stepping up to the plate at the moment and doing their jobs extremely well, and there is a good spirit there. It's been a rough 18 months for the club and we won't come out of it in a month, but there are signs that we can come out of it.

Understated. Reserved. Cautious. Hardly a chip off the old block.

Over at Leeds United, their demise as a once-great club is probably the most marked. Their decline set in after the European Cup final defeat in 1975, and all forms of success eluded them until they won the Second Division under Howard Wilkinson in 1989–90. A brief and spectacular revival saw them finish fourth in the top flight at the first time of asking, and they improved upon this by surprisingly winning the championship the following season, the last before the advent of the Premier League and the last time an English manager won his country's highest division.

But it was all downhill from there, and Wilkinson never recovered from overseeing a wretched display by Leeds against Aston Villa in the 1996 League Cup final. A 4–0 home defeat by Manchester United early in the 1996–97 season saw him walking the gangplank to be replaced by George Graham. Leeds' qualification for the UEFA Cup for the 1998–99 season sparked a brief revival in fortunes. European football was on the Elland Road agenda for five successive seasons, and it was looking like the good old days were back under the management of David O'Leary, who had been Graham's assistant until the Scot walked out in favour of Tottenham Hotspur. In 1999–2000, Leeds battled to the semi-finals of the UEFA Cup – their first semis in Europe in 25 years – only to fall to Turkish outfit Galatasaray.

The next season was one of which Clough would have been proud, with Leeds making the last four in the Champions League courtesy of thrilling victories over Lazio, Anderlecht and Deportivo. A goalless draw at home to Valencia in the first leg offered hope, but a comprehensive 3–0 defeat in the return in Spain shattered their dreams. Then . . . the plunge. A tame exit from the UEFA Cup at the hands of PSV Eindhoven in 2001–02 was bad enough, but this was followed by a similar surrender against Malaga the following season, which wiped Europe off the Leeds radar, possibly for years to come.

Once they were in the Champions League, heavy spending on players was undertaken to try to ensure that Leeds would be a permanent fixture in Europe's biggest club competition, but it was a gamble that backfired spectacularly. They failed to qualify, debts began to mount, two of their biggest players, Jonathan Woodgate and Lee Bowyer, were involved in a high-profile court case, the relationship between O'Leary and chairman Peter Ridsdale deteriorated, and soon Leeds were on a collision course with disaster.

O'Leary was dismissed and replaced by former England supremo Terry Venables, whose unhappy time at the club hit its low point when Woodgate was sold to Newcastle for £9 million against his manager's wishes. Venables' tenure was to last a mere eight months before he was sacked and replaced by Peter Reid, who was inheriting a rapidly deteriorating side but nevertheless engineered an escape from relegation, which had been looking more and more likely.

Ridsdale, meanwhile, had resigned from the Leeds board to be replaced by Professor John McKenzie, a local economics expert who was to preside over the dismissal of Reid following a shaky start to the 2003–04 season that saw crushing defeats by Leicester, Everton, Arsenal and Portsmouth. A once-steady ship was now rocking, and there were further significant developments when Gerald Krasner, an insolvency expert heading up a consortium, took the helm as chairman. He presided over a fire sale of the club's assets while caretaker manager Eddie Gray battled valiantly to produce the goods on the field, only for the club to be relegated after 14 years among the elite.

The drop cost Gray his job and Kevin Blackwell, who had been recruited by Reid as his number two, was handed his first managerial role. Despite the ongoing sale of players, with eyes constantly on the wage bill, Blackwell played the incoming transfer market shrewdly and settled the team to attain mid-table safety in 2004–05.

In January 2005, a takeover of the club was completed by former Chelsea chairman Ken Bates, who said:

I'm delighted to be stepping up to the mantle at such a fantastic football club. I see Leeds as a great club that has fallen on hard times. We have a lot of hard work ahead to get the club back where it belongs in the Premiership, and with the help of our fans we will do everything we can. It's going to be a tough job and the first task is to stabilise the cash flow and sort out the remaining creditors. But there is light at the end of a very long tunnel. For the past year it has been a matter of firefighting – now we can start running the club again.

Krasner gave his view on the takeover:

This deal ensures the medium- to long-term survival of the club, and I believe Mr Bates' proposals are totally for the benefit of the club. We are content that under Mr Bates Leeds United will continue to consolidate and move forward. When we took over Leeds United in March 2004, the club had a debt of £103 million. Since that date, my board has succeeded in reducing the debt to under £25 million. We worked tirelessly to solve all of the problems at Leeds United. Eighty per cent of the problems have already been overcome, and we came to this agreement with Mr Bates to secure its ongoing success.

Blackwell was given some financial clout in the summer of 2005 and brought in recognised strikers Rob Hulse, Richard Cresswell and Robbie Blake, as well as gifted USA winger Eddie Lewis. A top-six finish was achieved and after they saw off Preston North End in a fiery double-header in the play-off semi-finals, they were presented with the task of overcoming Watford in the final. But they had one of those days, lost comprehensively and were resigned to another season of trying to bring back the glory days.

A poor start to the following season saw Blackwell replaced by Dennis Wise, whom Bates had known from their days together at Chelsea, but he was always fighting an uphill battle. At the beginning of May 2007, with relegation looking certain, the club was declared insolvent and went into administration. As a result, Leeds were docked ten points by the Football League, sending the club into the third tier of English football for the first time in its history.

After a stormy few weeks during which United's survival at times looked uncertain, the administrators, KPMG, announced that the club had been sold to a consortium led by Ken Bates. Leeds were back under Bates' wing, and he was putting a positive spin on matters, commenting, 'Now we've got a clean start and a clean sheet of paper.' However, the club's troubles were far from over. At the beginning of August, Leeds were hit with a 15-point deduction because the club had been unable to meet the terms of the League's policy on insolvency.

Despite this penalty, and a mid-season change of manager when Wise controversially left to join Kevin Keegan at Newcastle United, being replaced by former Elland Road crowd favourite Gary McAllister, Leeds went on to secure a play-off place with one game to spare, only to lose 1–0 to Doncaster Rovers in the final at the new Wembley Stadium. McAllister's reign was short-lived, however, and he was sacked in December 2008 after a bad run that included the first loss to a non-league side in Leeds' history when they were beaten by Histon in the early stages of the FA Cup.

His replacement was Simon Grayson, a former player on Leeds' books who was then managing Blackpool. Again, a play-off spot was in the bag, but in May 2009 Millwall curtailed their ambitions in the semi-finals. For Leeds, it is proving a long way back.

The three clubs most famously managed by Clough do have something in common, although each for different reasons: all three marauded through the playing fields of Europe during the '70s and all, within a comparatively short time after Clough's departure, flirted with the ignominy of plying their trade in the third tier, with a return to European competition a dim and distant prospect. If Clough were to return from that great football stadium in the sky for a brief look at how his old clubs were faring five years after his death, his observations on Championship strugglers Nottingham Forest and Derby County might be, 'Get your bloody fingers out.' And on Coca-Cola League One club Leeds United, 'I told you so.'

17

PURE GENIUS

Who thought Derby County could be turned into League
champions; that any manager could bounce back from getting the
bullet after 44 days with a great club and go on to prove himself
among the best managers of all time; that what was done at Derby
could be repeated at Forest; that after winning one European Cup,
we could retain it; that a brash, self-opinionated young footballer,
cut down by injury in his prime, would go on to achieve more
impressive fame as a brash, highly successful manager?

Brian Clough, *Cloughie: Walking on Water*

Brian Clough is arguably the greatest manager the English game
has known. Wherever and whenever the debate is sparked
about who was better than whom, and why, it is impossible to
keep Clough's name out of the argument.

Peter Hampton says: 'From Clough's own point of view, of
course, his short stay at Leeds was fortuitous for his career
path, and easy money came his way with his severance making
him financially secure for life. Further, after his departure from
the club, he went on to be a hugely successful manager with
Nottingham Forest, and what he achieved there can never be
taken away from him. It was fantastic.

'I did feel, under Clough at Leeds, that the bunch of youngsters
of which I was a part would have been given a chance by him.

You got the notion that the kids would be nurtured by him because this was a time when the squad was ageing and, in all honesty, was ready for being broken up. Already there were changing faces, and those he brought in, O'Hare, McGovern and McKenzie, could have been mixed with the youngsters to form a much-changed Leeds United. I played with this trio in the reserves and each of them expressed a love for Cloughie, with two of them having been with him at Derby County.

'I often wonder what might have become of my own career had Clough stayed *in situ* at Leeds. I got the feeling that he rated me as a player, purely because if he didn't rate you, you were gone. I stayed. He wasn't one of those managers who would summon you to his office for a private chat to let you know what he thought about you; it was more that his actions spoke louder than words, and some were there one minute and gone the next. You could tell who he liked and disliked. In training, he would simply tell anybody he didn't like, "And you, young man, you can just bugger off. You're not wanted round here," whereas he'd leave alone those he wanted on board. He never said a bad word to me or, as far as I know, about me, and he was playing me regularly in the reserves, to the extent that I thought I was doing OK and would soon get a first-team opportunity.

'About the worst I ever got from him was one day when he looked me in the eye and said, "Young man, you're standing around like a spare prick at a wedding." This was in the dressing-room after the first of the pre-season games in 1974–75, an away fixture at Huddersfield, when I had been given a squad number and figured in the travelling party. I didn't make the team, however, and when he gave some of the big-name players a bollocking at half-time, I was pleased just to have been left well alone. After the game, however, Clough turned to me, the spare prick, and said, "Go and get some beers for these players." You don't know why he's singled you out for such a menial task. Perhaps it was a test of character; maybe he wanted to see how I would react. As a young lad, you've got two choices. You either break down and cry or you bat it back. All I know is that I did as I was told. Remember, this was the man who told one international footballer, "If you'd been a horse they'd have put you down long ago," and another world-famous player, "All you do is cheat and try to get the opposition into trouble," and a full title-winning squad, "You can all throw your medals in the bin because they were not won fairly."

'The day he was fired, I remember thinking, "Oh, crikey, here we go again. Now there'll be another manager to try to impress. Maybe the new guy will want me out." All sorts of things run through your mind.

'I followed Cloughie's career closely once he had left Leeds for Nottingham Forest. I think the whole country did. I played against his Forest side for Leeds in the semi-final of the League Cup in 1977–78. We'd lost the first leg 3–1 and in the second leg at Forest we went a goal up before again going down 4–2. Losing 7–3 on aggregate was a humbling experience! So I had first-hand experience of the team he built, and you've got to take off your hat to him for putting together such a dynamic squad. He had some terrific players and none better than his left-winger John Robertson. He was supremely talented, and they would get the ball to him as much as they could. I recall marking their right-winger Martin O'Neill and at times in the game he would be stood motionless. "Am I bloody invisible?" he joked a couple of times, his frustration at not getting the ball becoming more and more evident. He had been told to just stick out there on the right, hugging the touchline to try to stretch the defence, but I certainly cannot imagine Martin these days issuing instructions to his players to channel everything through just one individual.'

Hampton is best remembered by Leeds fans for making a substitute appearance during the 1975–76 season in a match against Burnley at Elland Road and hitting a spectacular winning goal. He remembers: 'Terry Yorath was booed by a section of the crowd in the first half, and they continued to give him a bad time until Jimmy Armfield took him off and put me on. Taffy waved two fingers at his tormentors on his way down the tunnel, and it was shortly after that that he was transferred to Tottenham. It just shows how one man's misfortune is another's opportunity. Where Terry had got himself into the supporters' bad books, that goal made me something of a folk hero for a time! Such is the uncertainty of this wonderful world we call football.'

Peter Lorimer concludes: 'Three decades on, we, as ex-players, all get on as old buddies. We meet regularly and love each other's company, and we still back the club to the hilt. Every home game, five or six lads go down and do the match-day hospitality, and we all want the club to succeed. We feel we gave the club its reputation. It lost it and we feel we want it back. And that's for everybody – the city and the fans.

'I doubt that Clough could ever have built that at Leeds. Again, when you talk to people who have played for him, you learn that there were little cliques here and there and a body of people in which this person didn't get on with that one and this little bunch didn't gel with that little crowd. We never had that at Leeds. We all got on with each other. Sure, there would be the odd little fallout in training and even during a match where there would be a verbal altercation. But this was never because you didn't like the person you were having a go at; it was heat-of-the-moment stuff that stayed in the moment and was forgotten about afterwards. In the showers later, you'd hear people saying, "Did you hear those two at it with handbags?" They'd make a joke of it. And this was all nurtured by Don Revie.

'The great thing about Don was his fostering of the family spirit within the club. He was like our second father, and his wife Elsie was like our second mother. The way they looked after us was fantastic. OK, he would use that philosophy to his advantage, with a little bit of conning of us here and there, but in the final analysis that's what management is about. Every player is different. Some need an arm round them, some need a bollocking, some need dropping from the team, some need sending away for a week's holiday because they are tired of the game and life itself is getting too much for them. The key with every good manager is to know which individual needs what treatment, and Don was a master at that.

'Where he had been the good shepherd tending his flock, keeping us all close together, his successor was the snarling fox who ripped at our throats. Let me say that it was certainly unknown to me that we had won anything by cheating. Indeed we were the club that suffered most from the very thing of which we stood accused by Clough. We had two European trophies snatched from our grasp at the whim of referees who performed as if they had taken to the field of play in cup finals in a frame of mind that was against us: one against AC Milan in Salonika where even the local Greek people booed the ref and he was later banned for life by UEFA after being convicted of match-fixing, and the other against Bayern Munich in Paris when so many soft decisions went their way and none ours that there were always suspicions, although nothing was proven. So the fact of the matter was that no team had been on the receiving end of cheating more than Leeds, and yet in Clough's book we were the great perpetrators of misdeeds.

'Clough was a total enigma. Eddie Gray remains one of my best friends, and he tells me of the life his brother Frank had under Clough at Nottingham Forest at a time when they won the European Cup. Eddie will ask Frank what Clough was like and the answer will come, "I don't know. He's hard to describe." Eddie persists and Frank volunteers, "Well, he didn't do anything tactically. He just used to come into the dressing-room with a ball before a game and say, 'You see this ball? Well that must be down there on the green part of the stadium. If God had wanted us to play football in the sky he'd have put grass up there.'"

'They'd win a game on a Saturday and he'd tell them to have until Wednesday off duty. Now Frank, who had been at Leeds and who had been used to working hard, would be gearing himself up for a day of torture on the players' return, and Clough would say, "Right, come on, get your tracksuits on, we're going to take the dog a walk on the banks of the River Trent." So they'd walk by the Trent with the boss's dog for an hour and walk back to the stadium for an hour and then he'd tell them to get off home. Clough did nothing really. He was a most unusual football manager. The afternoon before they played in the European Cup final in Switzerland he led his squad into a bar, produced two crates of beer and ordered the players to get stuck into them. Some of them protested that they didn't want an alcoholic drink ahead of such a big match, but he insisted they weren't going to leave until the contents had been consumed. By any stretch of the imagination, that is most unusual.

'Yet you talk to O'Hare and McGovern and others like Kenny Burns who played for him, and they loved him. They had every reason to love him, too, because of what he did for and with them. I have no doubt in my mind that Cloughie was a great manager, because you just do not win league titles with Derby and Nottingham Forest, with two European Cups thrown in, without having a degree of genius. He just was not a great manager of Leeds. On the discipline front, we and the players at nearly every other club were used to strict rules such as the avoidance of alcohol for 48 hours before a match. Suddenly you've got a guy saying, "Well, if you want a beer, then have a beer." In retrospect, who is right? Who is to say who is right and who is wrong?

'Another odd aspect of his management style was that where Don Revie would produce a dossier on every single player that we'd be facing in the next match, going into his abilities at thrown-ins, free kicks and corners, pace, movement, tackling and shooting and so on, Clough would just say, "Go out and do your stuff." Scientific it was not.

'In the end, I think it must have been a relief to Clough when he and Leeds parted company. It had been a case of him picking a team, us going out there and getting beaten . . . him picking a team, us going out there and getting beaten. And there he was. The biggest certainty was that he was going and, from our perspective, the sooner the better. Europe was on the horizon, and we did not want to have to go into this campaign with disharmony ravaging the club in the way that it was. You can't keep secrets at a football club, and it soon became known that he had gone up to Gordon McQueen and confided, "Right, we'll soon be rid of all these old guys and we'll build the club around you." That became a joke among the lads. "Ooooh, Gordon," we'd say, "I'm going to make you a star!"

'Clough tried working on the younger lads, but the fact was Giles went on playing for years, Hunter did, Bremner did. It wasn't the right time to be sending the club to the breaker's yard. It was getting near the time, but that was not it. How could it be, when we'd just won the title? Not only were we champions, he started with £2 million in the bank, which was a veritable fortune in those days. The club did not need any major restructure. There was plenty of young talent coming through that could have been blended with the experienced players on the books. For instance, you had McQueen coming in for Charlton, Terry Yorath coming in for Giles or Bremner, Frankie Gray for either of the full-backs. It was all there. A complete package.

'One of the abiding memories I have of Cloughie is the difficulty I and others had in trying to decipher whether he was being serious in some of the things he said or whether, in fact, it was just his humour. A common-sense interpretation would be that many of his rantings were too severe, and delivered without the faintest hint of a smile on his face, to be anything other than sincere. There was neither a joke at the end of it to soften the impact nor a conciliatory "But never mind . . ."

'Training under him often became irksome, too. You'd sit and wait for his arrival and wait and wait and wait. One day, he had his young son Nigel with him and there they were together, like a father plays with his boy, him in goal and Nigel shooting at him. We'd done all the warm-up and were ready for the training session, but he just ignored us as if we were not there for fully ten minutes. I don't know what point he was trying to make, but I do know that we had gone from such a well-drilled, professional outfit to something of a holiday camp.

'Maybe, though, his style of management was a good one.

One accusation that can never be levelled at Clough is that he was not successful. He was, and to some tune. Clough was perhaps even a brilliant manager, albeit only with players he had hand-picked and groomed, those who did what he said and danced to his tune.

'There were no goodbyes at Leeds. On our day off, we saw the pictures in the papers of him leaving in his Mercedes and stories of a pay-off, which he later admitted had set him up for life. This pay-off appeared to be a gesture by the board to get him out of the way as quickly as possible and with a minimum of fuss. It was a brushing under the carpet of a very messy situation created entirely by them.

'Jimmy Armfield was to come in a month later at a time when the lads' minds were focused on the fact that this would probably be the very last chance for the team that Revie had assembled to win the European Cup. We were in the last-chance saloon, and the most disturbing aspect of the dreadful start to the season was that those dreams of a last hurrah could soon be in tatters. Jimmy's immediate task was to pick up the pieces after Clough's short regime. He maintains to this day that he probably had the most difficult job of any manager at Leeds because he was the one who had to tell legends such as Billy Bremner, Norman Hunter and Johnny Giles that they had finished. He calls it his "dirty work".

'I will never know, I suspect, why Revie left in the first place. Did he leave because he found repellent the prospect of calling time on the careers of brilliant players he had nurtured over such a long period? Or did he leave because it was cosy and nice to quit as a manager who had just won the league title and walk straight into the England job? My leaning is towards the former argument. I think he realised that the time was dawning for the mould to be broken and that he simply could not face up to being the one to have to perform that unenviable task. I don't think the lure of the England job was such that he couldn't resist it; it was more that he saw it as a convenient way to avoid the inevitable crunch at Elland Road.

'I believe that Don was not built to be an international manager. He loved the day-to-day running of a club, and that was never going to be an aspect of managing the national team, where he would see his players once every three months for a couple of days. Indeed, when I have spoken to the players who played under him for England, they've confirmed that they could never get into his ways. His approach, they maintain, was too scientific, too intense for their liking.

'Once Clough was ensconsed at Nottingham Forest, he, of course, became a huge national figure through television. This, unfortunately, was not so much because of his achievements in the game as because he became notorious for coming out with outlandish statements and for his ritual humiliation of the people interviewing him. He almost became a parody of himself, saying controversial things that would leave people observing, "Well, that's Brian Clough for you." You could barely believe what you were hearing sometimes, but he got to the stage, I think, where every time he was doing a television interview or a newspaper article, he felt he had to go on the attack. And it didn't matter who was the victim of his verbal assaults. In this modern climate where people in football are fined for the merest hint of controversy in their behaviour or observations, he would have run out of money pretty damned fast. There was no praise. It was always swingeing criticisms of individuals, the game, the officials, the FA or UEFA or FIFA . . . anybody he had a mind to have a go at.

'There was always the suspicion that drink had taken him over, and in this regard I think the loss of Peter Taylor hit him hard. Peter appeared to be the one man who could sit him down and talk to him and rein in his excesses, but once they had parted company Cloughie seemed to go completely. The word in the game was that drink, unfortunately, was getting the better of him, and, really, he talked himself out of the England job by his constant criticism of the FA. He definitely would have been an England manager had it not been for the fact that the FA chiefs knew they would be unable to handle him.

'He was a character, and there is no denying that he did a fantastic job for both Derby and Forest, especially Forest. Nottingham is a relatively small city, and their achievements under him were out of proportion to a club of Forest's size. Clough's name will be forever written into the history of English football. But again, I feel it's worth pointing out that here in the twenty-first century people still talk about the great Leeds team and the great Liverpool team of the 1960s and '70s, but you'll never hear great things said about the Nottingham Forest side. Basically, it was a two-year thing that happened and then it was gone. He achieved great things and then, just as quickly, it disappeared. He turned it into something special and then he turned it into a circus. When the annals of football history are examined, people will say, "Bloody hell, where did Nottingham Forest suddenly come from for those two years?" Anybody who has won a European Cup has got to be rated as a top-ten achiever, but the thing with Clough was that he never built anything that lasted, not like Leeds, Liverpool or Manchester United. He was a quick-fix merchant who built his foundations on sand rather than rock, and the only explanation I can find for that is that if you were one of his players then there would be only a short timespan before you'd become thoroughly disillusioned by his mud-slinging and gratuitous criticism.

'Duncan McKenzie tells a funny story concerning a time he was playing in a practice match. At every twist and turn, Clough was on his case, criticising his passing, ball control, shooting, the lot. Impulsively, Duncan, who's a very funny guy anyway, stopped the game by picking up the ball and replied to the latest insult, "What do you want for 40 quid a week? Fucking Pelé?" Come to think of it, I wonder what insult Clough might have hurled at Pelé had he been a Leeds player.'

Eddie Gray observes: 'If you were able to go back in time and rerun the whole Clough saga, then maybe, given the man's phenomenal overall record, they should have given him more time. His career record was unbelievable. I have the greatest respect for him as a manager and for what he achieved in the game, but when he came to Leeds everything he did was wrong. If he had his time again, he would, I am sure, go about things more slowly. And perhaps with a little more passion.

'He certainly was not the character at Leeds that he became. Later, I loved listening to him and watching his antics. I mean, when he ran onto the pitch and slapped that young kid round the head. Well! I think he would like to have done that at Leeds with the players, but he would have been told where to go. And he didn't like that. He was used to bullying people. Once, when he was at Leeds, he phoned for one of the apprentices to take a cup of tea up to his office. When none was forthcoming after 15 minutes, he phoned back and berated the kid on the other end of the phone, demanding: "Who is this?"

'The kid, without giving his name, said, "Who is this?"

'"It's Brian Clough," he said. "Who's this?"

'Silence. Cloughie went mad, demanding to know who had failed the cup-and-saucer test. But he never did find out.

'Clough's record in the game easily puts him in the top five managers of all time. I can categorically state that on his performance at Leeds he would be in the bottom five managers of all time. What his genius was, I will never know, because I never saw it. And I don't think anybody really knows what made him such a giant of the game. Was it the fear factor? I doubt it. Strict discipline? He used to take the players for a pint before a game. There would be John Robertson sitting in the dressing-room smoking a fag before a game.

'Being perfectly honest, when I look at that Forest side, a smashing side, I would say that if they hadn't had a left-winger, they wouldn't have won anything. If you ask any of those Forest players who was the main man in the side – and Trevor Francis cost a record-breaking £1 million – they would say to a man that it was John Robertson. He was the man who created everything for them, while the rest worked hard. Before every game, Clough's instruction to all his players was "Just you get the ball and give it to the fat man." They would do as he said, and eight or ten times in a game Robbo would get the ball into the box across the face of goal in a very dangerous position for the opposition. Great player.

'At Leeds, I cannot think of one single attribute that I saw that would have made him a top manager. But he was. No doubt about it. The funny thing was I never fell out with Cloughie. I saw him when he was on the top table at a dinner in his honour – it was An Evening with Brian Clough or something like that – at Elland Road not long before he died. He was ill at the time and certainly did not look well. I asked him how he was doing and he was great, quite chatty, actually. Most of the other ex-players stayed away, having asked if I was attending, and when I said I was they said, "What would you want to go to that for?"

'"Because," I told them, "it's Cloughie – a great manager."

'And that's what he was. Whichever way you look at it, he was a bit like George Best: a genius but wayward. I knew George, and his family asked me to speak at his memorial service in Manchester. I spoke along with Sir Alex Ferguson and George's best mate down the years, the former Manchester United player David Sadler, and there was no doubting the deep affection in which George was held. You can say the same about another individual with alcohol-induced demons, Paul Gascoigne. Paul was meant to be up on the stage at a golf event I attended in North Yorkshire, and because of the state he was in, he had to be ushered off. All three, Brian, George and Paul, have appeared in public in inebriated states, but perhaps it is better to remember them for their wonderful contributions to our great game than for their flaws.

'In those 44 days, I don't think any Leeds United player really got to know Cloughie. But I would have loved to have got to know him, mostly to try to understand what made him tick and what made him behave in the way he did. I think the player closest to him was Allan Clarke. He was the one squad member who really appeared to get along with him and maybe the reason for that is that they were both similar characters. I think Clarkey tried to model himself on Cloughie when he became a manager at Barnsley, Leeds, Scunthorpe, Barnsley again and Lincoln. It was an "I'm the boss and don't you forget it" style.

'When Jimmy Armfield came in, he immediately showed some respect to the players. Where with Clough we couldn't win an argument, let alone a match, on the field, with Jimmy in charge, the same bunch of players got to the European Cup final. Enough said.

'I'm sure that if I sat next to Brian now and told him that at Leeds he got it wrong, the response I would get would be an unreserved agreement. With Brian, it all came down to one thing – his dislike of Don. When he first came, the first thing he did was to sling out the office furniture that had been Don's – the desk, the chair, the settee, the lot. Don had just taken delivery of a new Mercedes as his club car, and Cloughie wouldn't have it because it had been Don's. I think this dislike was mutual, by the way.'

Having witnessed one of his managers go on to take charge of England, Gray is adamant that, in Clough, there should have been a second. 'His record insists that he should have been England manager,' Gray says, 'but the FA were frightened of him. No disrespect to Nottingham Forest as a football club, but for Clough to have won two European Cups for them makes him a breed apart. Yes, he should have managed England. Of that I have no doubt.'

Gordon McQueen concludes: 'Cloughie rests peacefully in the knowledge that what he achieved with Derby and particularly Nottingham Forest will never be repeated – small-city, provincial clubs winning league titles and conquering Europe. But at Leeds, he was a man in too much of a hurry. The directors knew within a week of appointing Clough that they had made a mistake and very quickly regretted their actions.'

Joe Jordan concurs. 'The appointment of Brian Clough at Leeds was something I would never have expected to happen,' he says. 'It was something that never crossed my mind. Having said that, Clough did win the 1971–72 league title with Derby when Leeds were in the driving seat to do so. I think trying to beat Leeds became something of an obsession with him. That seemed to me to be at the root of his so-called hatred of the Yorkshire foe. When you put this into context, public criticism aimed at destabilising one of the superpowers when you are in direct competition with them kind of goes with the territory. Brian was a proud man and a winner, and by and large Leeds got the better of Derby over the years that they were slugging it out. That always took a bit of doing because Derby were a fantastic team under Clough.

'So as a title-winning manager, he probably had the credentials to take on the Leeds job, although we will probably never know the full extent of who else was considered for it and therefore whether the correct decision was made. It appears to me, however, to have been a case of the wrong man at the wrong club at the wrong time, though within a short time of leaving Leeds he proved to be a very good manager indeed.

'With Clough and Leeds, the chemistry was not right. In trying to understand that, it's hard to bring to mind a comparison in recent football history: a title-winning manager who joins a rival championship-winning club two years later, with a history of conflict between the clubs into the bargain. Building two clubs from the floor upwards is no mean feat, and that is what he did with Derby and Nottingham Forest. Maybe at Leeds, and this is just a thought, he found that the building work had long ago been completed.'

Terry Yorath says: 'In retrospect, I wish Clough had stayed, because if he'd been there for three years or so, I am sure Leeds would not have gone on the downward spiral that they did. Yes, a few people would have had to go, but he would have moulded the team he wanted into his ways and got the club onto the kind of solid footing that they have wished for many times since. Clough would have got over his early mistakes, such as bringing John McGovern and John O'Hare into a team in which, lovely lads that they were, they had no right to be. There were far better players already in the team.

'To have bought Duncan McKenzie was another mistake. That Leeds team had a certain way of playing that was very effective and had brought great results over a lengthy period of time. At its fulcrum were really top players like Bremner and Giles, who liked to get on top of the opposition quickly, grind out things and wear them down. The fans loved Duncan's flair but he was constantly pilloried by the other players for doing something flamboyant when the practical pass would have been far better for the team effort. You'd go a goal up in the traditional Leeds way and be working like stink to preserve the lead when Duncan would get the ball and set off on one of his mazy runs in which he would beat three players in spectacular fashion before losing the ball or giving it away.

'The signing of a player like Duncan, and I say this of someone I really liked and got along with, upset the Leeds apple-cart. Discipline, teamwork, endeavour and pragmatism were the bywords before he came into the club, and there was certainly no room in the team for a solo act. Duncan did have his good points. He had this instinctive ability to make people laugh, and he would lighten the gloom when one of the many dark clouds that descended during Clough's short reign appeared overhead. Someone like Duncan who can take the heat out of a tense situation with just one off-the-cuff comment is needed at every club, and I got along very well with him.

'But what was happening at Leeds was very dangerous. Under Revie, the disciplined way of going about things had become second nature, so that it never needed to be brought up in discussion. It was routine. There wasn't much hint of discipline under Clough, and when he was replaced by Jimmy Armfield what discipline was left went out of the club. Jim is a real gentleman who has had a wonderful lifetime in football and, just like everybody else in the game, I wouldn't say and nor would I listen to a bad word about him. I think the world of him. Many is the time I have been spellbound by his storytelling as he puffed away on his pipe, and when the definitive annals of English football history are written he will have his place in them, and rightly so. When he came over from Bolton to Leeds, he took over a club at which a day had not gone by under Clough without something happening. There was tension at board level, tension at management level, tension among the players, and all in all it was not a very nice place to be.

'I remember pretty early in Clough's reign we were playing Queens Park Rangers at home and I went in search of two spare tickets for the game. He even had to interfere in that. "I'm in charge of ticket distribution around here," he snapped when he learned of my quest. There was confrontation all the time. Soon there was a feeling among some of the players along the lines of "I'm not wanted here, so I'll go". Then word began to trickle down the line – this happens in football clubs – that those of a mind to leave should bide their time because this new liaison between Clough and Leeds might not last as long as was generally imagined. Then what had become inevitable duly happened, and he was gone in a puff of smoke.

'I don't think Jimmy Armfield could believe he was managing Leeds United, the reigning champions of English football. But the club's fortunes quickly turned around that season, certainly on the field, to the extent that we reached the European Cup final. Jimmy certainly had a calming effect on the place and the players were much more relaxed, but you'd be hard pushed to determine whether it was the players who got us to that final or Jimmy's management skills. Jimmy was not a Clough, nor a Revie. He had his own way of doing things. I had two seasons with him at Leeds before he decided I was dispensable and sold me to Coventry.'

Duncan McKenzie adds: 'I was only at Leeds under Cloughie for a few days before he got the sack, but when he got the boot he came up to me and said, "Young man, keep up those flicks, nutmegs and back heels. Never change." To hear someone like that say what he did made me feel great. Here was this guy who was a born winner and one of the best managers this country has ever produced saying such things. I remember Cloughie used to say to me, "What are you doing in our half? You're no good there. You're a liability! Get up there where you can score goals." Even when I left Leeds, Cloughie was still a part of me. He never left me alone! He came back to Leeds to try to get me, tried again when I had moved to Anderlecht and again when I was at Everton. It was pretty flattering that he showed faith in me.

'I saw him several times at Nottingham Forest a little later in life, and he would always greet me with some kind of caustic comment. I would give it back and we'd end up in howls of laughter. That's the relationship I had with him. In football terms, the man was a colossus. Our national team down the years has been the poorer for never having him as manager, but he knew and I think everybody knew that it would never have worked. You cannot take on the establishment and, as sure as night follows day, Clough would have done that. I suspect his stay at FA headquarters, had it happened, would have been appreciably shorter than his 44 days at Leeds.

'The fact is that he took football clubs from two smaller-sized cities barely geared up for things on such a grand scale – this wasn't London or Manchester or Liverpool – to the most enormous heights. He won consecutive European Cups with Nottingham Forest, and the vast majority of people would be hard-pressed to name you three players from those teams of his. That is pure genius.'

It is. And for most of his career, Clough was. Yet at least one club will never grasp the whys and wherefores of Old Big 'Ead. 'Brian Clough proved himself as one of the best managers this country has ever seen,' says Peter Hampton. 'It was a travesty that he never managed England, unlike his arch-rival Revie, and it is something of a farce that he and Leeds United should have wasted each other's time so badly.'

Leading the tributes to Brian Clough on the news of his death, aged 69, from stomach cancer in September 2004, his former Forest player, the then Celtic manager (now Aston Villa manager) Martin O'Neill said:

He was absolutely sensational and I don't think Brian would disagree with us either. He would be the first to say that he was the greatest of all time. But he was like England's version of Muhammad Ali. He had fantastic charisma, unbelievable charisma. Outwardly, he had this fantastic self-belief and self-confidence, but in truth I think sometimes he was as vulnerable as all of us.

One of the great myths of all time was that he was a manager and not a coach and seldom on the training ground. The fact is that every day was a coaching lesson from Brian Clough, and when he did come down to the training ground for a 20- to 25-minute spell, you'd pick up enough in that time to do you a lifetime. He coached during the course of games. His memory was phenomenal.

John [Robertson, O'Neill's assistant] and I were lucky that probably in that spell from 1975 to 1980 he was at his very best. He was bright. He was everything.

POSTSCRIPT

IN SEARCH OF BRIAN CLOUGH

I want no epitaphs of profound history and all that type of thing. I contributed, I hope they would say that, and I hope somebody liked me.

Brian Clough

It was in the winter of 1987 that the then editor of the *Daily Star*, Brian Hitchen, ended weeks of speculation when he emerged from his Fleet Street office onto the editorial floor and headed in my direction. 'Who's the new sports editor of the *Daily Star*, then?' he teased.

'I don't know, Brian. I've heard nothing,' I said.

'You don't know? What do you mean you don't know? You saw him in the mirror this morning when you were shaving!'

In the privacy of his office, he confirmed my appointment, saying, 'You've got the job. You're a national newspaper sports editor and I want you to make me a promise. Just promise that you'll enjoy every moment of it.'

There are those who might say that, over the next ten years, I took Brian far too literally, but I was determined to deliver the best for Brian and for the newspaper in terms of words and pictures and great sports columnists. Together, we introduced to the British newspaper industry the concept of the sports pull-out, including an eight-page horse-racing special called *Starform* in our Saturday editions and an eight-page football supplement in our Monday editions. I wanted new, celebrity columnists, and before long we had the brilliant northern trainer Jack Berry writing on horse racing, David 'Bumble' Lloyd on cricket, Mike 'Stevo' Stephenson on rugby league, Gareth Chilcott on rugby union and Barry McGuigan on boxing. All were household names with big personalities, and the only thing we were lacking as time went by was a really big name from the world of football.

There was no bigger name than Brian Clough, and his bold, brash, sometimes outlandish views, statements and observations were in perfect harmony with the tone of the newspaper. But before I could procure Clough's services, there were several obstacles to overcome. First, he was then a fixture in the sports pages of *The Sun* and no doubt the holder of a highly remunerative News International contract. There was the question of whether he would be prepared to write for a smaller audience and, further, whether he would be prepared to desert an organisation with which he was familiar for one that would involve a journey into the unknown. There was only one way to find out.

I tried to get in touch by phone through his secretary at Nottingham Forest, outlining my plans to her. When she returned my call, her helpful suggestion was that I fax through the contract that I had had drawn up by our legal department. She said she would come back to me once her boss had seen it. Over a frustrating period of ten days or so, my countless telephone calls failed to elicit anything approaching even a response, never mind a decision. But I was not going to be put off easily, and I decided the best course of action would be to present myself unannounced at Cloughie's place of work and simply see what happened.

On a bright Tuesday morning, I parked up at the famous City Ground on the banks of the Trent and headed for the main reception. As I pulled the door open, an approaching large, rotund figure asked the purpose of my visit. I told him I had come to see Brian Clough and the man, whom I knew to be the chairman, Maurice Roworth, asked, 'Do you have an appointment?' When I admitted that I didn't, he said: 'Look, I run this place, and if I want to see Mr Clough, *I* have to make an appointment.' This looked like it was going to be a fool's errand, but then, with impeccable timing, the man himself, in familiar green top, his manner bright and breezy, closed in on us. 'Morning!' he boomed and I wasted no time in introducing myself and explaining the purpose of my visit. 'Ah yes,' said Cloughie. 'The man with the golden handcuffs!'

A bemused and rather tetchy Roworth tried to engage his manager in conversation about a scheduled meeting, but Clough, sensing, I think, a bit of mischievous fun, completely ignored him and turned to me, saying, 'We're just getting ready for a bit of lunch. Do please join us. They do a lovely soup in the restaurant, and then there's beef baguettes and so on. Find a place in there and we'll be with you in a minute.' Well, hell. That was an unpredictably great start.

Soon, Clough and his assistant Ron Fenton were drawing up chairs beside me and we were immediately engaged in football banter. It was light-hearted, fun and ever so convivial, and though I hardly dared think it, the prospects of landing my big fish looked distinctly brighter at this stage than they had when I had set out up the M1 from London that morning. When we had finished lunch, I was invited to the inner sanctum, Clough's office, where we were greeted by the manager's dog, Dell. Clough instructed Fenton to summon one of the apprentice players to the office to collect Dell and take him for a walk, and soon the sound of approaching footsteps could be heard. But these footsteps were more of a shuffle. A knock at the door. A spotty young face in a tracksuit. 'You're limping!' boomed Clough. 'Limping? What the hell's wrong with you? Nothing. Young man, don't you ever, ever limp near me. Now take this dog for a walk. And I mean a long walk. I don't want to see you back here any time soon.' The young footballer blushed crimson and shook as he attempted to attach the dog's lead to its collar. He walked perfectly on the way out.

Sensing that there might be some business between Clough and I on the agenda, Fenton made his exit and, seizing the opportunity, I fished a copy of the contract out of my inside jacket pocket and asked if he had had a chance to read through it. He had been the perfect host all day, and now offered yet more hospitality, producing two crystal glasses into which he poured a good measure of whisky.

'I have thought about this,' he said, 'and I have a question for you. What is the length of your own contract at the *Daily Star*?'

'Twelve months,' I said, slightly bemused.

'Here's what I want you to do,' he replied. 'Go back to your employers and tell them that you are greatly undervalued by being given only a one-year contract and that your minimum requirement is a two-year contract. When you have a two-year contract, come back to me and I will be your columnist.'

This was pure genius on Clough's part. My interpretation was that he knew damn well that even a one-year contract was highly prized among journalists, much more familiar with one-month and three-month agreements, and that I wouldn't dare even to ask the Express Newspapers management for a longer period than twelve months, especially as I had only taken up my new role a few weeks previously. This strategy allowed Clough to turn me down without an out-and-out rejection. With the ball firmly in my court, he could turn round and say that I had not fulfilled my side of the bargain. He was, I realised, a politician of the highest order.

It's an old adage that sport and politics do not mix, but while Clough immersed himself in one of those subjects, he certainly had room in his life for the other. Indeed, he was twice approached by the Labour Party to stand for election. A brilliant perspective on this was provided by Barney Ronay in *The Guardian* in April 2007:

ANYONE WANT TO PLAY ON THE LEFT?

When football was the workers' game, it was the home of charismatic leftwingers like Bill Shankly and Brian Clough. Now, with the Premiership awash with TV money, the socialists seem to have disappeared. Do politics and the beautiful game just not mix any more?

Later this month Italian footballer Cristiano Lucarelli will be the celebrity guest of honour at a UCL seminar called Money, Politics and Violence. At first glance this seems an unlikely choice of speaker. It is tempting to speculate on Lucarelli's themes ('At the end of the day you're talking about a decay of the post-capitalist economy situation'), his insistence on taking the positives, giving 120 per cent and always remembering that left-leaning political theory is a funny old game.

Tempting, but in this case probably misguided. Lucarelli is an unusual footballer, a self-avowed communist and an oddity both in his own country and in the context of our ideologically neutral Premiership. At the top level at least, footballing socialists are an almost extinct breed. This is hardly surprising. The Premiership player lives a rarefied life. Alienated by celebrity and his own vertiginous wealth, bombarded with the tedious superlatives of a deeply introverted industry, it seems barely conceivable he might still be capable of making the distinctions required to call himself a socialist, a monetarist, a disciple of Chairman Mao, or anything else for that matter. Premiership football has very little political content; it's all on one note. As the former Scotland international Gordon McQueen says: 'Football is all about money and greed and everyone's involved in it.'

McQueen played for Leeds and Manchester United in the 1970s and '80s. He was also well known as a Labour Party supporter who wrote an article explaining his politics in the *Daily Mirror*. 'I came from a family and from an area that was and still is solid Labour,' he says now of his native Ayrshire. 'In fact, there were more communists than Tories. I just did what I was asked to do. I went to local meetings. I helped with fundraising.' McQueen was hardly a raving Trotskyite; just an everyday Labour man who also happened to be a professional footballer. This is something he believes is pretty much incompatible with the modern game.

'There are plenty of smashing lads involved now, but whether they could be bothered with something like that is a different story. The difference is they don't live in the real world. They're cosseted in a way we never were. I'd say 99 per cent are totally uninterested in politics.'

The players might not be interested, but in its own way modern British football is a deeply political affair. Just take a look at the Premiership to find out what 15 years of hot-housed free-market economics looks like. From the first BSkyB broadcast deal in 1992 the revenue from subscription television has utterly transformed the game. The new Sky and Setanta TV contract is worth £1.7 billion over three seasons, a significant amount of which will end up in the pockets of the men kicking the ball around. The escalation to a current average Premiership wage of £12,300 a week has been like an unplanned social experiment. The players have come to represent an acme of consumption, a brutally linear expression of a certain way of living. In our footballers we see a funfair mirror reflection of the same forces working on the people watching them from the stands. We don't admire them so much as aspire to their lifestyle, crave their large American cars and holiday homes in Dubai, bandy their salaries around with a Gollum-like mixture of avarice and disgust. The top tier of British football stands as an extreme expression of a certain kind of politics, rampant capitalism with the volume turned up to 11. A Premiership socialist? It might not even be possible.

This is all relatively new. We're not talking about golf here. Historically, football's politics, such as they are, have tended to loiter on the left wing. The majority of Premiership clubs have their roots in either a local church or a local pub. For 100 years these clubs existed as an extension of their local community, a living riposte – albeit an occasionally violent and shambolically administered one – to the Thatcherite notion that there is no such thing as society.

Bill Shankly is probably still British football's most celebrated socialist. Wisecracking, dapper and a charismatic orator, Shankly was a hugely successful manager of Liverpool through the '60s and early '70s. What seems most remarkable about him now is his insistence on talking politics, even while talking football: 'The socialism I believe in is everyone working for each other, everyone having a share of the rewards. It's the way I see football, the way I see life.'

Shankly traced his political beliefs to his upbringing in the Ayrshire mining village of Glenbuck. A childhood spent in areas dominated by heavy industry and trade union influence has been a common theme among football's senior socialists. Sir Alex Ferguson was a Govan shipyard shop steward before he became a player with Rangers. His backing for the Blair Labour leadership is well documented. At the last general election he posted a message on the government's website praising 'two brilliant barnstorming speeches from Tony and Gordon'. Ferguson, with his fine wines and his multimillion pound racehorse ownership disputes, has frequently been subjected to the familiar jibe of 'champagne socialism'. Football is fond of this kind of reasoning, based on the idea that those with socialist beliefs are expected to live exemplary altruistic lives, whereas rightwingers can pretty much do whatever they want. Nottingham Forest legend Brian Clough, a sponsor of the Anti-Nazi

League and a regular on picket lines during the miners' strike, had his own riposte. 'For me, socialism comes from the heart. I don't see why certain sections of the community should have the franchise on champagne and big houses.'

Clough was pretty much the standard-bearer for football socialism in the 1980s, a decade that saw the emergence of a new strain of rightwing footballer. Certainly something about Margaret Thatcher touched a chord with the aspirational pre-Premiership player, with his golfing sweaters, his sponsored Rover and his first intimations of the spiralling financial rewards that would reach frantic levels in the decades to come. The famous photo of Kevin Keegan and Emlyn Hughes cosying up to Thatcher on the Downing Street steps remains a pungent image. It wasn't just Keegan. Thatcherism mobilised footballers in unprecedented numbers. Coventry players Keith Houchen and Steve Ogrizovic campaigned for their local Tory candidate at the 1987 election. Footballers even managed to muscle their way in among all the Tarbies and Brucies at the grisly party glad-handings: Arsenal manager Terry Neill and star striker 'Champagne' Charlie Nicholas were among those to appear on stage at a Thatcher rally. For reasons that are still unclear, Thatcher herself was installed as honorary vice-president of Blackburn Rovers.

In the 20 years since, the footballing socialist has all but disappeared. Certainly, we've not had a lot to go on: Thierry Henry wearing a Che Guevara T-shirt; Diego Maradona smoking Montecristos with Fidel while detoxing in Cuba; Eric Cantona and his elusively loopy left-of-centre persona. 'Perhaps you may find it odd that I think happiness does not come from being able to buy a car that one wants,' he challenged in his autobiography, before reminding us that 'the woods are full of bows and arrows'.

This is a confusing time for any top-level footballer with a twitching of social conscience. The problem is, he often ends up looking a bit silly. Take Rio Ferdinand, for example. Ferdinand is an intelligent man. He lent his name to a campaign against knife crime in London. Peckham-raised, he discreetly offered his support in the aftermath of the Damilola Taylor murder. But somehow it seems that just making a bit of a difference isn't enough. Not when you're this important. 'I want to join forces with the Government,' he wrote in his autobiography, before going on to describe his plans for a countrywide rehabilitation of the nation's youth via his inspirational chain of Ferdinand-branded leisure centres, a vision of a brighter tomorrow he once tried to share with Gordon Brown after discovering they were staying in the same hotel ('unfortunately he had gone out for something to eat').

The suspicion is that socialism – in the everyday sense practised by the likes of McQueen – is simply incompatible with the life of the Premiership footballer. Leftwing sympathies are still present in isolated gestures. Liverpool player Robbie Fowler celebrated scoring in a European Cup-Winners' Cup game in 1997 by pulling up his shirt to reveal a T-shirt expressing support for striking Liverpool dockers. As a gesture it was widely appreciated. But solidarity only goes so far: Fowler is also English football's fourth-richest man, estimated to own almost 100 houses as part of a £28-million buy-to-let portfolio (inspiring the 'Yellow Submarine'-style terrace chant 'We all live in a Robbie Fowler house'). Wigan manager Paul Jewell's dad was a trade union activist in Liverpool. He keeps a pet tortoise called Trotsky.

And then there's Gary Neville, the man most people would pick out as an example of a modern footballing socialist. Neville's 'Red Nev' nickname was given to him by the tabloid press after his stewardship of a revolt in the England dressing-room over Ferdinand's punishment for missing a drugs test. It's not exactly flogging *Marxism Today* outside Sainsbury's, but the nickname has stuck.

Neville is one of the Premiership's more thoughtful players. He has called on his colleagues not to use agents, although having always been represented by his father makes this an easy position to adopt. He signed up to the recent initiative for footballers to donate a day's wages to a nurses' hardship fund. He might even, you never know, see himself as a socialist. Still, you come up against the insurmountable stumbling block of his profession. In Neville we can see an intelligent man placed in an unintelligent situation. Earning £80,000 a week for playing football places him on one side of a very real divide, whatever his potential leftwing leanings. The old distinction of champagne socialism doesn't really do it justice, unless perhaps we're talking about taking an Olympic swimming pool-sized Jacuzzi in the stuff every morning. Which is possibly something Neville might be planning to do in the £3-million home with golf course, gym, pools, stables and a cinema he is having built in Lancashire. Clough is right. Socialism doesn't necessarily exclude you from living in a big house; but there are limits to everything.

Does any of this matter? Certainly, football's central relationship, that between fans and players, seems to have suffered some collateral damage. The working man's ballet is now very much the middle-class man's ballet, too. Nothing wrong with that, of course, but the speed with which the demographic of football's target market has shifted is unprecedented. Not least in the idea of actually having a target market in the first place. Andy Lyons is editor of *When Saturday Comes*, the UK's only independent national football magazine. *WSC* began as a fanzine in 1986, at a time when following football was a relatively marginalised activity. 'There used to be a sense of a shared experience of being a football supporter,' Lyons says. 'This has splintered now, due in part to the sheer weight of numbers of the Sky generation of new supporters.'

Various forces have been working on this relationship between supporters and players: the repackaging of the game as televised entertainment and the dilution of the idea of a geographical fanbase; the hyper-inflationary hikes in ticket prices and the emphasis on football as a corporate hospitality product. Going to watch a game at Arsenal's new Emirates ground feels more like attending a stadium rock concert or visiting the Ideal Home exhibition. Your relationship to everyone else inside the stadium has changed. You're united by consumer choice. The people performing in front of you are skilled entertainers.

This is not necessarily what football's traditional consumers (formerly 'fans') actually want. A feature of some recent Liverpool home games has been a habit among home fans of a concerted holding up of scarves en masse and singing of their traditional anthems in a self-consciously 'Liverpool Kop' manner. Always a club tradition at bigger games, at every home game it is a relatively new thing, fetishising the club's own past, perhaps out of a sense of nostalgia for a still-present but undeniably fragile sense of footballing community. This feeling of a collective identity is what sustained football through its lean years. Will it still be there when they come again?

British football is ahead of the rest of the world here. Lyons believes that in other countries players are not only more openly political, but possibly also have a greater bond with their supporters. 'You find in countries where the working classes tend to be more political, such as Argentina, where there is still a strong trade union movement, there tends to be more of a sense of communal identity,' he says. 'Society is perhaps based around older social patterns that no longer exist here, such as heavy industry. In among these, football is one of the forces that bind people together.'

There are plenty of examples of political South American footballers. The World Cup-winning Brazilian striker Romario is a high-profile supporter of the progressive President Lula and has also assisted with projects to relieve poverty in the favelas. Italian club Internazionale were persuaded by their Argentinian captain Xavier Zanetti to donate €5,000 (£3,400) to help Zapatista rebels in Mexico. 'We believe in a better, unglobalised world enriched by the cultural differences and customs of all the people,' Zanetti said, possibly surprising some of his teammates in the process.

Where all this leaves us is hard to say. Is it really impossible to be a socialist and a top-level footballer? Probably, in the hard line 'property is theft' sense of the word; the bar has simply been raised too high. But then, all of this is very new. There is no precedent for the Premiership, outside of the transcontinental sporting conferences of the US – never exactly a hot-bed of leftwing politics and, what with the market-led sports 'franchise' system, certainly not an environment where the social bond between supporters and club is valued.

It would be nice to see someone trying, however. In the future, perhaps a few of our footballers might be willing to challenge their environment, rather than simply accepting its rewards. Former England goalkeeper David James made the relatively radical suggestion last week that players might be paid only on a performance-related basis. This might not exactly be up there with Paul Breitner, a West German World Cup-winner in 1974, who combined a mastery of attacking full-back play with growing a bushy beard, espousing Marxism. But James' notion of footballers-as-estate-agents at least goes pleasingly against the tide. It's an acknowledgment that there might be another way. And, like Lucarelli, who cuts a slightly cartoonish figure with his Che Guevara T-shirts and clenched-fist salutes, it's also appealingly silly; a counter to the po-faced sense of entitlement that has too often been the Premiership player's defining trait. This is only football, after all. It doesn't have to mean anything. But it's usually much more fun when it tries.

With Clough's rejection of me and the *Daily Star* confirmed beyond doubt, I was back on the M1 and in a no-win situation. It's a poor strategist, however, who has no plan B, and I turned my attentions instead to the Liverpool goalkeeper Bruce Grobbelaar, who, like Clough, was larger than life and would certainly add some colour to our pages. This was much more straightforward. We met one evening in a city-centre restaurant in Liverpool and the contract was signed between courses there and then.

The ink on the contract was barely dry when, on 15 April 1989, Liverpool met Nottingham Forest at Sheffield Wednesday's Hillsborough stadium in an FA Cup semi-final. In the most tragic event in British football history, 96 Liverpool fans were crushed to death in unforgettably traumatic scenes, with the match having got as far as the sixth minute before police ordered it to be stopped. The disaster was to dominate both the front and back pages of the newspapers for months to come, and almost the first words Grobbelaar produced for the *Daily Star* formed his own heart-rending account of those terrible events as they unfolded in front of him from his place in the Liverpool goal. The Zimbabwean was so badly traumatised that he had great difficulty writing this first-hand account, but he summoned the courage, strength and compassion, in a deeply touching piece, to paint a picture of his adopted city in mourning.

In view of Clough committing what he later admitted was a serious error of judgement when, in his autobiography, he wrote of the Hillsborough disaster, 'I will always remain convinced that those Liverpool fans who died were killed by Liverpool people,' I have often wondered since whether fate intervened to save me from a whole heap of embarrassment. But that was Clough: enigmatic, unpredictable, controversial.

It would be remiss of me not to record here my own admiration for Brian Clough, as a man, a manager, a personality and a character. In a modern world rife with blandness, political correctness, denial of culpability and abdication of responsibility among those in positions of power, he is sorely missed. I adored him. English football was much the richer for his impossible-to-ignore presence, and it misses now the likes of himself, Ron Atkinson and Tommy Docherty, men who knew how to entertain off the field as well as on it and felt it incumbent upon themselves so to do.

I feel much the same about that incredible Leeds United team of the early 1970s. They were fabulous. Quite possibly the best England has ever produced. You did not have to be a supporter to appreciate their brilliance.

The fact that the best manager in England and the best team in England failed to hit it off was a great shame and something of a mystery. But I offer up my own conclusion: the day they first crossed paths, an irresistible force met an immovable object.

WHERE ARE THEY NOW?

DAVID HARVEY

Leeds' last big season of achievement coincided with a huge stroke of misfortune for David Harvey. He was injured in a car crash to the extent that he missed the European Cup final against Bayern Munich, replaced by his understudy David Stewart. Stewart did little wrong, but Leeds were beaten 2–0 by Bayern Munich in Paris.

Harvey's 16th and last Scotland appearance came in 1976. He stayed at Leeds until 1980 and then went to play in Canada with the Vancouver Whitecaps. He returned to Leeds in 1983, after the club had been relegated. By the time he left in 1985, he had played under three of his old teammates – Allan Clarke, Eddie Gray and Billy Bremner.

Harvey played for Bradford City under another old Leeds mate, Trevor Cherry, and then drifted into non-league football until retirement. Now 61, he works as a farmer and postman on Sanday in the Orkney Islands. Statistically, he is Scotland's most successful post-war goalkeeper.

PAUL REANEY

Now 64, Reaney is still involved in football, running half-term coaching sessions for children at a leisure resort in Norfolk.

BILLY BREMNER

Bremner finally left Leeds United in the late summer of 1976 to join Hull City. He had played 772 games for Leeds, putting him second behind Jack Charlton in the club's all-time list. Though winding down his career, Bremner emerged as a big success at Hull over two years before he joined Doncaster Rovers, managing an admirable four seasons there before retiring at the age of 39. In 1978, Bremner became manager of Doncaster Rovers, where he stayed for seven years.

He then succeeded ex-teammates Allan Clarke and Eddie Gray as manager of Leeds, aiming to restore happier days to the club after their relegation in 1982. However, they did not achieve promotion to the top flight and Bremner was sacked in September 1988.

At the beginning of December 1997, he suffered a heart attack at his Doncaster home in the small village of Clifton, South Yorkshire, and was rushed to hospital but died two days before his 55th birthday. He was voted Leeds' greatest ever player, with a statue standing outside Elland Road in his honour.

GORDON McQUEEN

McQueen, a central defender who was only 22 when Clough arrived at Elland Road, was harshly sent off against Barcelona in the European Cup semi-final of 1974, and he would miss the subsequent defeat to Bayern Munich due to suspension. He would go on to sign for Manchester United for £495,000, winning one FA Cup, and was awarded 30 caps for Scotland. Now 56, he is a European scout at Middlesbrough.

TERRY COOPER

Leeds' left-back, now 64, had a career in management at the two Bristol clubs, Birmingham and Exeter. He is presently a scout at Southampton Football Club.

TREVOR CHERRY

Although he missed half of the season in 1975 due to injury, Cherry recovered in time to help Leeds in their European Cup campaign as it progressed towards the semi-finals against Barcelona. Cherry marked Dutch legend Johan Cruyff out of each leg as Leeds reached the final, but after he missed subsequent league matches through suspension, manager Jimmy Armfield did not recall him for the final.

In 1976, Cherry succeeded Billy Bremner as captain of Leeds and won his first England cap. He continued to play for Leeds until 1982, the year in which the club was relegated under the management of his former teammate Allan Clarke. Now 61, the ex-England captain runs a promotions and hospitality company in his home town of Huddersfield, as well as a waste-paper company and a five-a-side football centre. He tried to buy Leeds in 2004.

PETER LORIMER

The European Cup final defeat to Bayern Munich was the turning point for the great Revie team and for Peter Lorimer too as one by one the major players left the club. Lorimer, who also made his 21st and final Scotland appearance in 1975, was still not 30 and continued to play as an experienced head amidst a new generation of Leeds United players. Mediocrity summed up the rest of the 1970s for Leeds United and Lorimer left in 1979, no longer a regular player, to try his luck in the North American Soccer League.

The 62 year old writes a column in the club's programme and is a summariser for Yorkshire Radio. A fans' representative on Leeds' board, he also runs the Commercial Inn pub in the city.

PAUL MADELEY

Leeds' Mr Utility spent his entire 17-year career at Elland Road. He later ran a sports shop and entered his family's DIY business. Now 64, he has suffered from ill health and in 2004 was diagnosed with Parkinson's disease.

JOE JORDAN

Having fought his way into the squad, and after playing in the European Cup final, Jordan would ultimately follow many of the great players of that era and leave for pastures new, signing for Manchester United in 1978 for £350,000. At Old Trafford, he would make 135 league appearances and play in the 1979 FA Cup final. In 1981, he made the dream move to AC Milan.

With more than fifty caps for his country, including two World Cup finals, Jordan has been inducted into the Scottish Football Hall of Fame. Now 57, he was caretaker manager at Portsmouth but followed Harry Redknapp to Tottenham, where he is assistant manager.

JOHNNY GILES

Giles was outstanding in Leeds' European campaign of 1974 but was no longer an automatic fixture in the side. After appearing in the 1975 final in Paris, Giles accepted an offer in June 1975 from West Bromwich Albion to become their player-manager, while still playing for and managing the Irish national team. This legend of the Revie era left Leeds after 12 years, 521 appearances and 114 goals.

At 68, he continues to work in journalism and is a leading football analyst on Irish radio station NewsTalk 106. In 2007, Giles successfully took legal action against the author and publishers of *The Damned United* over the portrayal of his actions at the time of Brian Clough's tenure.

DUNCAN McKENZIE

One of Clough's successes, Duncan McKenzie's career would actually flourish at other clubs, most notably Everton, where his performance against Liverpool in the 1977 FA Cup semi-final is still admired by fans. Now 58, he has worked as a newspaper columnist and radio commentator, as well as being a successful after-dinner speaker.

TERRY YORATH

The midfielder, father of television presenter Gabby Logan, would leave Leeds in 1976, signing for Coventry City for £125,000, playing 99 games and scoring 3 goals. A spell at Tottenham Hotspur in 1979 followed and then Yorath completed his playing career with Vancouver Whitecaps in 1983. He won 42 caps for Wales.

Yorath has managed Bradford City, Swansea, Cardiff and Sheffield Wednesday, as well as being assistant at Huddersfield. He was in charge of the Welsh national team – just failing to win them admission to the 1994 World Cup finals. He has also managed Lebanon. Now aged 59, he manages non-league Margate.

INDEX

INDEX